A SOCIOLOGY OF
GLOBALIZATION

Contemporary Societies Series

Jeffrey C. Alexander, Series Editor

Andrew Abbott   *Methods of Discovery: Heuristics for the Social Sciences*

Arne Kalleberg   *The Mismatched Worker*

Judith Lorber   *Breaking the Bowls: Gender Theory and Feminist Change*

Douglas Massey   *Strangers in a Strange Land: Humans in an Urbanizing World*

Saskia Sassen   *A Sociology of Globalization*

Michael Schudson   *The Sociology of News*

Steven Seidman   *The Social Construction of Sexuality*

Bryan Turner   *The New Medical Sociology: Social Forms of Health and Illness*

Forthcoming

Craig Calhoun   *The Public Sphere*

Michael J. Shanahan and Ross Macmillan   *Biography and the Sociological Imagination: Contexts and Contingencies*

David Snow and Sarah Soule   *A Primer on Social Movements*

A SOCIOLOGY OF GLOBALIZATION

Saskia Sassen

COLUMBIA UNIVERSITY

CONTEMPORARY SOCIETIES
Jeffrey C. Alexander
SERIES EDITOR

 W. W. NORTON & COMPANY ✺ NEW YORK LONDON

W. W. Norton & Company has been independent since its founding in 1923, when William Warder Norton and Mary D. Herter Norton first published lectures delivered at the People's Institute, the adult education division of New York City's Cooper Union. The Nortons soon expanded their program beyond the Institute, publishing books by celebrated academics from America and abroad. By mid-century, the two major pillars of Norton's publishing program—trade books and college texts—were firmly established. In the 1950s, the Norton family transferred control of the company to its employees, and today—with a staff of four hundred and a comparable number of trade, college, and professional titles published each year—W. W. Norton & Company stands as the largest and oldest publishing house owned wholly by its employees.

Composition by PennSet, Inc.
Manufacturing by Quebecor World—Fairfield Division.
Production manager: Jane Searle.
Series design by Beth Tondreau Design.

Library of Congress Cataloging-in-Publication Data
Sassen, Saskia.
  Sociology of globalization / Saskia Sassen.
    p. cm. — (Contemporary societies)
  Includes bibliographical references and index.

ISBN 13: 978-0-393-92726-9 (pbk.)
ISBN 10: 0-393-92726-1 (pbk.)

1. Globalization—Social aspects. I. Title. II. Series.

JZ1318.S28 2006
303.48'2—dc22

2006040138

W. W. Norton & Company, Inc., 500 Fifth Avenue, New York, NY 10110-0017
www.wwnorton.com

W. W. Norton & Company Ltd., Castle House,
75/76 Wells Street, London W1T 3QT

2 3 4 5 6 7 8 9 0

Contents

PREFACE

This small book seeks to map a very large subject, and to do so without sacrificing the complexity of that subject. One result is that the reader is regularly invited to find more of everything—details, evidence, bibliographical references—in this author's other books. I am a captive of my long-standing determination to raise the level of complexity in the study of globalization.

I owe much to the many different audiences that have heard me lecture on just about all the topics in this book. Their questions and contestations helped shape and sharpen my thinking. Each chapter began as a public lecture, and I thank my hosts for giving me the opportunity: Columbia University's Schoff Memorial Lectures, the Theodore Hesburgh Lectures in Ethics and Politics (University of Notre Dame), the Keck Lecture (Amherst College), the Alexander von Humboldt Lecture (University of Nijmegen), the Simmel Lectures (Humboldt University), the Annual Review of International Political Economy Lecture, and even, most unexpectedly for one like myself, the Annual Lecture of the Society for Sparsely Populated Areas. In addition to these lectures, portions of the texts in this book come from the recently published *Territory, Authority, Rights: From Medieval to Global Assemblages*. I want to thank Princeton University Press for allowing me to use portions of Chapters 7, 8, and 9.

I want to thank Jeff Alexander for asking me to write this book. It became an opportunity to explore the potential contributions of sociologists who never had globalization in mind. The possibility of this potential lies in the particular conceptualization of the global advanced in this book: the global is in good part constituted inside the national and hence becomes susceptible to being studied, at least in part, through existing sociological work, including data sets and methods. Seen this way, much old and new sociology actually contains conceptual, methodological, and empirical elements that can help advance the sociological study of globalization.

Karl Bakeman, Rebecca Arata, and Abigail Winograd made all the difference in getting the book done. A very big thank you goes to several students at the University of Chicago. Most especially, I want to thank Geoff Guy for his assistance with the sociological literature. Rachel Harvey and Danny Armanino were great research assistants at all stages of the project. They responded promptly to my requests, no matter where I was in the world—which for them meant being available at all times of day and night. Finally, Richard Sennett, Hilary Koob-Sassen, Rut Blees Luxemburg, and Fausto Sassen Blees were, as always, a source of much affection and laughter.

All errors are mine. This holds especially for this book. My attempts to explore the potential contributions to a sociology of globalization in scholarship that did not have this subject in mind, opens up the possibility of errors of interpretation—or, more interestingly, the possibility of new interpretations and new debates on old texts.

A SOCIOLOGY OF GLOBALIZATION

Chapter One
INTRODUCTION

TRANSNATIONAL PROCESSES such as economic, political, and cultural globalization confront the social sciences with a series of theoretical and methodological challenges. Such challenges arise out of the fact that the global—whether an institution, a process, a discursive practice, or an imaginary—simultaneously transcends the exclusive framing of national states yet partly inhabits national territories and institutions. Seen this way, globalization is more than the common notion of the growing interdependence of the world generally and the formation of global institutions. But if the global, as I argue, partly inhabits the national, it becomes evident that globalization in its many forms directly engages two key assumptions in the social sciences. The first is the explicit or implicit assumption about the nation-state as the container of social process. The second is the implied correspondence of national territory with the national—the assumption that if a process or condition is located in a national institution or in national territory, it must be national. Both assumptions describe conditions that have held, albeit never fully, throughout much of the history of the modern state, especially since World War I, and to some extent continue to hold. What is different today is that these conditions are partly but actively being unbundled. Different also is the scope of the unbundling.

Conceiving of globalization not simply in terms of interdependence and global institutions but also as inhabiting the national opens up a vast and largely unaddressed research agenda. The assumptions about the nation-state as container of social process continue to work well for many of the subjects studied in the social sciences and have indeed allowed social scientists to develop powerful methods of analysis and the requisite data sets. But they are not helpful in elucidating a growing number of questions about globalization and the large array of transnational processes turning up on the research and theorization agenda of the social sciences. Nor are those assumptions helpful in developing the requisite analytics. Thus methods and conceptual frameworks that rest on the assumption that the nation-state is a closed unit and that the state has exclusive authority over its territory cannot fully accommodate the critical proposition organizing this book: The fact that a process or an entity is located within the territory of a sovereign state does not necessarily mean it is national or of the type traditionally authorized by the state (foreign tourists, embassies, etc.); it might be a localization of the global. Whereas most such entities and processes are likely to be national, there is a growing need for empirical research to establish the status of what is in turn a growing range of possible instances of the global. Much of what we continue to categorize as national may well be precisely such instances. Developing the theoretical and empirical specifications that allow us to accommodate such conditions is a difficult and collective effort.

This book seeks to contribute to the collective effort by mapping an analytic terrain for the study of globalization that can encompass this more complex understanding. It includes, but also moves beyond, understandings of globalization that focus only on growing interdependence and self-evidently global institutions. Thus part of the research entails detecting the presence of globalizing dynamics in thick social environments that mix national and non-national elements. This framing of the global allows us to use many of the research techniques and data sets in the social sciences that were developed with national and subnational settings in mind. But we still have to develop new conceptual frameworks for *interpreting* findings—frameworks that do not assume that the national is a closed and exclusive system. Surveys of factories that are links in global commodity chains, in-depth interviews that decipher individual imaginaries about globality, and ethnographies of national financial centers—all expand the analytic terrain for understanding global processes. Such expansion opens up the research agenda for the social sciences in general and, perhaps especially, for more sociological and anthropological types of questions.

What is it, then, that we are trying to name with the term *globalization*? In my reading it involves two distinct sets of dynamics. One involves the formation of explicitly global institutions and processes, such as the World Trade Organization (WTO), global financial markets, the new cosmopolitanism, and the International War Crimes Tribunals. The practices and organizational forms through which such dynamics operate constitute what is typically thought of as global. Although they are partly enacted at the national scale, they are to a large extent novel and self-evidently global formations.

The second set of dynamics involves processes that do not necessarily scale at the global level as such yet, I argue, are part of globalization. These processes take place deep inside territories and institutional domains that have been constructed largely in national terms in much of the world, though by no means in all of it. Although localized in national—indeed, in subnational—settings, these processes are part of globalization in that they involve transboundary networks and entities connecting multiple local or "national" processes and actors, or the recurrence of particular issues or dynamics in a growing number of countries or localities. Among these entities and processes I include, for instance, cross-border networks of activists engaged in specific localized struggles with an explicit or implicit global agenda, as is the case with many human rights and environmental organizations; particular aspects of the work of states—for example, the implementation of certain monetary and fiscal policies in a growing number of countries, often with enormous pressure from the International Monetary Fund (IMF) and the United States, because those policies are critical to the constitution of global financial markets; and the fact that national courts are now using international instruments—whether human rights, international environmental standards, or WTO regulations—to address issues where before they would have used national instruments. I also include more elusive emergent conditions, such as forms of politics and imaginaries that are focused on localized issues and struggles shared by other localities around the world, with all participants increasingly aware of this situation; I call these noncosmopolitan globalities.

When the social sciences focus on globalization, it is typically not on this second type or set of processes and institutions but rather on the self-evidently global scale. The social sciences have made important contributions to the study of this global scale by establishing that multiple globalizations exist and by making it increasingly clear that the dominant form of globalization—the global corporate economy—is but one of several. Political science—specifically, international relations (IR)—has a strong canonical framing of the international, with the national state as a key actor. The strength itself of this canon poses difficulties when it comes to opening up to the possibility of global formations and their multiscalar character. The same can be said for sociology. The strength of its research methods and data sets has rested to a large extent on the type of closure represented by the nation-state. This holds in particular for the more quantitative types of sociology, which have been able to develop increasingly sophisticated methods predicated on the possibility of closed data sets. Though using very different methods and hypotheses, applied economics is similarly conditioned on data sets that presume closure in the underlying reality. On the other hand, although still maintaining similar assumptions about the nation-state, more historically inflected forms of sociology have made significant contributions to the study of international systems; notable here is the work on world-systems and cross-border migrations.

Economic and political geography, more than any of the other social sciences, has contributed to the study of the global, especially through its critical stance on scale. It recognizes the historicity of scales and thus resists the reification and naturalization of the national scale that is so present in most of social science. Anthropologists have contributed studies of the thick and particularistic forces that are also part of these dynamics, thereby indirectly alerting us to the risks of exclusively scalar analytics that disregard these complex environments. Without wanting to generalize, I will suggest that the analytic and interpretive tools of these two disciplines have been at an advantage when it comes to studying the global both in its conventional understanding as interdependence and in the more expanded approach developed in this book, notably its subnational scaling. Despite these advances in the social sciences, there is still much work to do, at least some of which entails distinguishing the various scales that get constituted through global processes and practices and the specific contents and institutional locations of this multiscalar globalization.

There are conceptual and methodological consequences to the approach developed in this book. Most important, my approach incorporates the need for the detailed study of particular national and subnational formations and processes and their recoding as instantiations of the global. This means that we can use many of the existing data sets and technologies for research, but we need to situate the results in different conceptual architectures. These architectures require new categories that do not presuppose the customary dualities of national/global and local/global. Examples of these categories are transnational communities, global cities, commodity chains, and space-time compression. This terminology arises partly out of an attempt to name conditions that are novel, have assumed novel forms, or have become visible because of the unsettlement of older realities. Older analytic categories may be used, but in ways that differ from those for which they were designed. Familiar sociological categories—such as race, gender, cities, immigration, and social connectivity—in principle can incorporate the analytics emerging from this conceptual reorganization. The category of denationalization that I use in this book and developed elsewhere (Sassen 1996, 2006a) captures an increasingly common effect arising from the interactions of the global and the national. A critical element in this interaction is the highly institutionalized nature and the sociocultural thickness that characterize the national. Structurations of the global inside the national therefore entail a partial, typically highly specialized and specific denationalization of particular components of the national.

OUTLINE OF THE BOOK

The next chapter and the final chapter introduce what are probably the least familiar material and analytics. The effort in those chapters is to expand the analytic terrain within which globalization may be situated as an object of study. The aim in Chapters Two and Eight is experimental rather than to ground globalization in the existing scholarship. Readers who are unfamiliar with the subject might consider skipping Chapter Two. At the heart of the book are chapters that explore the existing specialized scholarship in sociology in order to understand what it might contribute to the sociology of globalization. Most of the scholars whose work I discuss have never written about globalization. That is precisely the point, and it parallels the effort here and in Chapter Two to expand the analytic terrain within which to examine globalization. In this case the effort is to expand the scholarship we might bring to bear on core issues of a sociology of globalization. Chapters Three through Seven do this by addressing the state, cities, migrations, and emergent global classes. Those are core categories in sociology. The scholarship discussed in those chapters helps us explore different types of research and theorization practices in the study of the global.

Chapter Two
ELEMENTS OF A SOCIOLOGY
OF GLOBALIZATION

THIS CHAPTER DEVELOPS the theoretical and methodological elements of a more sociological study of the globalizing and denationalizing dynamics introduced in Chapter One. Critical among these elements are questions of place and scale. The global is generally conceptualized as overriding or neutralizing place and as operating on a self-evidently global scale. A focus on places, scales, and diverse meanings of the national helps us explore types of research and theorization practices not usually included in the study of the global. Furthermore, studying global processes in terms of these three elements touches on traditional objects of study in sociology: social structures, practices, and institutions. In later chapters, I examine how sociology provides a variety of concepts and methodological tools for apprehending the complexity and diversity of globalization as constituted by specific empirical referents, notably cities and states. Yet while particular attention is given to a sociological perspective, the questions addressed in this chapter are clearly not confined to sociology. Constructing the object of study in this type of effort often means operating at the intersection of multiple disciplinary forms of knowledge and techniques for research and interpretation.

Global formations may have existed for centuries. Sociologists have made some of the most important contributions to the study and theorization of such formations (Abu-Lughod 1989; Arrighi 1994; King 1990; Wallerstein 1974). Their character has varied across time and space. So today we can identify novel formations or novel traits in old formations, and sociologists have made some significant contributions to their study (Albrow 1996; Sklair 1991; Robinson 2004). Today's global formations are diverse both as social forms and as normative orders. For instance, as social forms the global capital market and the international human rights regime are starkly different, and so are their normative orders. For social scientists the research agenda consists largely of exploring this diversity, to capture the differences rather than only show the parallels. Capturing the specificity and variability of global formations makes for richer and more complex research findings. It also contributes to a more sociological perspective insofar as the aim is to capture different patterns of social relations. Thus many of the emerging global formations are partially or completely novel institutional orders or systems of relations. Further, institutionalized forms will tend to have distinct subcultures, formal and informal rules, regulatory regimes, assemblages of social actors, and power logics.

Each of the four sections of this chapter is concerned with identifying critical dynamics for understanding globalization sociologically. Thus each one focuses on a rather sharply defined instance of the challenge that today's global dynamics present to social science research. Each is, then, an opportunity to explore theoretical and methodological questions. In their aggregate these sections do not cover all the questions that need to be raised but rather get at some of the foundational ones.

The first section develops the notion of scalar hierarchies. It considers the traditional scalar hierarchy, which is centered on the nation-state, and focuses on its current destabilizing under the impact of novel dynamics and technologies. It uses this destabilizing effect as one window on the question of what is different today. Taking off from this view, the second section examines the meaning of the subnational in a global, partially digital world. The third section carries this view further to examine how subnational entities can exit the nested hierarchies organized around the national state and its role as the supposedly exclusive actor in international relations. The focus here is on the networks that connect cities across borders and can increasingly bypass national states. This holds especially for global cities, of which there are about forty in the world. These networks constitute one of the critical global formations today, as they include a rapidly growing range of actors and activities, including such diverse cases as the global network of a firm's affiliates, transnational migrant networks, and international terrorist networks. This type of focus helps open up the analysis to the possibility that subnational levels might matter to the process of constituting global social forms. It gives us an analytic bridge between the global scale, still an elusive notion, and the more familiar concept of the local in terms of the city or the immigrant community, for example. And it has the effect of disaggregating the global into particular cross-border circuits connecting specific localities, thereby partially bringing the vague notion of the global to the more concrete notion of networks of places.

The fourth section considers the implications that this articulation of the global in and through the national and the subnational has for national states. This consideration expands the analytic terrain for understanding the global by showing it to be partially constituted through the denationalizing of particular components of what have been constructed as national territories and institutional domains. Thereby we open up the national—a key sociological concept—for research on globalization. The national state is clearly a key actor and an institutional order at play in these articulations of the global with the national and the subnational.

THE DESTABILIZING OF OLDER HIERARCHIES OF SCALE

Global processes and formations can be, and are, destabilizing the scalar hierarchy centered in the national state. Previously the formation of the national state destabilized older hierarchies of scale, which typically were constituted through the practices and power projects of past eras, such as the colonial empires of the sixteenth and subsequent centuries and the medieval towns that dominated long-distance trading in certain parts of Europe in the fourteenth century. Most notable today is what is sometimes seen as a return to older imperial spatialities for the economic operations of the most powerful actors: the formation of a global market for capital, a global trade regime, and the internationalization of manufacturing production. It is of course not simply a return to older forms. It is crucial to recognize the specificity of today's practices and the capabilities enabling them. This specificity is in part a result of the fact that today's transboundary spatialities have to be produced in a context in which most territory is encased in a thick and highly formalized national framework marked by the exclusive authority of the national state. The preeminence of the national scale and of the exclusive authority of the state over its territory is, in my reading, one of the key contexts for understanding the specificity of the current phase of globalization. This preeminence of the national brings with it a necessary participation of national states in the formation of global systems (Sassen 1996, chaps. 1 and 2; 2006a).[1]

The global project of powerful firms, the new technical capabilities associated with information and communications technologies (ICTs), and the growth of supranational components in state work are beginning to constitute strategic scalings beyond that of the national. Among these are subnational scales such as the global city and supranational scales such as global markets. These processes and practices partially destabilize the scale hierarchies that expressed the power relations and political economy of an earlier period. These were—and, to a large extent, continue to be—organized in terms of institutional size and territorial scope: from the international down to the national, the regional, the urban, and the local, with the national functioning as the articulator of this particular configuration. That is, the crucial practices and institutional arrangements that constituted the system occurred at the national level. Notwithstanding different origins and starting times around the world, the history of the modern state can be read as the work of rendering national just about all crucial features of society: authority, identity, territory, security, law, and market. Periods preceding those of the ascendancy of the national state saw rather different types of scalings, with territories typically subject to multiple systems of rule rather than to the exclusive authority of a state.

Today's rescaling dynamics cut across institutional size and the institutional encasements of territory produced by the formation of national states. This rescaling does not mean that the old hierarchies disappear but rather that novel scalings emerge alongside the old ones and that the former can often trump the latter. Older hierarchies of scale constituted as part of the development of the nation-state continue to operate, but they do so in a far less exclusive field than they did in the recent past. This holds even when we factor in the hegemonic power of a few states, which meant—and continues to mean—that most national states were not—and still are not—fully sovereign in practice.

Existing theory is not enough to map today's multiplication of practices and actors contributing to these rescalings. Included are a variety of nonstate actors and forms of cross-border cooperation and conflict, such as global business networks, the new cosmopolitanism, nongovernmental organizations (NGOs), diasporic networks, and such spaces as global cities and transboundary public spheres. IR theory is the field that to date has had the most to say about cross-border relations. But current developments associated with various mixes of globalization and the new ICTs point to the limits of IR theory and data. Several critical scholars (Taylor 2000; Cerny 2000; Ferguson and Jones 2002; Rodney Brace Hall and Thomas J. Biersteker 2002; Walker 1993) have shown us how the models and theories of IR remain focused on the logic of relationships between states and the scale of the state at a time when we see a proliferation of nonstate actors, cross-border processes, and associated changes in the scope, exclusivity, and competence of state authority over its territory. Theoretical developments in other disciplines may prove important. Especially relevant, as I mentioned above, is geography and its contributions to critical analyses of scale, unlike other social sciences, which tend to take scale as a given and the national scale as a naturalized condition.

A second feature is the multiscalar character of various globalization processes. A financial center in a global city is a local entity that is also part of a globally scaled electronic market. We might think of this as an instance in which the local is multiscalar. Obversely, the WTO is a global entity that becomes active once it is inserted into national economies and polities and can thus be conceived of as an instance in which the global is multiscalar. These instances cannot easily be accommodated by older nested hierarchies of scale, which position everything that is supranational above the state in the scalar hierarchy and everything that is subnational beneath the state. A more complex multiscalar configuration is the new type of operational space used by multinational firms: it includes as key components both far-flung networks of affiliates and concentrations of strategic functions in a single location or in a few locations (for example, Taylor, Walker, and Beaverstock 2002; Ernst 2005).[2] Perhaps most familiar here is again the bundle of conditions and dynamics that marks the model of the global city (Sassen 1991). In its most abstract formulation this is captured in what I see as one of the key organizing hypotheses of the global-city model—to wit, that the more globalized and the more digitized the operations of firms and markets become, the more their central management and specialized servicing functions (and the requisite infrastructures and buildings) become strategic and complex, thereby benefiting from agglomeration economies. To varying extents these agglomeration economies are still delivered through territorial concentrations of multiple resources—that is, they are mostly delivered through cities. This variety of multiscalar dynamics points to conditions that cannot be organized as a hierarchy, let alone as a nested hierarchy. It is a multiscalar system operating across scales and not, as is so often said, merely scaling upward as a result of new communications capabilities.[3]

In the next section, I examine this multiscalar character that the local and the global are assuming. I do so by focusing in particular on subnational instances, as those are less familiar than explicitly global formations and, furthermore, lend themselves especially well to sociological studies.

The Subnational: A Site for Globalization

Studying the global, then, entails a focus not only on that which is explicitly global in scale but also on locally scaled practices and conditions that are articulated with global dynamics. And it calls for a focus on the multiplication of cross-border connections among localities in which certain conditions recur: human rights abuses, environmental damage, mobilization around certain struggles, and so on. Furthermore, it entails recognizing that many of the globally scaled dynamics, such as the global capital market, are actually partially embedded in subnational sites (financial centers) and move between these differently scaled practices and organizational forms. For instance, the global capital market is constituted through both electronic markets with a global span and locally embedded conditions—that is, financial centers and all they entail, from infrastructure to systems of trust.

A focus on such subnationally based processes and dynamics

of globalization requires methodologies and theorizations that engage not only global scalings but also subnational scalings as components of global processes. This juxtaposition has the effect of conceptually destabilizing the mostly implicit model of a state-centered nested scalar hierarchy. Studies of global processes and conditions that are constituted subnationally have some advantages over studies of globally scaled dynamics, but they also pose specific challenges. They make possible the use of long-standing quantitative and qualitative research techniques in the study of globalization. They provide a bridge for using the wealth of national and subnational data sets as well as specialized scholarship, such as that of area studies. As indicated earlier, however, both sub- and supranational studies need to be situated in conceptual architectures that are not quite those held by the researchers who generated these research techniques and data sets, as their efforts for the most part had little to do with globalization.

One central task we face is decoding particular aspects of what is still represented or experienced as national, which may in fact have shifted away from what historically has been considered or constituted as national. This task, then, is in many ways a research and theorization logic that is the same as that developed in studies of the global city. But whereas today we have come to recognize and code a variety of components of global cities as part of the global, this categorization does not hold for a growing number of other subnational domains we should include in the globalization research agenda. In this book I focus on a range of globalizing or denationalizing dynamics that are still coded and represented as local and national.

Three instances serve to illustrate some of the conceptual, methodological, and empirical issues in this type of study. The first one concerns the role of place in many of the circuits that constitute economic and political globalization. A focus on places allows us to unbundle globalization in terms of the multiple specialized cross-border circuits on which different types of places are located. In Chapter Seven I discuss a particular version of this unbundling: the emergence of forms of globality centered on localized struggles and actors that are part of cross-border networks; this is a form of global politics that runs through local rather than global institutions.

Perhaps the most highly developed scholarships on the role of place and global circuits are those on global cities and on commodity chains. Research on global commodity chains focuses on networks of labor and production processes whose final result is a finished commodity (Gereffi and Korzeniewicz 1994); they are constituted by sets of interorganizational networks of households, business enterprises, and particular state components, all of which share a focus on the production of a given commodity. While research on global commodity chains focuses largely on circuits, work on global cities draws attention to strategic places in the global economy. Global cities are subnational places in which multiple global circuits intersect and thereby position these cities in several structured cross-border geographies, each of which typically has a distinct scope and is constituted in terms of distinct practices and actors. For instance, at least some of the circuits connecting São Paulo to global dynamics are different from those connecting Frankfurt, Johannesburg, or Mumbai (Bombay). Furthermore, specific sets of overlapping circuits contribute to the constitution of distinctively structured cross-border geographies. We are, for instance, seeing the intensifying of older transnational hegemonic geographies—for example, the increase in transactions among New York, Miami, Mexico City, and São Paulo (see Ramos Schiffer 2002; Parnreiter 2002)—as well as newly constituted geographies—for example, the articulation of Shanghai with a rapidly growing number of cross-border circuits (Gu and Tang 2002; Wasserstrom 2004; Rowe and Kuan 2004). This type of analysis produces a different picture of globalization from one centered on global markets, international trade, or the pertinent supranational institutions. It is not that one type of focus is better than the other but that the supranational focus—the most common by far—is not enough.

A second instance, partially connected to the first, is the role of the new interactive technologies in repositioning the local, thereby inviting us to make a critical examination of how we conceptualize the local. Through the new technologies a financial services firm becomes a microenvironment with a continuous global span. And so, too, do resource-poor organizations or households. These microenvironments can be oriented to other microenvironments located far away, thereby destabilizing the notion of context, which is often associated with that of the local and with the notion that physical proximity is one of the attributes or markers of the local. A critical reconceptualization of the local along these lines entails at least a partial rejection of the notion that local scales are inevitably part of nested hierarchies of scale running from the local to the regional, the national, and the international.

The third instance concerns a specific set of interactions between global dynamics and particular components of national

states. The crucial conditionality here is the partial embeddedness of the global in the national, of which the global city is
perhaps most emblematic. My main argument is that insofar as
specific structurations of the global inhabit what historically
has been constructed and institutionalized as national territory,
they engender a variety of negotiations between the global and
the national. One set of outcomes evident today is what I
describe as an incipient, highly specialized, and partial denationalization of specific components of national states.

In all three instances the question of scaling takes on a specific content. The content involves practices and dynamics that,
I argue, pertain to the global yet are taking place at what historically has been constructed as the scale of the national. With
few exceptions, most prominent among which is a growing
scholarship in geography, the social sciences have not had critical distance—that is, have not historicized—the scale of the
national. The consequence has been a tendency to take it as a
fixed scale and reify it and, more generally, to neutralize the
question or at best to reduce scaling to a hierarchy of size. Associated with this tendency is the often-uncritical assumption
that these scales are mutually exclusive and—most pertinent
for my argument here—that the scale of the national and that
of the global are mutually exclusive. A qualifying variant that
allows for mutual imbrications, though of a limited sort, can be
seen when scaling is conceived as a nested hierarchy.[4]

Finally, the three instances described above go against the
assumptions and propositions that are now often described as
methodological nationalism. But they do so in a distinct way.
Crucial to the critique of methodological nationalism is the
need for transnationalism because the nation-as-container cate-

gory is inadequate given the proliferation of transboundary dynamics and formations (for example, Taylor 2000; Beck and Beck-Gernsheim 2001; Beck 2000; Robinson 2004). What I am focusing on here is, rather, yet another set of reasons for supporting the critique of methodological nationalism: the fact of multiple and specific structurations of the global within what has been constructed historically as national. Furthermore, I posit that because the national is highly institutionalized and thick, structurations of the global inside the national entail a partial, typically highly specialized and specific denationalization of particular components of the national.

The new networks connecting cities through a variety of activities and novel institutions are an example of a global scaling constituted through subnational places and their increasingly intense cross-border transactions.

THE CROSS-BORDER NETWORK OF GLOBAL CITIES

When economic activity becomes globalized, it partly reshapes existing orders and contributes to the formation of novel ones. It does so through the practices of economic actors (global firms and markets) and the development of particular value regimes (deregulation of the economy). Exploring these changes requires new conceptual architectures; one example is the model of the global city. As the global economy has expanded over the last two decades, we have seen the formation of a growing network of global cities, now numbering about forty, through which national economic wealth and processes have been articulated with a proliferation of global circuits for capital, investment, and trade. This network of global cities constitutes a space of power that contains the capabilities needed for the global operations of firms and markets. It partially cuts across the old North-South divide and constitutes a geography of centrality that today also incorporates major cities of the global South even though the hierarchy in this geography of centrality is quite sharp. At its most concrete level this new geography is the terrain on which multiple globalization processes assume material and localized forms. An examination of global cities and their networks helps us understand how spatial and organizational centrality is institutionalized in the global economy (see in general Abu-Lughod 1999; Short and Kim 1999; Sachar 1990; Allen, Massey, and Pryke 1999; Matthew J. O. Scott 2001; Marcuse and Van Kempen 2000; Gugler 2004; Taylor 2004; Harvey 2007; Fujita et al. 2004).[5]

Choosing how to name a configuration has its own substantive rationality. Choosing the term *global city* (Sassen 1991; Sassen-Koob 1982, 1984) was a knowing choice. It was an attempt to name a difference: the specificity of the global as it gets structured in the contemporary city.[6] I did not choose the obvious alternative, *world city*, because it has precisely the opposite attribute: it refers to a type of city that we have seen over the centuries (for example, Braudel 1984; Peter Hall 1966; King 1990) and most probably in much earlier periods in Asia or in European colonial centers (Gugler 2004). Most of today's major global cities are also world cities, but there may well be some global cities that are not world cities in the full, rich sense of that term. Exploring these issues is partly an empirical question; furthermore, as the global economy expands and incorporates additional cities into its various networks, it is quite possible that a growing number of global cities will not be world cities. Thus the fact that Miami developed global-city functions beginning in the late 1980s (Nijman 1996) does not make it a world city in the older sense of the term.

I have proposed five hypotheses to help explain the importance of cities in the institutionalization of global economic processes. In the first four the effort was to qualify what was emerging in the 1980s as a dominant discourse on globalization, technology, and cities, which posited the end of cities as important economic units or scales. One tendency in that account was to take the existence of a global economic system for granted. My effort was to recover the actual work of implementing and managing a global economy and, in so doing, to recover the importance of cities for this work.

A first hypothesis was that the greater the geographic dispersal of economic activities along with their simultaneous integration through telecommunications, the greater the growth and importance of central corporate functions. The more dispersed a firm's operations across different countries, the more complex and strategic are the managing, coordinating, servicing, and financing of a firm's network of operations.

Second, the more complex these central functions become, the more likely the headquarters of large global firms "outsource" them. Headquarters buy a share of their central functions from highly specialized service firms: accounting, legal, public relations, programming, and telecommunications, among others. Thus while even ten years ago the key site for the production of these central-headquarter functions was the headquarters of a firm, today there is a second key site: the specialized firms contracted by headquarters to produce some of these central functions or components of them. This pattern is especially prevalent among firms involved in global markets and nonroutine operations. But increasingly the headquarters of all firms are buying more such inputs rather than producing them in-house.

The third hypothesis is that the more complex and globalized a specialized service firm's markets are, the more its central functions are subject to agglomeration economies. The complexity of the services they need to produce, the uncertainty of the markets they are involved with either directly or through the headquarters for which they are producing the services, and the growing importance of speed in all these transactions, all produce a mix of conditions that constitutes a new agglomeration dynamic. The mix of firms, talent, and expertise in a broad range of specialized fields makes a certain type of urban environment functions as an information center. Being in a city becomes synonymous with being in an extremely intense and dense information loop.

A fourth hypothesis, derived from the preceding one, is that the more headquarters outsource their most complex, nonstandardized functions, particularly those subject to uncertain and changing markets and speed, the freer they are to opt for any location because less of the work that is done in the headquarters is subject to agglomeration economies. Thus the key sector specifying the distinctive production advantages of global cities is the highly specialized and networked services sector.[7]

The fifth hypothesis is that insofar as these specialized service firms need to provide a global service (through a global network of affiliates or some other form of partnership) there is a strengthening of cross-border city-to-city transactions and networks. At the limit this may well be the beginning of the formation of transnational urban systems. The growth of global markets for finance and specialized services, the need for transnational service networks due to sharp increases in international investment, the reduced role of the government in the regulation of international economic activity, and the corresponding ascendancy of other institutional arenas, notably global markets and corporate headquarters—all of these factors point to the existence of a series of transnational networks of cities. A corollary is that major business centers in the world today draw their importance from these transnational networks. There is no such entity as a single global city—and in this sense there is a sharp contrast with the erstwhile capitals of empires.

Central to these hypotheses about the organizational architecture of the global economy is the proposition that this economy contains both the capabilities for enormous geographic dispersal and mobility and pronounced territorial concentrations of resources necessary for the management and servicing of that dispersal. The management and the servicing of much of the global economic system take place in this growing network of global cities and cities or regions that are better described as having a limited number of global-city functions. The growth of global management and servicing activities has in turn brought with it a massive upgrading and expansion of central urban areas even as large portions of these cities fall deeper into poverty and experience infrastructural decay. Although this role involves only certain components of urban economies, it has contributed to a repositioning of cities both nationally and globally. The intensity of transactions among these cities, particularly through the financial markets, investment, and contracting for services, has increased sharply, and so have the orders of magnitude involved. We can see here at least the incipient formation of transnational urban systems. To a large extent, the major business centers in the world today draw their importance from these transnational networks which, in turn, signals a division of functions.

A transnational urban system is in part an organizational structure for cross-border transactions. There have long been cross-border economic processes—flows of capital, labor, goods, raw materials, travelers—and in that sense there is nothing new about today's emerging interurban networks. But over the centuries there have been enormous fluctuations in the degree of openness or closure in the organizational forms within which these flows have taken place. In the last hundred years the interstate system came to provide the dominant organizational form for cross-border flows in much of the world, with national states as the key actors. It is this condition that began to change dramatically in the 1980s and grew rapidly in the 1990s as a result of privatization, deregulation, the new information technologies, the opening up of national economies to foreign firms, and the growing participation of national economic actors in global markets. The organizational architecture for cross-border flows that emerges from these rescalings and articulations is only partially ensconced in, and at times increasingly diverges from, the interstate system. The key articulators now include not only national states but also firms and markets whose global operations are facilitated by new policies and cross-border standards produced by willing or not-so-willing states (for example, Panitch 1996; Gill 1996; Ferguson and Jones 2002; Rodney Bruce J. Hall and Thomas J. Biersteker 2002; Harvey 2007; Taylor 2004).

The growth of networked cross-border dynamics among global cities includes a broad range of domains—political, cultural, social, and criminal. There are multiple empirical referents for these nonstate forms of articulation, which we can disaggregate into particular components. One type of empirical referent is economic, including the growing number of cross-border mergers and acquisitions, the expanding networks of foreign affiliates, and the growing number of financial centers that are becoming incorporated into global financial markets. There is also a proliferation of specialized global circuits for economic activities that both contribute to these new scales and are enhanced by their emergence. A second type of empirical referent is the growing range of cross-border transactions among immigrant communities and communities of origin and a greater intensity in the use of these networks once they become established, including economic activities that had been unlikely until now. We also see greater cross-border networks for cultural purposes, both economic and artistic, as in the growth of international markets for art and a transnational class of curators, and for nonformal political purposes, as in the growth of transnational networks of activists organized in support of environmental causes, human rights, and so on. These are largely city-to-city cross-border networks, or at least it appears at this time to be simpler to capture the existence and modalities of these networks at the city level. The same can be said for the new cross-border criminal networks, whether they are linking drug dealers, terrorists, or traffickers in people. These and other processes explain why a growing number of cities are playing an increasingly important role in directly linking their national economies and societies with global circuits. As cross-border transactions of all kinds grow, so do the networks binding particular configurations of cities (for example, Taylor 2004; Amen et al. 2006; Lo and Yeung 1996). This growth in turn contributes to the formation of specific cross-border geographies that connect particular sets of cities.

The outcome is a rescaling of the strategic sites that articulate the new system. With the partial unbundling, or at least weakening, of the national as a spatial unit come conditions for the ascendancy of other spatial units and scales (for example, Taylor 1995; Sum 1999; Brenner 1998; 2004; Harvey 2007). Among these are subnational scales, notably cities and regions; cross-border regions encompassing two or more subnational entities; and supranational entities such as global electronic markets and free-trade blocs. The dynamics and processes that get territorialized or are sited at these diverse scales can in principle be regional, national, and global. This rescaling carries consequences for governing the flows and transactions circulating through the particular or general networks of cities, global and otherwise.

Although these networks are partially embedded in national territories, existing national frameworks cannot necessarily regulate their functions. Regulatory functions have increasingly shifted toward a set of emerging or newly invigorated cross-border regulatory networks and the development of an array of standards by which world trade and global finance may be organized. Specialized, often semi-autonomous regulatory agencies and the specialized cross-border networks they are forming are taking over functions once encased in national legal frameworks, and standards are replacing rules in international law.

This last point touches on a crucial theme running through

this book: the theoretical and empirical challenges of studying global phenomena located within the nation-state. Studying global cities and their cross-border networks brings the empirical issues to the fore. Because global cities are located within national territories, the movement of various flows among these cities eventually "touches down" in the national sphere as well. Mapping this empirically can be difficult because most data sets relating to cross-border flows focus on the movement of capital, information, people, and other entities among nation-states, not among individual cities. Thus there is a need for constructing new sets of data to trace these flows. The most significant contribution to this effort has been by Peter Taylor and his colleagues through the setting up of GaWC. Most recently, Alderson and Beckfield (2004) have developed yet another methodology and data set to get at these types of questions. (See also the debate in the *American Journal of Sociology* 2006).

In constructing the new data sets, we can use the qualitative and quantitative methods employed by the social sciences, including sociology. Researchers have begun to address this challenge by studying these global formations as either nodes (Alderson and Beckfield 2004) or flows between nodes (Taylor 2004; see Sassen 2002a for examples of both approaches). Individual nodes can reveal how components of a single city, such as firms and markets, are articulated with the wider network (Gu and Tang 2002; David R. Meyer 2002; Taylor, Walker, and Beaverstock 2002). Research using qualitative methods can delve into the specific globalizing cultures of cities (for example, Krause and Petro 2003; Hill 2007; Peterson 2007) and the daily work and politics involved in the production and maintenance of a global city (for example, Simmonds and Hack 2000; Rutherford 2004; Samers 2002; Amen et al. 2006). Research on the cross-border networks of global cities has explored the links among these cities and has sketched a hierarchy of the system (David A. Smith and Michael Timberlake 2002; Taylor, Walker, and Beaverstock 2002). Using quantitative methods, researchers have explored the flows between cities using data on air traffic (David A. Smith and Michael Timberlake 2002), inter- and intrafirm links (Taylor, Walker, and Beaverstock 2004), and information flows (Mitchelson and Wheeler 1994). Constructing a more complete picture of these cross-border networks and their nodes will require more research, however. Sociology in particular and the social sciences in general, with their diverse qualitative and quantitative methodologies, can help specify these emergent global formations by using both older data sets and constructing new data sets in ways that avoid methodological nationalism.

Denationalized State Agendas and Privatized Norm Making

Each section in this chapter has drawn attention to the problems of treating the global-national as a mutually exclusive duality. The importance of strategic places such as global cities in capturing global processes and the possibility of localities interacting directly with global networks are cases that problematize the notion of a global-national duality. The global economy to a large extent materializes in national territories; its topography moves between digital space and places in national territories. Global cities are locations in which the global economy is in good part organized, serviced, and financed. Global processes do not need to move through the hierarchies of national states; they can directly become articulated with certain kinds of localities and local actors.

Although none of these circumstances alters the geographic boundaries of the national state's territory, they do change the meaning of the state's exclusive authority over that territory. As institutions, national states are becoming deeply involved in the implementation of the global economic system. This repositioning of the state raises the issue of whether there are particular conditions that make execution of this role in the current phase distinct and unlike what it may have been in earlier phases of the world economy. While this is in many ways a question of interpretation, I argue that there is indeed something distinctive about the current period. That is, the current role of the state is not new, but it has been transformed.

The work of states, or the raison d'etat—the substantive rationality of the state—has had many incarnations over the centuries, each of which has had consequences. Today the conditionalities for and the content of specific components of the work of states have changed significantly compared with those of the period immediately preceding the post–World War II decades. Some of those changes are typically captured by the image of the current neoliberal or competitive state as compared with the welfare state of the postwar era. We have, on the one hand, the existence of an enormously elaborate body of law, developed in good measure over the last hundred years, that secures the exclusive territorial authority of national states to an extent not seen in earlier centuries. On the other hand, we see considerable institutionalizing, especially in the 1990s, of the "rights" of non-national firms, the deregulation of cross-border transactions, and the growing influence or power of some of the supranational organizations. If securing these rights, options, and powers entailed even a partial relinquishing of components of state authority as constructed over the last century, then we can posit that this process sets up the conditions for a transformation in the role of the state. It also signals a necessary engagement by national states in the process of globalization (Aman 1998; Sassen 1996).

This changed condition of the state is often explained in terms of a decrease in regulatory capacities resulting from some of the basic policies associated with economic globalization. We generally use terms such as *deregulation* and *financial and trade liberalization* to describe the changed authority of the state in a broad range of markets and economic sectors, and over its national borders. This shifting authority also includes the privatization of public-sector firms. The problem with such terms is that they capture only the withdrawal of the state from regulating its economy. They do not register all the ways in which the state participates in setting up the new frameworks through which globalization is furthered. Nor do they capture the associated transformations inside the state. These are precisely my two concerns.

The new geography of power confronting states entails, therefore, a far more differentiated process than notions of an overall decline in the significance of the state suggest. Instead we are seeing a repositioning of the state in a broader field of power and a reconfiguring of the work of states. This broader field of power is constituted in part by the formation of a new private institutional order linked to the global economy and in part by the growing importance of a variety of institutional orders engaged with various aspects of the common good broadly understood, such as the international network of NGOs and the international human rights regime. Analyzing this geography of power requires capturing and conceptualizing a specific set of operations that takes place within national institutional settings but is geared to non-national or transnational agendas, whereas once they were geared to national agendas.

This understanding of the state raises two crucial questions. The first question concerns the nature of this engagement:[8] is the role of the state simply one of reducing its authority (for example, as suggested by terms such as *deregulation* and *privatization* and, in general, *less government*), or does it also require the production of new types of regulations, legislative items, court decisions—in brief, the production of a series of new "legalities"?[9] The second question explores how various types of states navigate their engagement with global processes. Some states, specifically the United States and the United Kingdom, produce the design for these new legalities—that is, particular aspects of the law derived from Anglo-American commercial law and accounting standards—and impose them on other states, given the interdependencies at the heart of the current phase of globalization. This in turn creates and imposes a set of specific constraints on all participating states.[10] Legislative items, executive orders, adherence to new technical standards, and so on, have to be produced through the particular institutional and political structures of each of these states.[11]

The first question requires an exploration of the engagement of the state with global processes. One of the roles of the state vis-à-vis economic internationalization has been to negotiate the intersection of national law and the activities of foreign economic actors—whether firms, markets, or supranational organizations—in its territory as well as the overseas activities of national economic actors. In the case of the United States, legislative measures, executive orders, and court decisions have enabled foreign firms to operate in the United States and for the United States to have internationalized markets.

The case of central banks can be used to illustrate this mix of national institutions and global policies. Central banks are national institutions that address national matters. Yet over the last decade they have become the institutional home within the national state for monetary policies that are necessary to further develop a global capital market and, indeed more generally, a global economic system. The new conditionality of the global financial system—the requirements that need to be met for a country to become integrated into the global capital market—contains as one of its key elements the autonomy of central banks from presidents or prime ministers.[12] This autonomy facilitates the task of instituting a certain kind of monetary policy, one privileging low inflation over job growth even when a president may prefer it the other way around, particularly at reelection time. While securing central-bank autonomy has certainly cleaned up a lot of corruption, it has also been the vehicle for one set of accommodations on the part of national states to the requirements of the global capital market. A parallel analysis can be made of ministries of finance (or the Treasury in the United States), which have had to impose fiscal policies aimed at reducing state social expenditures, yet another conditionality of economic globalization.

This accommodation of the interests of foreign firms and investors under conditions in which most of a country's institutional domains have been constructed as "national" entails negotiation.[13] The mode of this negotiation in the current phase has tended in a direction that I describe as a denationalizing of several highly specialized national institutional components.[14] My hypothesis here is that as of the 1980s some components of national institutions, even though formally national, are not national in the sense in which state practice has constructed the meaning of that term since the emergence of the so-called regulatory state, particularly in the West. Though imperfectly implemented and often excluding national minorities, Keynesian policies aimed at strengthening the "national" economy and "national" consumption capacity, and at raising the educational level of the "national" workforce, are good illustrations of this meaning of the national. There are clearly enormous variations among countries in the extent to which such a national policy project existed and the actual period of time during which it was implemented. The key issue today, however, is that state policies and the work of states have altered various elements of what has traditionally been considered a territorially and institutionally exclusive national state.

How do states handle this engagement with the global? Crucial to my analysis is the fact that the emergent, often imposed consensus in the community of states on furthering globalization is not merely a political decision: it entails specific types of *work* by a large number of distinct institutions in each country. In this sense, the consensus forces states to engage in actual work. It is not merely the taking of a decision. Furthermore, this work has an ironic outcome insofar as it destabilizes some aspects of state power: the state can be seen as incorporating the global project of its own shrinking role in regulating economic transactions. The state here can be conceived of as representing a technical administrative capacity that cannot be replicated at this time by any other institutional arrangement; furthermore, this capacity is backed by military power, which for some states is a global power. Seen from the perspective of firms operating transnationally, the objective is to ensure the functions traditionally exercised by the state in the national realm of the economy, notably guaranteeing property rights and contracts, only now extended to foreign firms as well. How this gets done may involve a range of options. To some extent this work of guaranteeing is becoming privatized, as is signaled, for instance, by the growth of international commercial arbitration and by key elements of the new kinds of privatized authority.[15] The U.S. government as the hegemonic power of this period has led or forced other states to adopt these obligations toward global capital and in so doing has contributed to strengthening the forces that can challenge or destabilize what have historically been constructed as state powers.[16]

Regardless of whether the focus is on individual states or the emergent consensus in the community of states, a set of strategic dynamics and institutional transformations is at work. These dynamics and transformations may incorporate a small number of state agencies and units within departments or a small number of legislative initiatives and executive orders and yet have the power to institute a new normativity at the heart of the state. This is especially so because these strategic sectors are operating in complex interactions with private, transnational, and powerful actors. It is happening to varying degrees in a growing range of states, even as much of the institutional apparatus of states remains basically unchanged. (The inertia of bureaucratic organizations, which creates its own version of path dependence, makes an enormous contribution to continuity.) What we see at work here is the incipient and partial denationalization of specific, typically highly specialized state institutional orders and state agendas. From the perspective of research, I have argued that this transformation entails the need to decode what is "national" (as historically constructed) about these particular specialized institutional orders inside national states (Sassen 2006a, chap. 4).

The mode in which this participation by the state has evolved has been toward strengthening the power and legitimacy of privatized and denationalized state authorities. The outcome is an emergent order that has considerable governance capabilities and structural power. This institutional order contributes to strengthening the advantages of certain types of economic and political actors and to weakening those of others. It is extremely partial rather than universal, but it is strategic in that it has undue influence over wide areas of the broader institutional world and the world of lived experience. Further, this order is not fully accountable to formal democratic political systems. While partially embedded in national institutional settings, it is distinct from them.

There are several features we can identify in this new private institutional order at the heart of several national state institutions. First, the distinctive features of this new, mostly but not exclusively private institutional order in formation are its capacity to privatize what was heretofore public and to denationalize what were once national authorities and policy agendas. This capacity to privatize and denationalize entails specific transformations of the national state—or, more precisely, of some of its components. Second, this new institutional order has normative authority—a new normativity that is not embedded in what has been and to some extent remains the master normativity of modern times, raison d'état. Instead, this normativity comes from the world of private power yet installs itself in the public realm and in so doing helps denationalize national state agendas. Third, particular institutional components of the national state begin to function as the institutional home for the operation of powerful dynamics constitutive of what we could describe as global capital and global capital markets. In so doing, these state institutions help reorient their particular policy work or broad state agendas toward the requirements of the global economy. These features then raise a question about what is national in these institutional components of states linked to the implementation and regulation of economic globalization (for data and sources, see Sassen 2006a, chap. 5).

Geared toward governing key aspects of the global economy, both the particular transformations inside the state and the emergent privatized institutional order are partial and incipient but strategic. Both have the capacity to alter possibly crucial conditions for "liberal democracy" and for the organizational architecture of international law, its scope, and its exclusivity. In this sense both have the capacity to alter the scope of the authority of states and the interstate system, the crucial institutional domains through which the "rule of law" is implemented. We are not seeing the end of states but, rather, that states are not the only or the most important strategic agents in this new institutional order and, second, that states, including dominant states, have undergone profound transformations in some of their key institutional components. Both these trends are likely to add to the democratic deficit and further strengthen the "legitimacy" of certain types of claims and norms, notably those of global economic actors.

In brief, my argument is that the *tension* between a) the necessary though partial location of globalization in national territories and institutions and b) an elaborate system of law and administration that has constructed the exclusive national territorial authority of sovereign states, has been partially negotiated through, first, processes of institutional denationalization inside the national state and the national economy and, second, the formation of privatized intermediary institutional arrangements that are only partially encompassed by the interstate system. These arrangements are, in fact, evolving into a parallel institutional world for the handling of cross-border operations.[17] In terms of research this means, among other tasks, establishing what are the new territorial and institutional conditions under which national states operate.

CONCLUSION

This chapter focuses on critical global processes and dynamics that evince multiple sociological features. We can distinguish very broadly three major objects of study. One consists of the endogenizing or localizing of global dynamics, producing a concrete and situated object of study, such as particular types of places—global cities and silicon valleys. A second consists of formations that although global are articulated with particular actors, cultures, or projects, producing an object of study that requires negotiating a global and a local scale, such as global

markets and global networks. A third consists of the denationalizing of what has been constructed historically as national
and may continue to be experienced, represented, and coded as
such; this process produces an object of study that is contained
within national frames but needs to be decoded, such as state
institutions that are key producers of policy instruments
needed by global economic actors. These three types of instances capture distinct social entities and have diverse origins.
They are not necessarily mutually exclusive, however.

Cutting across these diverse processes and domains is a research and theorization agenda. The following chapters develop
this agenda by bringing together different strands of rapidly
growing scholarships in several disciplines, some focused on
self-evidently global processes or conditions and others on local
or national processes or conditions. But all contribute to capturing the more social aspects of these conditions, and in that
sense they contribute to a sociological analytics. This agenda is
driven by at least some of the following major concerns.

At the most general level, a first concern is establishing
novel or additional dimensions of, respectively, the spaces of
the national and of the global. Specific structurations of what
we have represented as the global are actually located deep inside states and other national institutions and, more generally,
in territories encased by national legal, administrative, and cultural frameworks. In fact, what has been represented (and to
some extent reified) as the scale of the national contains a simultaneity of scales, spaces, and relations, some national in the
historic sense of the term, some denationalized or in the process
of becoming so, and some global.

A second major concern is with critical examinations of how

we conceptualize the local and the subnational in ways that allow us to detect those instances—even when they might be a minority of all instances—that are in fact denationalized and multiscalar even when they are represented and experienced as "simply local." The multiscalar versions of the local examined in later chapters have the effect of destabilizing the notion of context, which is often predicated on that of the local, and the notion that physical proximity is one of the attributes or markers of the local. Furthermore, a critical reconceptualizing of the local along these lines entails at least a partial rejection of the notion that local scales are inevitably part of the nested hierarchies of scale running from the local to the regional, the national, and the international. Localities or local practices can constitute multiscalar systems, operating across scales and not merely scaling upward as a result of new communications capabilities.

A third major concern is how to conceptualize the national, especially the specific interactions between global dynamics and particular components of the national. The crucial conditionality here is the partial embeddedness of the global in the national, of which the global city is perhaps emblematic and one of the most complex instances. My main argument is that this embeddedness engenders a variety of negotiations insofar as specific structurations of the global inhabit and partly denationalize what historically has been constructed and institutionalized as national. This type of focus brings to the fore the particularities of each state when it comes to its interaction with global forces. Even though most states have wound up implementing policies that support economic globalization, those actions do not preclude institutional differences in the process of accommodation. Some states will have resisted and others promptly acquiesced. Understanding this interaction of global and national forces demands detailed studies of the particular ways in which different countries have handled and institutionalized this negotiation.

Chapter Three
THE STATE CONFRONTS THE GLOBAL ECONOMY AND DIGITAL NETWORKS

THE SCHOLARSHIP ON THE STATE AND GLOBALIZATION contains three basic positions: one finds that the state is victimized by globalization and loses significance; a second finds that nothing much has changed and states basically keep on doing what they have always done; and a third, a variant of the second, finds that the state adapts and may even be transformed, thereby ensuring that it remains the critical actor and does not decline. There is research to support critical aspects of each of these positions, partly because much of their difference hinges on interpretation. But notwithstanding its diversity, this scholarship tends to share the assumption that the national and the global are mutually exclusive.

Given the effort in this book to expand the analytic terrain on which the question of globalization may be mapped, the broader research and theorization agenda needs to address aspects of globalization and the state that are lost in those dualized accounts of their relationship. Although many components of each are indeed mutually exclusive, there is a growing, often specific set of components that does not fit this dual structure. As was pointed out in the preceding chapter, this is evident, for instance, with critical components in the work of ministries of finance and central banks (called, respectively, the Treasury and the Federal Reserve in the United States) and with the increasingly specialized technical regulatory agencies, such as those concerned with finance, telecommunications, and competition.

Factoring in these types of conditions amounts to a fourth position, in addition to the three referred to above. Whereas this fourth approach does not necessarily preclude all the propositions in the other three, it is nonetheless markedly different in its foundational assumptions. For instance, in my research I find that far from being mutually exclusive, the state is one of the strategic institutional domains in which critical work on the development of globalization takes place. This development does not necessarily produce the decline of the state, but neither does it keep the state going as usual, nor does it merely produce adaptations to the new conditions. The state becomes the site for foundational transformations in the relationship between the private and the public domains, in the state's internal balance of power, and in the larger field of both national and global forces within which the state now has to function (Sassen 2006a, chaps. 4 and 5).

The first section of this chapter introduces a number of conceptual issues that arise from the sociological scholarship on the state, one that has not been much concerned with globalization. The focus is particularly on the fourth trend specified above, as it is far more open to sociological approaches and data. It is here that sociology could make a big difference in the development of methods, theory, and data on the state and globalization. One way of conceiving synthetically of the broad and probably growing range of processes comprised by this fourth approach is to emphasize the denationalizing of specific forms of state authority due to the partial location of global processes in national institutional orders. The second section of the chapter discusses key features of the locational and institutional embeddedness of the global economy; it develops issues raised in Chapter Two. The third section sketches out the particular substance and conditionality of this new mode of authority, which though housed or located in national state capacities and institutions, is not national in the way we have come to understand this feature of states over the last century. The empirical focus for much of the examination is confined to states under the so-called rule of law, especially the United States. The final section explores this new mode of state authority in the case of the Internet and other digital networks that largely do not fit in established jurisdictions.

HOW TO STUDY THE STATE IN A GLOBAL CONTEXT

A number of scholars have addressed various dimensions of the state's participation in global processes. Some (for example, Krasner 2004; Fligstein 2001; Evans 1997) argue that globalization is made possible by states and that hence not much has changed for states and the interstate system. The present era is merely a continuation of a long history of changes that have not altered the fundamental fact of state primacy (Mann 1997). Both the "strong" and the "weak" versions of neo-Weberian state theory (Skocpol 1985; Evans 1997) share certain dimensions of this conceptualization of the state. Although acknowledging that the primacy of the state may vary given different structural conditions between state and society, these authors tend to understand state power as basically denoting the same conditions throughout history: the ability to implement explicitly formulated policies successfully. A second type of literature (Panitch 1996; Gill 1996; Mittelman 2000) interprets deregulation and privatization as the state's incorporation of its own shrinking role. In its most formalized version this position emphasizes the state's constitutionalizing of its diminished role. In this literature, economic globalization is not confined to the act of capital crossing geographic borders, as is captured in measures of international investment and trade, but is in fact conceptualized as a politico-economic system. A third, growing literature emphasizes the relocation of national public governance functions in private entities within both, the national and global orders, as well as in supranational organizations (for example, Hall and Biersteker 2002; Dezalay and Garth 1996; Cutler et al. 1999). Key institutions of the supranational system, such as the WTO, and private bodies, such as the International Chamber of Commerce, are emblematic of this shift. Cutting across these types of literature are the issues raised earlier in this chapter, of whether states are declining, whether they are remaining as strong as they have ever been, or whether they have changed but as part of an adaptation to the new conditions rather than on account of a loss of power.

Sociologists such as those mentioned above have not focused on the question of globalization and the state. But much in their work can illuminate critical aspects of the state that are helpful in developing a more sociological approach to that question. The focus developed in this chapter emphasizes the work of states in the development of a global economy and, to a lesser extent, other forms of globalization. The consequences for the state that such work entails are diverse and can be interpreted in more than one way—for instance, some interpretations might conceive of some consequences as intended and others as unintended. Here I will focus in particular on types of state work that I interpret as producing a denationalizing of particular components of state authority, which nonetheless remain inside the state rather than shifting to the private or global institutional domains, as is typically emphasized in the pertinent scholarship. Tilly's historical distinction between the national state and "the state" as such is helpful in this regard. Whereas states are "coercion-wielding organizations that are distinct from households and kinship groups and exercise clear priority in some respects over all other organizations within substantial territories," *national* states are distinguished by "governing multiple contiguous regions and their cities by means of centralized, differentiated, and autonomous structures" (1990, 1–2). The centralized national state acts as an interface between national and supranational forces and as a "container" for the former (Brenner 1999; Agnew 2005; Ó' Riain 2000). This distinction makes analytic room for the possibility of yet another mode of stateness—the denationalized state (whether partly or fully so). Delimiting the national state as one particular form of state allows more analytic freedom in conceptualizing those processes, and opens up a research agenda.

A first step in this type of analysis is to establish the state's position to recover the ways in which the state participates in governing the global economy in a context increasingly dominated by deregulation, privatization, and the growing authority of nonstate actors. A key organizing proposition is the embeddedness of much of globalization in national territory—that is, in a geographic terrain that has been encased in an elaborate set of national laws and administrative capacities. The embeddedness of the global requires at least a partial lifting of these national encasements and hence signals a necessary participation by the state, even when it concerns the state's own withdrawal from regulating the economy. Like Tilly's definition, nearly all sociological definitions of the state from Max Weber on emphasize a territorial dimension of state power. To the extent that this emphasis entails a conception of territory associated with the "national state," it follows that existing state capacities are oriented toward a univocally national society. Even Mann (1986, 26–27), who is otherwise enormously sensitive to the multiple spatialities of the exercise of power in social life, defines the state largely as an organization exercising political power and enforcing cooperation within a bounded territory. Subjecting the "national" to empirical observation opens up the research agenda. This territorial dimension means that as states have participated in the implementation of the global economic system, they have in many cases undergone significant transformations. The accommodation of the interests of foreign firms and investors entails a negotiation. This negotiation includes the development inside national states—through legislative acts, court rulings, executive orders—of the mechanisms necessary for the reconstitution of certain components of national capital into "global capital" and the accommodation of new types of rights or entitlements for foreign capital in what are still national territories that in principle are under the exclusive authority of their states.[1]

Such an approach is one way of expanding the analytic terrain for mapping globalization—it extends that terrain deep into highly specialized components of the national state. The particular transformations it uncovers inside the state are partial and incipient but strategic. For instance, they can weaken or alter the organizational architecture for the implementation of international law insofar as such law depends on the institutional apparatus of national states. Furthermore they have created the conditions whereby some parts of national states actually gain relative power (Sassen 1996, chaps. 1 and 2) as a result of that participation in the development of a global economy. Disaggregating "the" state along these lines makes it apparent that certain wings of the state become more, not less, powerful due to their functional importance in the global economy. This dynamic must be distinguished on the one hand from Skocpol's (1979, 1985) position, which emphasizes the structural independence of the various components of the state and their internal rationalization, and on the other hand from a world-system perspective, which would treat "state power" as monolithically resulting from placement in the structural hierarchy of world economies. States do not meekly confront their changing environments; rather, they actively engage with them and try to maintain their position of power (Datz 2007). This process involves both the modification of existing capacities to new situations (Datz 2007; Weiss 1998) and, potentially, the attempt by state actors to link into the global economy, to claim jurisdiction over the various tasks involved in globalization, thereby securing their own power (Sassen 2006a, chaps. 4 and 5). (For an illuminating model of this process involving professional groups, see Abbott 1988.) As particular components of national states become the institutional home for some of the dynamics that are central to globalization, they undergo a change that is difficult to register or name. In my own work I have found useful the notion of an incipient denationalizing of specific components of national states—that is, components that function as such institutional homes. The question for research then becomes what is actually "national" in some of the institutional components of states linked to the implementation and regulation of economic globalization. Returning to Tilly's (1990) historical distinction, I would argue that today we see partial and highly specialized shifts from a national state to a state *tout court* in a growing number of countries. The hypothesis here would be that some components of national institutions, even though formally national, are not national in the sense in which we have constructed the meaning of that term over the last hundred years.

This partial, often highly specialized, or at least particularized, denationalization can also take place in domains other than that of economic globalization, notably the recent incarnation of the human rights regime, in which national courts can be used to sue foreign firms and dictators or to grant undocumented immigrants certain rights (Sassen 2006a, chaps. 6 and 9). Denationalization is thus multivalent: it endogenizes global agendas of many different types of actors, not only corporate firms and financial markets but also human rights regimes. In discussing the state as a site for the pursuit and articulation of strategies, Jessop (1990, chap. 9) argues that any coherence to the state can be only temporary and grounded in a hegemony of particular groups. Therefore, numerous compromises with subaltern groups are necessary, and there exists the possibility of entrenchment of nondominant groups within certain components of the state apparatus. Applied to the kinds of methodological questions that concern me here, Jessop's distinctions open up the state to detailed empirical research.

These trends toward a greater interaction of national and

global dynamics are not new. There have been times in the past when they may have been as strong in certain aspects as they are today. For instance, there was a global capital market at the beginning of the twentieth century. Furthermore, in many ways state sovereignty was never absolute but was always subject to significant fluctuations. Thus Arrighi and Silver (1999, 92–94) argue that historically "each reaffirmation and expansion of legal sovereignty was nonetheless accompanied by a curtailment of the factual sovereignty that rested on the balance of power" among and within states (93). "Furthermore, the crisis of national sovereignty is no novelty of our time. Rather, it is an aspect of the stepwise destruction of the balance of power that originally guaranteed the sovereign equality of the members of the Westphalian system of states" (94).

Nonetheless, after almost a century of a strengthening national state, since the late 1980s we have seen a considerable institutionalizing of the "rights" of non-national firms, the deregulation of cross-border transactions, and the growing influence or power of some supranational organizations. If securing these rights, options, and powers entailed even a partial relinquishing of components of state authority as constructed over the last century, then we can posit that it sets up the conditions for a necessary engagement by national states in the process of globalization. Furthermore, we need to understand more about the nature of this engagement than is represented by concepts such as deregulation. It is becoming clear that the role of the state in the process of deregulation involves the production of new types of regulations, legislative items, and court decisions (Picciotto 1992; Cerny 2000; Panitch 1996)—in brief; the production of a series of new "legalities." The background condition here is that the state remains the ultimate guarantor of the "rights" of global capital—that is, the protection of contracts and property rights and, more generally, a major legitimator of claims. (See also Fligstein 1990, 2001.)

To apply the phraseology of Skocpol, Evans, and Rueschemeyer (1985) to the global domain, we can say that the state maintains its level of capacity (albeit with some transformations) even as it may lose some of its autonomy. We might want to do research to determine whether these capacities are being deployed in accordance with the functional logic of capital or with that of projects articulated within the state and, if so, what parts of the state. To some extent this work of guaranteeing is becoming privatized, as is signaled by the growth of international commercial arbitration (Dezalay and Garth 1996) and by key elements of the new privatized institutional order for governing the global economy (Cutler 2002), subjects addressed later.

There is a second articulation of the state and globalization, one predicated on the sharply unequal power of states. State scholarship has been dominated by largely western-centered analytical categories. A growing critical scholarship (often referred to as post-colonial studies) seeks to decenter state analysis onto a larger historical map. It does so in very diverse ways. Thus Chakrabarty (2000) constucts the notion of "provincializing Europe" as a way of incorporating the different trajectories of statehood in other parts of the world and thereby "globalizing" knowledge (not simply attacking European-centered knowledge). Mbembe (2001) posits the "banality of power" in Africa and contests the categories—oppression and resistance, autonomy and subjection, and state and civil society—that have marked social theory in the late twentieth century.

In fact some states, particularly the United States and the United Kingdom, are producing the design for the new standards and legalities needed to ensure protections and guarantees for global firms and markets. Those two states are by far the most powerful producers of new standards and legalities insofar as most of them are derived from Anglo-American commercial law and accounting standards. Hence a limited number of states, often functioning through the supranational system, are imposing the standards and legalities which will have to be produced through the particular institutional and political structures of the other states. In terms of research and theorization this is a vast, uncharted terrain: it means examining how that production takes place and gets legitimated in different countries. One possible outcome is considerable cross-national variations (which would then need to be established, measured, and interpreted). In Meyer's (1997) framework, national variations notwithstanding, there is a recurrent set of institutional arrangements, models that shape states, institutions, and individual actors collectively producing a kind of rationalized order. Another outcome might be production of "institutional isomorphism" (see the essays in Powell and DiMaggio 1991). Here Meyer's work can be seen as providing a missing link. While work such as that collected in Powell and DiMaggio analyzes the structural causes of the emergence of formal similarities among organizations across widely separated areas and the mechanisms of power and legitimation underlying those causes, it tends to assume that organizations already exist within a shared structural field. Thus, once these organizations are mutually relevant, structural forces can act on each one to shape it to a common mold. In the situations analyzed here, it is not immediately clear whether the various relevant organizations exist within the same organizational fields, and whether much of the work they perform is oriented specifically toward making them co-present with a common (global) field or space. Here it is important to emphasize again that the emergent, often imposed consensus in the community of states to further globalization is not merely a political decision: it entails specific types of work by a large number of distinct state institutions in each of these countries. This is an underresearched process, one that would lend itself to comparative cross-national studies. Clearly the role of the state will vary significantly depending on the power it has internally and internationally (see Krasner 2004 and comments).

A crucial part of the argument is the fact of the institutional and locational embeddedness of globalization. Specifying this embeddedness has two purposes. One is to provide the empirical specification underlying my assertion that the state is engaged in the implementation of global processes rather than serving as a "victim" of them. Establishing embeddedness of the global in the national in turn feeds the proposition about the denationalizing of particular state functions and capacities as this engagement by the state proceeds. The second purpose is to signal that given this embeddedness, the range of ways in which the state might be involved could in principle be far more diverse than those at play today, which are largely confined to furthering economic globalization. Jessop (1990), though not necessarily focused on globalization, provides an illuminating theoretical perspective for conceptualizing how these possibilities are either reinforced or selected against by the structures of the state. Conceivably state involvement could address a whole series of global issues, including the democratic deficit in the multilateral system governing globalization.[2]

In the immediately following sections of this chapter I elaborate on features of today's global economy that point to locational and institutional embeddedness.

THE LOCATIONAL AND INSTITUTIONAL EMBEDDEDNESS OF THE GLOBAL ECONOMY

There are three features of the global economy I want to emphasize here. First, the geography of economic globalization is strategic rather than all-encompassing, and that is especially so when it comes to the managing, coordinating, servicing, and financing of global economic operations. This geography differs from that of the world-system perspective, which defines a global economy by a continuous division of labor between states (Wallerstein 1974). Differentiation between center and periphery no longer largely comprises a differentiation between different production processes or places in commodity chains; rather, the differentiation is largely functional and cuts across the spatialities presupposed in Wallerstein's framework. By defining the world economy as basically a relationship between territorial states, Wallerstein forecloses the possibility of conceptualizing globalization as anything but the expansion of the world economy to include new states; the possibility of a reconstitution of the spatiality of global capitalism is rendered invisible (Brenner 1999, 57–60; 2004). The fact that it is strategic is significant for a discussion of the possibilities of regulating and governing the global economy. Second, the center of gravity of many of the transactions that we refer to in an aggregate fashion as the global economy lies in the North Atlantic region. This concentration facilitates the development and implementation of convergent regulatory frameworks and technical standards and enables a convergence around "Western" standards. If the geography of globalization were a diffuse condition at the planetary scale, one involving equally powerful countries and regions with a much broader range of differences than those evident in the North Atlantic, the question of its regulation might well be radically different. Third, the strategic geography of globalization is partially embedded in national territories—that is, in global cities and Silicon Valleys.

The combination of these three characteristics suggests that states may have more options for participation in the governing of the global economy than much of the focus on the loss of regulatory authority allows us to recognize. There is a growing scholarship that emphasizes both globalization and regulation. Research by Gereffi (1994, 1999) emphasizing the cross-border organization of production and marketing points to a type of arrangement that could enable regulation. It transcends some of the limitations of the classical world-system perspective in that Gereffi's "commodity-chains" take place across multiple borders and the primary axes of differentiation is *functional*. Nonetheless, the basic criteria for structural differentiation remain somewhat static—assembly, manufacturing, retailing, and so on. To the extent that new possibilities for spatially distributing these tasks emerge, it is basically a function of technological change (for example, information technology allowing for the dispersal of production) and changes in the structure of market demand (mass production versus flexible specialization). Since these conditions are basically defined as a given in the commodity-chains scholarship, the most the state can do is attempt to maximize its position within a given hierarchy: it can try to "upgrade" its position. In this analysis, then, the constitutive role of the state vis-à-vis the global economy remains relatively difficult, and hence so do its potential capacities for global economic governance.

There are sites in this strategic geography where the density of economic transactions and the intensity of regulatory efforts come together in complex, often novel configurations. Two of these sites are the focus of this section. They are foreign direct investment, which for the most part consists of cross-border mergers and acquisitions, and the global capital market, undoubtedly the dominant force in the global economy today. These two processes also make evident the enormous weight of the North Atlantic region in the global economy. Along with trade, they are at the heart of the structural changes constitutive of globalization and the efforts to regulate it. Both foreign direct investment and the global capital market bring up specific organizational and regulatory issues that help highlight the regulatory role of states (Helleiner 1999; Pauly 2002; Eichengreen 2003).[3] There has been an enormous increase in the complexity of management, coordination, servicing, and financing for firms operating worldwide networks of factories, service outlets, and/or offices and for firms operating in cross-border financial markets. For reasons I discuss in greater detail in Chapter Four this increase in complexity has brought about a sharp growth in control and command functions and their concentration in a cross-border network of global cities. These growth and locational patterns in turn contribute to the formation of a strategic geography for the management of globalization. Nowhere is this as evident as in the structure of the global capital market and the network of financial centers. Elsewhere I have examined this institutional order as the site of a new type of private authority (Sassen 1996, chap. 2).

The empirical patterns of foreign direct investment and global finance show the extent to which their centers of gravity lie in the North Atlantic region and, but to a far lesser extent, in China and Japan (Sassen 2006b, chap. 2). The northern transatlantic economic system (specifically, the links among the European Union, the United States, and Canada) represents the major concentration of processes of economic globalization in the world today. This concentration holds whether one looks at foreign direct investment flows in general, cross-border mergers and acquisitions in particular, overall financial flows, or the new strategic alliances among financial centers. At the turn of the millennium this region accounted for 66 percent of worldwide stock market capitalization, 60 percent of inward foreign investment stock and 76 percent of outward foreign investment stock, 60 percent of worldwide sales in mergers and acquisitions, and 80 percent of purchases in mergers and acquisitions. There are other major regions in the global economy: China, Japan, Southeast Asia, and Latin America. But except for some of the absolute levels of capital resources in Japan and the purchases of U.S. dollars by China, they are dwarfed by the weight of the northern transatlantic system.

This heavy concentration in the volume and value of cross-border transactions raises a number of questions. One concerns its features, such as the extent to which there is interdependence and, thereby the elements for a cross-border economic system. The weight of these transatlantic links needs to be considered against the weight of older zones of influence for each of the major powers—particularly, the Western Hemisphere in the case of the United States; Africa, and central and eastern Europe in the case of the European Union.

The United States and individual E.U. members have long had often intense economic transactions with their zones of influence. Some of these have been reinvigorated in the new economic policy context of openness to foreign investment, privatization, and trade and financial deregulation. In my reading of the evidence, both the relations with their respective zones of influence and the relations within the Northern transatlantic system have changed. The transnational economic system centered in the North Atlantic system includes an emerging system of rules and standards, and articulations with a growing worldwide network of sites for investment, trade, and financial transactions. It is through this incorporation in a North Atlantic–centered hierarchical global network that the relations with their zones of influence are now constituted. Thus although the United States is still a dominant force in Latin America, several European countries have become major investors in Latin America as well, on a scale far surpassing past trends. And although several E.U. countries have become leaders in investment in central and eastern Europe, U.S. firms are playing a greater role there than they ever played before.

What we are seeing today is a new grid of economic transactions superimposed on the old geoeconomic patterns. The latter persist to varying extents, but they are increasingly submerged in this new cross-border grid, which amounts to a new, though partial geoeconomics. The decline of the import-substitution model of development can be seen as symptomatic of this shift. Under this model, the state as interface between national and international economies set up a number of protections for infant industries until they were ready to compete. A high position in the global hierarchy was associated with high value-added manufacturing work, and the goal was a complete development of national space. By contrast, the advent of export-led development resulted in the creation of specialized spaces within national territories—export-processing zones and kindred arrangements—that only imperfectly aligned with the old categories of national and international economies. The paradigmatic cases of this form of development in East Asia did not accomplish this transformation solely through acquiescence to market logic; rather, the strong role of the state has been well documented. From these local innovations within an old economic-spatial hierarchy, traces of the new order emerged. Analysis of these hierarchies cannot be confined to classifications that identify its structural positions and their occupants. Rather, we must know how these outcomes are produced, reproduced, and transformed. The new configurations are particularly evident in the organization of global finance and, though less so, in direct foreign investment, especially cross-border mergers and acquisitions. (I discuss the evidence in Sassen 2006b.)

Worldwide Networks and Central Command Functions
There are clearly strong dispersal trends contained in the patterns of foreign investment and capital flows in general. These

include the offshoring of factories, the expansion of global networks of affiliates, franchises and subsidiaries, and the formation of global financial markets with a growing number of participating countries. What is left out of this picture is the other half of the story. This worldwide geographic dispersal of factories and service outlets takes place through highly integrated corporate structures with strong tendencies toward concentration in control and profit appropriation. The North Atlantic system is the site for most of the strategic functions involved in managing and coordinating the new global economic system.

Elsewhere (Sassen 2001) I have shown that when the geographic dispersal of factories, offices, and service outlets through cross-border investment takes place within integrated corporate systems, mostly multinational corporations, central functions also grow; we can see a parallel trend with financial firms and markets. The evidence shows that the more globalized firms become, the more their central functions grow—in importance, in complexity, and in the number of transactions they make.[4] The specific forms assumed by globalization over the last decade have created particular organizational requirements. The emergence of global markets for finance and specialized services and the growth of investment as a major type of international transaction have contributed to the expansion in command functions and in firms' demands for specialized services.[5]

We can make this growth of headquarter work more concrete by considering some of the staggering figures involved in the worldwide dispersal and by imagining the extent to which parent headquarters must engage in coordination and management. For instance, by the late 1990s there were almost half a million foreign affiliates of firms worldwide, most of them belonging to North American and western European firms; by 2004 this number had risen to almost a million (Sassen 2006b: chap. 2).[6] There has been a greater growth in foreign sales through affiliates than through direct exports: in 1999 foreign sales were $11 trillion through affiliates and $8 trillion through the worldwide export of goods and services. This growth has of course also fed the intrafirm share of "free" cross-border trade. The data on foreign direct investment show clearly that the United States and the European Union are the major receiving and sending regions in the world. Finally, the transnationality index of the largest transnational firms shows that many of the major firms in these regions have over half their assets, sales, and workforce outside their home country.[7] Together, these diverse data sets provide a fairly comprehensive picture of this combination of dispersal and growth of central functions.

The globalization of a firm's operations brings with it the massive task of coordination and management. This is not new, but the work has grown over the last two decades and has become more complex. Furthermore, dispersal of a firm's operations does not occur through a single organizational form; rather, behind the numbers lie many different organizational forms, hierarchies of control, and degrees of autonomy. The globally integrated network of financial centers is yet another form of this combination of dispersal and growing complexity of central management and coordination functions.

Of importance to this analysis is the dynamic that connects the dispersal of economic activities with the ongoing weight and growth of central functions. In terms of sovereignty and globalization this means that an interpretation of the impact of globalization as creating a space economy that extends beyond the regulatory capacity of a single state is only half the story; the other half is that central functions are disproportionately concentrated in the national territories of the highly developed countries.

By central functions, I do not mean only top-level headquarters; I am referring to all the top-level financial, legal, accounting, managerial, executive, and planning functions necessary to run a corporate organization operating in more than one country and, increasingly, in several countries. As discussed earlier, these central functions are partially embedded in headquarters but are also in good part embedded in what has been called the corporate-services complex—that is, the network of financial, legal, accounting, and advertising firms that handle the complexities of operating in more than one national legal system, national accounting system, advertising culture, and so on, and do so in the face of rapid innovations in all those fields. Such services have become so specialized and complex that headquarters increasingly buy them from specialized firms rather than produce them in-house. These agglomerations of firms producing central functions for the management and coordination of global economic systems are disproportionately concentrated in the highly developed countries—particularly, though not exclusively, in global cities. Such concentrations of functions represent a strategic factor in the organization of the global economy.

One argument I am making here is that it is important analytically to distinguish between the strategic functions for the global economy or for global operations and the overall corporate economy of a country. The global control and command functions are partially embedded in national corporate structures but also constitute a distinct corporate subsector, which can be conceived of as part of a network that connects global cities across the globe. These networks are not defined by a global division of labor in the production of commodities and by the resulting market-based trade transactions; rather, the "members" of these networks divide up the work of reproducing the global economy, that is, the structures of global management and control. Much as the state could once be seen as institutionally central to the reproduction of a regime of accumulation—in other words, as pivotal to a mode of regulation—the distribution of strategic functions to global cities can be seen as the rearticulation of a mode of regulation contributing to a new global regime of accumulation.

Regulation theory, basically a form of institutionalism, would likely have difficulties grasping this form of global regulation, for two reasons. First, the spatialities constituting these modes of operation/regulation are not easily matched with specific institutional scales, most of which are still national. Second, absent the emergence of a single global institutional frame capable of structuring world-economic relations, it is unclear whether regulation theory is capable of detailing the actual mechanisms whereby structure is reproduced. So far only potential elements of such a system have emerged, largely from relatively "local" practices in these global cities. Regulation theory is better equipped to detail the functioning of an already existing national institutional structure; it is less well equipped to explain the constitution of that structure and its deployment to a global scale. For the purposes of certain kinds of inquiry, these distinctions may not matter; for the purposes of understanding the global economy, they do.

These distinctions matter for questions about the regulation of cross-border activities. If the strategic central functions—both those produced in corporate headquarters and those produced in the specialized corporate-services sector—are located in a network of major financial and business centers, the question of regulating what amounts to a key part of the global economy is not the same as it would be if the strategic management and coordination functions were as widely distributed geographically as are the factories, service outlets, and affiliates. Regulation of these activities is evolving along lines of greater specialization and greater cross-border scope than most current state-centric national regulatory systems can comfortably accommodate today. In my reading, a crucial issue for understanding the question of regulation and the role of the state in the global capital market is the ongoing embeddedness of this market in networks of financial centers operating within national states; these are not offshore markets. This gives states some grip over global finance. The North Atlantic system contains an enormous share of the global capital market through its sharp concentration of leading financial centers.[8] Furthermore, as the system expands through the incorporation of additional centers into this network—from eastern Europe, Latin America, and so on—the question of regulation also pivots on the existence of dominant standards and rules—that is, those produced by the economies of the North Atlantic. In brief, studies that emphasize deregulation and liberalization do not sufficiently recognize an important feature, one that matters for the analysis here: the global financial system has reached a level of complexity that requires the existence of a cross border network of financial centers to service the operations of global capital (Sassen 2006a, chap. 7). Each financial center represents a massive and highly specialized concentration of resources and talent, and the network of those centers constitutes the operational architecture for the global capital market.

It might be interesting at this point to recall Arrighi's (1994) argument that the restarting of a cycle of accumulation derives from local entrepreneurial innovations. As a local system manages to draw profits toward itself, it becomes a model for other systems in the world economy: it exercises a hegemonic leadership function. Power accrues to this territorial region because of its superior performance, not because of its strategic positioning within a global capitalist system. Hence, in this analysis the basic dynamics hold for each of the phases of the world economy, and spatial differentiation is primarily a function of market and competitive efficiency. But within each phase also, Arrighi brilliantly lays out the dynamics of its growth and its downfall; the ascendance of finance is the key indicator of decline. If we do not pay attention to these conditions for the production and reproduction of structural dynamics within each phase, we are limited in theorizing the level of change within a system.[9] In examining the structuring of key features of the current phase of the global economy, I emphasize on the one hand the production of strategic resources and capabilities and on the other hand the fact that global cities do not simply compete with one another. Together they provide a critical networked infrastructure for the management and control of global chains of transactions, each with considerable specificity of functions. The result is multiple divisions of labor among cities, contributing to distinctive articulations of the global economy beyond the core-periphery articulation.

State Regulatory Capacities

The existence of such a strategic geography on the organizational side of the global economy is a significant factor in the question of how the state can and does participate in the implementation of the global corporate economy. Regulation is one angle from which to approach this question. The orders of magnitude and the intensity of transactions in the North Atlantic system facilitate the formation of standards even in the context of what are, relatively speaking, strong differences between the United States and continental Europe in their legal, accounting, anti-trust, and other rules. It is clear that even though these regions have more in common with each other than with much of the rest of the world, their differences matter when it comes to the creation of cross-border standards. But shared Western standards, in combination with enormous economic weight, have facilitated the circulation of U.S. and European standards and their imposition on transactions involving firms from other parts of the world. There is a sort of globalization of Western standards. Much has been said about the dominance of U.S. standards, but European standards are also evident—for instance, in the mostly administrative anti-trust procedures being developed in central and eastern Europe, which contrast with the litigation-oriented U.S. system.

Foreign direct investment and the global capital market are at the heart of a variety of regulatory initiatives. The growth of foreign direct investment has brought with it a renewed concern with questions of extraterritoriality and competition policy, including the regulation of cross-border mergers. The growth of the global capital market has brought with it specific efforts to develop the elements of an architecture for its governance: international securities regulation, new international standards for accounting and financial reporting, and various other provisions. Each has tended to be ensconced in fairly distinct national regulatory frameworks: foreign direct investment in anti-trust law, and global finance in national regulatory frameworks for banking and finance.[10]

National states participate in the framing of cross-border regimes. In my current research on the United States, I am extricating from what has been constructed as "U.S. legislative history" a series of legislative items and executive orders that can be read as both accommodations on the part of the national state and its active participation in producing the conditions for economic globalization. This is a history of microinterventions, often minute transformations in our regulatory or legal frameworks that facilitated the extension of cross-border operations of U.S. firms. It is clearly not a new history, neither for the United States nor for other Western former imperial powers (for example, the "concessions" to trading companies under British, Dutch, and other colonial regimes). Yet I argue that we can identify a new phase, one with very specific instantiations of this broader feature.[11] Among the first of these new measures in the United States, and perhaps among the best known, are the tariff items passed to facilitate the internationalization of manufacturing, which exempted firms from import duties on the added value of reimported components assembled or manufactured in offshore plants. I date this microhistory of legislative and executive interventions to the late 1960s, with a full crystallization of various measures facilitating the global operations of U.S. firms and the globalization of markets in the 1980s, and continuing vigorously into the 1990s. The International Investment Survey Act of 1976, the implementation of International Banking Facilities in 1981, the various deregulations and liberalizations of the financial sector in the 1980s, and the implementation of global standards in the 1990s, are but the best-known landmarks in this microhistory.

Furthermore, the new types of cross-border collaborations among specialized government agencies concerned with a growing range of issues emerging from the globalization of capital markets and the new trade order are yet another aspect of this participation by the state in the implementation of a global economic system. A good example is the heightened interaction in the last three or four years among competition policy regulators from a large number of countries. This has been a period of reinvigorated work on competition policy because economic globalization puts pressure on governments to work toward convergence, given the diversity of laws affecting competition and enforcement practices (Portnoy 2000). This convergence around specific issues of competition policy can coexist with ongoing, often enormous differences among the countries involved when it comes to laws and regulations affecting components of their economies that do not intersect with globalization. There are numerous other instances of this highly specialized type of convergence: regulatory issues concerning telecommunications, finance, the Internet, and so on.

It is, then, a very partial type of convergence. But regulators of different countries often begin to share more with each other than they do with colleagues in their home bureaucracies.

What is of particular interest here is that today we see a sharp increase in the work of establishing convergence.[12] We can clearly identify a new phase in the last ten years. In some sectors there has long been an often elementary convergence, or at least a coordination of standards. For instance, central bankers have long interacted with one another across borders, but today we see an intensification in those transactions, which becomes necessary in the effort to develop and extend a global capital market. And the increase of cross-border trade has brought with it a sharpened need for convergence in standards, as is evident in the vast proliferation of regulatory standards issued by the International Standards Organization (ISO).

Although this strategic geography of globalization is partly embedded in national territories, this embedding does not necessarily mean that existing national regulatory frameworks can regulate those functions. Two trends are evident, one recognized, the other not. Much attention has been devoted to the trend for regulatory functions to increasingly shift toward a set of emerging or newly invigorated cross-border regulatory networks and the development of an array of standards by which to organize world trade and global finance. Specialized, often semi-autonomous regulatory agencies and the specialized cross-border networks they are forming are taking over functions once encased in national legal frameworks, and standards are replacing rules in international law. The question for research and theory is whether this mode of regulation is sufficient and whether state participation may emerge again as a more significant factor for the ultimate workability of some of the new regulatory regimes. The second trend, discussed below, is that the state participates in this new regulatory apparatus, but only under very specific conditions.

NATIONAL STATES IN THE GLOBAL ECONOMY: DENATIONALIZED PARTICIPATION

The representation of economic globalization in the two preceding sections of this chapter is quite different from many of the standard accounts. For the purposes of this discussion, two of the features of globalization discussed above are especially significant. One feature is that the global economy needs to be produced, reproduced, serviced, and financed. It is not simply a heightening of interdependence or a function of the power of multinational corporations and financial markets. Rather, it takes a vast array of highly complex functions to ensure its existence. These have become so specialized that they can no longer be contained in the functions of corporate headquarters. Global cities are strategic sites for the production of these specialized functions to run and coordinate the global economy. Inevitably located in national territories, global cities are the organizational and institutional space for the major dynamics of denationalization. Although such processes of denationalization—for instance, certain aspects of financial and investment deregulation—are institutional and not geographic, the geographic location of many of the strategic institutions—financial markets and financial services firms—means that these processes are embedded geographically. The second feature, partly connected to the first, is that the global economy to a large extent materializes in national territories. Its topography moves between digital space and national territories. This movement requires a particular set of negotiations, one that has the effect of leaving the geographic boundaries of the national state's territory unaltered but transforms the institutional encasements of that geographic fact—that is, the state's territorial jurisdiction or, more abstractly, its exclusive territoriality. The work of states in producing part of the technical and legal infrastructure for economic globalization has involved a change in both the exclusivity of state authority and the composition of the work of states.

Economic globalization entails a set of practices that destabilizes another set of practices—that is, some of the practices that have come to constitute national state sovereignty. Implementing today's global economic system in the context of national territorial sovereignty has required multiple policy, analytic, and narrative negotiations. These negotiations have typically been summarized or coded as "deregulation." Yet there is much more going on in these negotiations than the concept of deregulation captures. The encounter of a global actor—a firm or market—with one or another instantiation of the national state can be thought of as a new frontier. It is not merely a dividing line between the national economy and the global economy. It is a zone in which politico-economic interactions produce new institutional forms and alter some of the old ones. Nor is it just a matter of reducing regulations. For instance, in many countries the need for autonomous central banks in the current global economic system has required a thickening of regulations in order to delink central banks from the influence of the executive branch of government and from deeply "national" political agendas.

The sociological literature on the state has mostly not focused on state work in the implementation of a global corporate economy. But it has made important contributions to the analysis of state work in the implementation of markets. Many of those contributions are useful in beginning to develop the necessary sociological categories. Existing research on state capacity has theorized the structural underpinnings of the ability of the state to *intervene* in social and economic life (Skocpol 1979; Skocpol and Finegold 1982; Skocpol 1985; Evans 1995; see also Block 1977). As explicit intervention has become delegitimated and states have "submitted" to the necessities of market logics, it has become unclear whether this conceptualization can fully explain the role of the state in contemporary economic life. From this perspective the contemporary state can be little more than a tool for the organization of interests of the ruling class: the autonomy of the state has evaporated as economic actors have become stronger. However, ongoing research in economic sociology has advanced a modified view of the relationship between states and markets, one that is more capable of theorizing the specific functionalities of the contemporary state. Rather than assuming a mutual externality or dualism of state and economy, authors of this research have argued that states play a constitutive role in market formation; hence states do not only "intervene" in markets and the economy (Block 1994). Moreover, markets and their "needs" and "logics" do not exist in complete autonomy from the state but are embedded in the institutional structure and stability provided by the state (Fligstein 2001). The safeguarding of private property, the enforcement of contracts, and so on, depend on the existence of a legitimate public authority. The determination of such rules and structures comprises a distinctly political project. These functions are provided by states but seem better conceptualized in terms of the provision of a secure environment for capital than in terms of the attainment of the specific state-defined goals that figure centrally in mainstream research on the state. Nevertheless, the kinds of capacities theorized by Skocpol and her followers remain critical; the state remains the primary executor of legitimate authority within territorial spaces. Hence the capacity of states to perform specific tasks, such as controlling inflation or enforcing contracts, constitutes the mechanics of the economic system. But the state must be seen as strategic in this system in two senses: not only because of its centralization of legitimate power and authority and resulting capacity to accomplish specific tasks, but also in its provision of an institutional location for the creation of an overarching framework for economic action (Jessop [1990] provides a way of thinking about this that is very different from Fligstein's.)

In my own research I have sought to address these issues by examining whether such state participation in constituting a global corporate economy actually produces a particular, perhaps novel, type of authority or power for specific state institutions. That is, state participation may raise the power of some state entities—for instance, central banks and ministries of finance—even as it sharply reduces the power of others, such as the welfare system. Skocpol (1985, 17) argues that state capacities may not be evenly distributed across different policy domains. In other words, as certain segments of government attain a higher level of organization than others, their relative capacity will vary. Although policy consequences are seen to

flow from this unevenness, the sources of the structural unevenness of internal state development have been relatively unex-
plored, as they are presumed to result from changes in the
structural conditions underlying state autonomy. Weiss (1998)
provides some tools for theorizing about these differences by
arguing that specific capacities are developed in order to address specific tasks or problem areas. Unevenness, therefore, results not only from the relative power of the state and society
but also from the types of problems facing the state and society
(Weiss 1998, 9–10). The form of the state, or the development
of its specific capacities, depends more on the development of a
state's function than on its structure. It is continually emergent
and recomposed as specific state organizations engage with
changing problem situations. I have found that the weight of
both national and foreign private interests in this specific work
of the state becomes constitutive of novel state capacities and a
new type of state authority, a hybrid that is neither fully private nor fully public (Sassen 2006a, chaps. 4 and 5). One possible interpretation is that we are seeing the incipient formation
of a type of state authority and practice that entails a partial denationalizing of the national state.

This conceptualization also introduces a twist in the analysis of private authority because it seeks to detect the presence of
private agendas inside the state or, in other words, inside a domain represented as public. However, because it emphasizes
the privatization of norm-making capacities and the enactment
of those norms in the public domain, it differs from an older
scholarly tradition on the captured state that focused on the co-
optation of states by private actors. Likewise, it differs from the
tradition that would analyze the emergence of an autonomous

class of state managers (Skocpol and Finegold 1982), thus seeing public policy in terms of the actions of this quasi-public group with its own private interests. (It is important to note that these writers are well aware that state managers have only an autonomous influence in specific conjunctures.) The combination of an articulated set of interests of state elites and the successful reproduction of their control of state power constitutes an important mechanism of path dependencies resulting from the development of specific capacities, forms of expertise, or cognitive constraints built into "policy paradigms" (for example, Peter A. Hall 1989; Hall and Soskice 2001; Dobbin 1994). These path dependencies may limit the mutability of state capacity. But here I am less concerned with the specific public and private interests controlling components of state power than with the projects embodied in, and the functions realized through the exercise of, state power. As the public functions of norm making and rule making become increasingly subordinated to technical standards that enable corporate globalization, we can observe the emergence of a substantively private agenda within the boundaries of a formally legitimate public authority. The articulation of this private agenda within the state does not depend solely on the formal representation of private interests. In this regard, then, my position is not comfortably subsumed under the proposition that nothing much has changed in terms of state power, nor can it be subsumed under the proposition of the declining significance of the state.

An important methodological assumption here is that focusing on economic globalization can help us disentangle some of these issues precisely because in strengthening the legitimacy of claims by foreign investors and firms, economic globalization adds to and renders visible the work of accommodating their rights and contracts in what remain basically national economies. The state is a strategic site for globalization not only in the sense of embodying the capacities to accomplish particular goals because of its centralization of coercive power but also in the sense of providing a domain in which "strategies" of collective action may be articulated (Jessop 1990). *Strategy* here refers not only to the action of individuals or collective subjects but also to the many ways in which collective action may be coordinated: what will be impermissible, how benefits will be distributed, and so on. Jessop (1990) develops this notion in terms of "strategies of accumulation." These strategies manifest themselves not in any one particular policy but as the coherence of a set of policies; it is through examination of these manifestations that one may uncover the more general strategies in this case, concerning foreign capital. However, these dynamics can also be present when privatization and deregulation concern native firms and investors, even though in much of the world privatization and deregulation have been constituted through the entry of foreign investors and firms.

The discussion thus far suggests that some of the key features of economic globalization allow for a broader range of forms of state participation than is generally recognized in analyses of the declining significance of the state. Peter Hall and David Soskice (2004), for instance, find significant competitive possibilities in social democratic states, thus undermining common claims that there is no alternative to market-structured social relations. There are at least two distinct issues here. One is that the current condition, marked by the ascendancy of private authority, is but one possible mode of several in which the state could be articulated. Hence entities such as the Schumpeterian workfare state (Jessop 1990), the competition state (Cerny 1990), and so on, should be thought of only as tendencies within contemporary development and not as necessary outcomes or predictions. The other issue is that the current condition leaves room for new forms of participation by the state as well as new forms of cross-border state collaboration in the governing of the global economy (see, for example, Aman 1995, 1998). Among them are forms of state participation aimed at recognizing the legitimacy of claims for greater social justice and democratic accountability in the global economy, although both would require administrative and legal innovations.[13] The effort here, then, is not so much to show the enormous power and authority amassed by global markets and firms but to detect the particular ways in which the power and authority of the state can and do shape and reshape those forms of private economic power. A key implication is that in the context of economic globalization a new type of state authority may well arise out of such particular instances and that it could also be used for non-corporate aims.

A distinct angle from which to view some of these issues is brought up by the new digital capabilities of the global corporate world, which are generally seen as escaping state jurisdictions and hence providing a sort of counterfactual argument to the one developed thus far, which emphasizes state powers.

Digital Networks, State Authority, and Politics

The rapid proliferation of global computer-based networks and the digitization of a broad array of economic and political activities enabling them to circulate in these networks raise questions about the effectiveness of current framings for state authority and democratic participation.[14] In a context of multiple partial and specific changes linked to globalization, these forms of digitization have enabled the ascendancy of subnational scales, such as the global city, and supranational scales, such as global markets, where before the national scale was dominant. The critical issue in this section arises from the fact that these rescalings do not always parallel existing formalizations of state authority. As I have discussed, today's rescaling dynamics cut across institutional size and the institutional encasements of territory and authority produced by the formation of national states (Taylor 2000; Ruggie 1993; Robinson 2004). At its most general these developments raise a number of questions about their impact on the regulatory capacities of states and their potential for undermining state authority as it has come to be constituted over the last two centuries. More analytically, we might ask whether these developments signal new types of imbrications of authority and place.

These questions can be explored by focusing on how digitization has enabled the strengthening of older non-state actors and spaces and the formation of novel ones capable of engaging the competence, scope, and exclusivity of state authority. The particular empirical cases discussed here are global finance and electronic cross-border activism, in both of which digitization has been transformative. To some extent these cases are overdetermined in that they entail multiple causalities and contingencies. By focusing on digitization, I do not mean to posit a single causality. On the contrary, digitization is deeply caught up with other dynamics that often shape its development and uses; in some cases it is completely derivative, a mere instrumentality of the other dynamics in play, and in some cases it is constitutive of new domains (Benkler 2006). One key assumption is that understanding the imbrications of digitization and politico-economic processes requires recognizing the embeddedness of digital space and resisting purely technological readings of the technical capacities involved.

This section develops these issues through an examination of three dynamics. The first is the relationship between state authority and the Internet, a necessary introduction to a subject weighed down by assumptions about the built-in capacities of the Internet to override existing relations of law to place, notably the much-noted fact that firms, individuals, and NGOs can elude government control when operating in cyberspace. The second is the relationship between state authority and the global capital market, particularly in regard to the fact that this market is not only largely electronic and de facto supranational but also enormously powerful. The third, to be examined in Chapter Seven, is the formation of types of global politics that run through the specificities of localized concerns and struggles yet can be seen as expanding democratic participation beyond state boundaries. I regard these politics as noncosmopolitan versions of global politics, a view that in many ways raises questions about the relation of law to place that are opposite those raised by global finance. My effort in the next sections is to map a conceptual problematic rather than to provide all the answers.

State Regulation and the Internet

The condition of the Internet as a decentralized network of networks has contributed to strong notions about its built-in autonomy from state power and its capacity to enhance democracy from the bottom up by strengthening both market dynamics and access by civil society.[15] At the core of the Internet are so-called Internet exchanges, national backbone networks, regional networks, and local networks, all of which are often privately owned. On October 24, 1995, the U.S. Federal Networking Council made the following resolution concerning the definition of the term *Internet:*

> "Internet" refers to the global information system that (i) is logically linked together by a globally unique address space based on the Internet Protocol (IP) or its subsequent extensions/follow-ons; (ii) is able to support communications using the Transmission Control Protocol/Internet Protocol (TCP/IP) or its subsequent extensions/follow-ons, and/or other IP-compatible protocols; and (iii) provides, uses, or makes accessible, either publicly or privately, high level services layered on the communications and related infrastructures described herein.[16]

Thus whereas in principle many of the key features of the Internet do indeed have this capacity to enhance democracy and openness, its technology also suggests possibilities for significant control and the imposition of limitations on access.

Although it is certainly the case that in many ways the Net escapes or overrides most conventional jurisdictions (Post 1995; Rogers 2004), this fact does not necessarily imply the absence of regulation and/or control. Much of the literature on this issue operates at two very different levels. One is a generalized set of notions that is still rooted in the earlier emphasis on the Internet as a decentralized space in which no authority structures can be instituted. The other is a rapidly growing technical literature, in good part stimulated by the growing importance of Internet addresses and the system of registering domain names, along with the associated legal and political issues those have engendered. A fact too often left out of the generalized commentaries on the Internet is that at least three factors constitute a de facto management of the Internet. The first is government authority through technical and operational standard-setting for both hardware and software. The second is the growing power of large corporate interests in shaping the growing orientation of the Internet toward privatizing capabilities. And the third is a kind of central authority that has long overseen some of the crucial features of the Internet having to do with addresses and numbers-granting and the system of domain names. These three conditions do not signal that regulation is ipso facto possible. They merely signal that the representation of the Net as escaping all authority or oversight is inadequate (Goldsmith and Wu 2006; Mueller 2004).

Boyle (1997), among others, has examined how the built-in set of standards that constitute the Internet undermines claims that the state cannot regulate it. Indeed, he argues that the state's regulatory agenda is already partially contained in the design of the technologies. Thus the state can regulate the Internet in this case even though it does not do so via sanctions. Boyle in fact alerts us to the fact that privatized and technologically based rule enforcement would take policing away from the scrutiny of public law, freeing states from some of the constitutional and other constraints restricting their options. Such absence of constraints on state action can be problematic even in the case of states that operate under the rule of law, as examples of abuse of power by various government agencies in the United States make clear.[17]

The second de facto "regulatory" condition is the power of private corporate interests in shaping the activity space of the Internet. In this shaping lies a kind of control. It makes clear that the question of democratic governance of the Internet goes far deeper than the types of bodies set up to govern it. Beyond governance, the actors shaping the development of the Internet diverge sharply, ranging from the original group of computer scientists who developed the open and decentralized features of the Internet to multinational corporations concerned with the protection of intellectual property rights. Most recently there has been a strengthening of civic and political groups concerned with the extent to which private corporate interests are shaping Internet access and development. One of the most radical critiques comes from Lovink (2003), who finds that the original open Internet culture has lost its capacity to enable civil society full access and that the only way forward is via a new culture. (See also Thierer and Crews 2003.)

One central issue that captures these divergent interests is that Internet software development since the mid-1990s has focused on firewalled intranets for firms, firewalled tunnels for firm-to-firm transactions, identity verification, trademark protection, and billing. The rapid multiplication of this type of software and its growing use on the Internet overall reduce the publicness of the Net and risk orienting much of the capability represented by the Internet toward corporate and, more broadly, commercial interests. This trend is especially significant if there is less production of software aimed at strengthening the openness and decentralization of the Internet, as was the case in the Internet's earlier phases. Since 1995–1996 political and technical developments have brought about what may be interpreted as an increase in controls (Lessig 1999; Dean et al. 2006). Prior to 1995 users could more easily maintain their anonymity while online and it was difficult to verify users' identity, thereby ensuring better protection of privacy. The architecture of the Internet inhibited "zoning"—any technique that facilitates discrimination in access to or distribution of some good or service.[18] Since then, with the drive to facilitate e-commerce, the situation has changed: the architecture of the Internet now facilitates zoning.[19] These conditions inevitably play a role in current efforts at Internet governance.

The third element constituting a de facto management of the Internet is the existence of an originally informal and now increasingly formalized central authority governing the Internet's key functions.[20] The nature of this authority is not necessarily akin to that of a regulatory authority but it is a gatekeeping system of sorts and raises the possibility of oversight capacities that will increasingly demand considerable innovation in our concept of what constitutes regulation.[21] The establishment of the Internet Corporation for Assigned Names and Numbers (ICANN) in the summer of 1998, now the group charged with overseeing the Net's address system, represents a formalization of the earlier authority.[22] It was basically started as a group of insiders with fairly loose and ineffective bylaws. By early 1999, it had implemented conflict-of-interest rules, opened up some board meetings to the public, and worked toward developing a mechanism to elect board members in an effort to build in more accountability.[23] Setting up ICANN has by no means solved all problems,[24] and ICANN is today the subject of growing debate among various digital sub-cultures, many of which see ICANN as a deeply undemocratic regulatory apparatus largely dominated by U.S. interests, notably large corporations.[25] (See Klein 2004; Siochru et al. 2002.)

What I want to emphasize here is that these trends signal the existence of Internet management. Perhaps more important, they show us the necessity for, as we might say, fair governance if we are to ensure that public interest issues also shape Internet development. Market forces alone will not ensure that the Internet contributes to the strengthening of democratic institutions, as many a commentator has assured us. As the Internet has grown, become more international, and gained in economic importance, there appears to be growing concern that a more organized and more accountable system is needed.

The debate about the Internet is somewhat divided on the question of whether it can be governed at all.[26] Simplifying what is a partially overlapping set of positions, one might say that for some the Internet is an entity that can be subjected to a governance mechanism, whereas for others there is no such entity but rather a decentralized network of networks that at best can lend itself to the coordination of standards and rules. Among those who consider the Internet a single entity, much of the concern has focused on the establishment of a system of property rights and other such protections and the means for enforcing them. The disagreement has centered on how to administer and enforce such a system. For some (for example, Foster 1996) it would be necessary to attach such a system to a multilateral organization, notably the International Telecommunication Union or the World Intellectual Property Organization, precisely because there is no global trademark law, only national law, whereas the Internet is a global entity. This arrangement would ensure recognition by member governments. For others, however, the mechanisms for governance would come from the institutions of the Internet itself. Gould (1996), for example, argues that there is no need for outside institutions to be brought in but contends that Internet practices could produce a sort of constitutional governance pertaining exclusively to the realm of the Internet. A third type of proposal was developed by Mathiason and Kuhlman (1998), who suggest the need for an international framework convention agreed on by governments; such a framework convention could parallel the UN framework Convention on Climate Change.

On the other hand, those experts who consider that there is no such entity as the Internet, but only a decentralized network of networks, argue that there is no need for any external regulation or coordination. Furthermore, the decentralized nature of the system would make external regulation ineffective. But there tends to be agreement with the proponents of governance as to the need for a framework for establishing a system of property rights. Gillett and Kapor (1996) argue for the functionality of diffused coordination mechanisms; furthermore, the authority of such coordination, they posit, could be more easily legitimated in distributed network environments like the Internet than in more traditional settings, and increasingly so given a stakeholder community that is becoming global. Mueller (1998) strongly argues against both an Internet regulatory agenda and the policing of trademark rights. He is critical of the very notion of the term *governance* when it comes to internetworking, as it is the opposite of what ought to be the purpose, which is that of facilitating internetworking. He argues that too much debate and effort have focused on restricting the ability to internetwork (see also Mueller 2004).

In what is at this time one of the most systematic examinations of the various perspectives, Pare (2003) argues that neither approach offers much insight into the processes actually shaping the governance trajectory of the Internet; he focuses particularly on the addressing system. Nor can these approaches account for the operational structures of the organizations currently responsible for managing the core functions of internetworking (at both the national and international levels) or the likelihood of their survival.[27] One important issue is the role of the actual features of the technology in shaping some of the possibilities or forms of governance or coordination (Pare 2003, chap. 5; Latham and Sassen 2005; Rogers 2004; Mueller 2004). Transnational electronic networks create a set of jurisdictions different from those of territorially based states. Hence there is little purpose in trying to replicate territorially based regulatory forms for the Internet. One possibility is that various dimensions of internetworking, including Internet addressing, could be governed by decentralized emergent laws that eventually could converge in common standards for mutual coordination. For authors emphasizing the technology question, the Internet is a regulated environment, given the standards and constraints built into the hardware and software. Thus Reidenberg (1996) agrees that the Internet undermines territorially based regulatory governance. But new models and sources of rules have been, and continue to be, created out of the technical standards and their capacity to establish default boundary rules that impose order in network environments (see also Lessig 1999; Goldsmith and Wu 2006). Technical standards can be used as instruments of public policy, and in this regard Reidenberg (1998) posits the emergence of a *lex informatica*. For those of us working on the global economy today, this viewpoint is clearly reminiscent of the older *lex mercatoria*, a concept that is now being revived in the context of economic globalization and privatization.

The public-access Internet is only one portion of the vast new world of digital space, and in my reading, much of the power to undermine or destabilize state authority attributed to the Internet actually comes from the existence of private dedicated digital networks, such as those used in wholesale global finance. To this I turn now.

Distinguishing Public-access and Private Digital Space

Many assertions about digital dynamics and potentials actually involve processes happening in a type of private digital space that is radically different from the public-access Internet (whether free or for a fee). I consider this a serious though fairly common confusion. Most wholesale financial activity and other significant digital economic activities take place in private digital networks.[28] This is a type of private space that, at one end, can include privatized Internet spaces such as firewalled sites and tunnels and, at the other, dedicated networks.

Private digital networks make possible forms of power other than the distributed power we associate with public digital networks. The financial markets illustrate this possibility well. The three properties of electronic networks—decentralization, simultaneity, and interconnectivity—have produced sharp increases in the orders of magnitude of the global capital market.

In a narrow technical sense we can interpret such increases as an outcome similar to the sharp increase in the number of transactions individuals can have in a given amount of time using the Internet compared with what might be the case with other technologies, such as faxing. However, given that digital networks dedicated to financial activities are embedded in a specific social field—the financial sector—the result of these technical features is increased capital concentration rather than increased distribution. At the same time, the limits of the context are set by the transformative impact of digitization on the sector itself: more instability and risk.

One of the key outcomes of digitization for finance has been the jump in orders of magnitude. There are basically three ways in which digitization has contributed to this outcome. The first is in the use of sophisticated software, a key feature of the global financial markets today and a condition that in turn has made possible an enormous amount of innovation. It has raised the level of liquidity and has increased the possibilities for liquefying forms of wealth hitherto considered nonliquid.[29] Such liquefying can require enormously complex instruments; the possibility of using computers not only facilitated the development of those instruments but also enabled their widespread use insofar as much of the complexity could be contained in the software. The second way in which digitization has affected finance lies in the features of digital networks that maximize the implications of global-market integration by producing the possibility of simultaneous interconnected flows and transactions. Since the late 1980s, a growing number of financial centers have become globally integrated as countries have deregulated their economies. This nondigital condition has increased the impact of the digitization of markets and instruments.

Third, because finance involves transactions rather than simply the flow of money, the particular technical properties of digital networks have assumed added meaning because the number of transactions that can be executed within a given time frame can be multiplied with every additional participant. Elsewhere I have examined organizational complexity as a key variable allowing firms to maximize the utility or benefits they can derive from digital technology (Sassen 2001, 115–16); in the case of financial markets, complex instruments can have that same effect (Sassen 2006a, chap. 7).

The combination of these conditions has contributed to the distinctive position of the global capital market regarding other components of economic globalization. One indicator is the actual monetary values involved; another, though more difficult to measure, is the growing weight of financial criteria in economic transactions, sometimes referred to as the financialization of the economy. From 1980 to 1995, the period that launches a new global phase, the total stock of financial assets increased three times faster than the aggregate gross domestic product (GDP) of the twenty-three most highly developed countries that formed the Organisation for Economic Cooperation and Development (OECD) for much of that period, and the volume of trading in currencies, bonds, and equities increased about five times faster (Woodall 1995). This aggregate GDP stood at $30 trillion at the end of the 1990s, whereas the worldwide value of internationally traded derivatives was over $65 trillion. By 2004, that value had risen to $290 trillion. To put these figures in perspective, it is helpful to compare them to the value of other major components of the global economy, such as the value of cross-border trade (approximately $11 trillion in 2004) and global foreign direct investment stock ($8 trillion in 2004). Foreign exchange transactions were ten times as large as world trade in 1983 but seventy times larger in 1999 and over eighty times larger by 2003 even though world trade had itself grown sharply over that period.[30]

In brief, the deregulation of domestic financial markets and the global integration of a growing number of financial centers, computers, and telecommunications technologies have contributed to an explosive growth in financial markets.[31] The high degree of interconnectivity in combination with instantaneous transmission signals the potential for exponential growth.[32] The increase in volume per se may be secondary in many regards. But when the volume can be deployed—for instance, to overwhelm national central banks, as happened in 1994 in Mexico and in 1997 in Thailand—then the fact of the volume itself becomes a significant variable. Furthermore, when globally integrated electronic markets could enable investors to rapidly withdraw well over $100 billion from a few countries in Southeast Asia in the 1997–1998 crisis and the foreign currency markets had the orders of magnitude to alter exchange rates radically for some of those currencies, the fact of digitization emerged as a significant variable that went beyond its technical features.

These conditions raise a number of questions concerning the impact of this concentration of capital in global markets which allow for high degrees of circulation in and out of countries (see Sassen 2006a, chap. 5, for a discussion). Does the global capital

market now have the power to "discipline" national governments—that is, to subject at least some monetary and fiscal
policies to financial criteria—whereas in the preceding period
it could not quite do so? How does such a power affect national
economies and government policies more generally? Does it alter the functioning of democratic governments? Does this kind
of concentration of capital reshape the accountability relation
that has operated through electoral politics between governments and their people? Does it affect national sovereignty?
And finally, do these changes reposition states and the interstate system in the broader world of cross-border relations? The
responses to these questions vary, with some scholars finding
that in the end the national state still exercises the ultimate authority in these matters (Helleiner 1999) and others seeing an
emergent power gaining at least partial ascendancy over national states (Panitch 1996).

If the formation of a global capital market represents a concentration of power that is capable of influencing national governments' economic policy and by extension other policies, one
of the key issues concerns norms. In my reading, today's global
financial markets are not only capable of deploying raw power
but also have produced a logic that becomes integrated into national public policy and sets the criteria for "proper" economic
policy.[33] The operational logic of the capital market contains
criteria for what leading private interests today consider sound
financial policy, and these criteria have been constructed
as norms for important aspects of national economic policy
making going far beyond the financial sector as such. This dynamic has become evident in a growing number of countries as
they became integrated in the global financial markets. For

many the norms have been imposed from the outside. As has been said often, some states are more sovereign than others in these matters.[34] Some of the more familiar elements that have become norms of "sound economic policy" include the new importance attached to the autonomy of central banks, anti-inflation policies, exchange-rate parity, and the variety of items usually referred to as IMF conditionality.[35]

Digitization of financial markets and instruments played a crucial role in raising the orders of magnitude of the global capital market, the extent of its cross-border integration, and hence its raw power. Yet this process was shaped by interests and logics that typically had little to do with digitization per se, even though it was crucial. This analysis makes clear the extent to which these digitized markets are embedded in complex institutional settings. In addition, while the raw power achieved by the capital markets through digitization facilitated the institutionalizing of certain finance-dominated economic criteria in national policy, digitization alone could not have achieved this policy outcome.

One crucial implication of this particular type of embeddedness of global finance is that the supranational electronic market space, which operates in part outside any government's exclusive jurisdiction, is actually only one type of space for this digitized industry. The other type of space is marked by the thick environments of actual financial centers, places in which national laws continue to be operative, albeit often in profoundly altered forms. The embeddedness of private economic electronic space entails the formation of massive concentrations of infrastructure, not just worldwide dispersal, and a complex interaction between digitization and more situated transactions, which are much more subject to direct state authority. The notion of global cities captures this particular embeddedness of global finance in actual financial centers.[36] In the case of private digital spaces such as those described here for global finance, this embeddedness carries significant implications for theory and politics, specifically, for the conditions through which governments and citizens can act on this new electronic world.

In brief, the private digital space of global finance intersects in at least two specific ways with the world of state authority and law. One is through the introduction of new types of norms, those reflective of the operational logic of the global capital market, into national state policy. The other is through the partial embeddedness of even the most digitized financial markets in actual financial centers, an intersection that in part returns global finance to the world of national governments. Global digitized finance makes legible some of the complex and novel imbrications of law and place and the fact that it is not simply an overriding of national state authority. It consists, rather, of both the use of that authority for the implementation of regulations and laws that respond to the interests of global finance *and* the renewed weight of that authority in the case of financial centers.

Chapter Four
THE GLOBAL CITY: RECOVERING PLACE AND SOCIAL PRACTICES

THE MASTER IMAGES in the currently dominant account of economic globalization emphasize hypermobility, global communications, and the neutralization of place and distance. There is a tendency to take the existence of a global economic system as a given, a function of the power of transnational corporations and global communications. This emphasis brings to the fore both the power and the technical attributes of the global corporate economy. A sociological inquiry needs to go beyond givens and attributes. It needs to examine the making of these conditions and the consequences of this making.

The capabilities for global operation, coordination, and control contained in the new information technologies and in the power of transnational corporations need to be produced. By focusing on the production of these capabilities, we add a neglected dimension to the familiar issue of the power of large corporations and the new technologies. The emphasis shifts to the practices that constitute what we call economic globalization and global control: the work of producing and reproducing the organization and management of both a global production system and a global marketplace for finance under conditions of economic concentration. A focus on practices draws the categories of place and production process into the analysis of economic globalization. These are two categories easily overlooked in accounts centered on the hypermobility of capital and the power of transnationals. Developing categories such as place and production process (even in finance) does not negate the centrality of hypermobility and power. Rather, these categories bring to the fore the fact that many of the resources necessary for global economic activities are not hypermobile and are indeed deeply embedded in places such as global cities and export-processing zones, and so are many global work-processes.

Why is it important to recover place and production in analyses of the global economy, particularly as they are constituted in major cities? It is because they allow us to see the multiplicity of economies and work cultures in which the global information economy is embedded. They also allow us to recover the concrete, localized processes through which globalization takes shape and to argue that much of the multiculturalism in large cities is as much a part of globalization as is international finance. Finally, focusing on cities allows us to specify a geography of strategic places at the global scale, places bound to one another by the dynamics of economic globalization. I refer to this as a new geography of centrality, and one of the questions it engenders is whether this new transnational geography is also the space for new transnational politics. Insofar as an economic analysis of the global city recovers the broad array of jobs and work cultures that are part of the global economy, though typically not marked as such, it allows us to examine the possibility of new forms of inequality arising from economic globalization. And it allows us to detect new types of politics among traditionally disadvantaged workers; that is, it allows us to understand in its empirical detail whether operating in this transnational economic geography as it materializes in global cities makes a difference to the disadvantaged. This politics of the disadvantaged would be a politics arising from economic participation in the global economy by those who hold the "other" jobs in that economy, whether factory workers in export-processing zones in Asia, workers in garment sweatshops in Los Angeles, or janitors on Wall Street.

The specific sociological question organizing the examination of these kinds of issues is whether we are actually seeing new social forms among old social conditions. Thus power, capital mobility, economic and political disadvantage, homelessness, gangs—all existed long before the current phase of globalization. But are the types of power, mobility, inequality, homelessness, professional classes and households, gangs, and politics that we saw emerge in the 1980s sufficiently distinct from those of the past that they are actually novel social forms even though in a general sense they look the same as they always have? My argument is that many are indeed new social forms because they arise out of the specificity of the current phase. Thus the empirical details of these social forms are also a window into the features of the current globalization phase.

These are the subjects addressed in this chapter. The first section examines the possibility that the city, a complex type of place, has once again become a lens through which to examine major processes that unsettle existing arrangements. The second section examines the role of place and production in analyses of the global economy. Based on this recovery of place-based activities in a global economy, the third section posits the formation of new cross-border geographies of centrality and marginality constituted by these processes of globalization. Returning to the consequences of these processes for the specific types of places involved in these geographies, the fourth section discusses some of the elements that suggest the formation of a new sociospatial order in global cities. The fifth section examines particular localizations of the global by focusing on immigrant women in global cities. The final section considers the global city as a nexus where these various trends come together and produce new political alignments.

THE CITY: ITS RETURN AS A LENS FOR SOCIAL THEORY

The city has long been a strategic site for the exploration of many major subjects confronting society and sociology. But it has not always been a heuristic space—a space capable of producing knowledge about some of the major transformations of an epoch. In the first half of the twentieth century the study of cities was at the heart of sociology. This is evident in the work of Georg Simmel, Max Weber, Walter Benjamin, and most prominently, the Chicago school, especially Robert Park and Louis Wirth, both deeply influenced by German sociology; and, though writing later, Henri Lefebvre. These sociologists confronted massive processes—industrialization, urbanization, alienation—in a new cultural formation they called urbanity. For them studying the city was not simply about studying the urban. It was about studying the major social processes of an era. Since then the study of the city, and with it urban sociology, have gradually lost their privileged roles as lenses through which to view the discipline and as producers of key analytic categories. There are many reasons for this change, most important among which are the particular developments of method and data in sociology in general. Critical is the fact that the city ceased serving as the fulcrum for epochal transformations and hence as a strategic site for research on nonurban processes. Urban sociology became increasingly concerned with what came to be called social problems.

Today, as we begin a new century, the city is once again emerging as a strategic site for understanding some of the major new trends reconfiguring the social order. The city, together with the metropolitan region, is one of the spaces where major macrosocial trends materialize and hence can be constituted as an object of study. Among these trends are globalization, the rise of the new information technologies, the intensification of transnational and translocal dynamics, and the strengthened presence and voice of specific types of sociocultural diversity. Each of these trends has its specific conditionalities, content, and consequences. The urban moment is but one moment in a number of often complex multisited trajectories, and this raises an important question: can the sociological study of cities produce scholarship and analytic tools that help us understand the broader social transformations under way today, as it did early in the preceding century? One critical issue here is whether these larger transformations evince sufficiently complex and multivalent urban instantiations to allow us to construct such instantiations as objects of study. The urban moment of a major process is susceptible to empirical study in ways that other phases of such a process might not: The financial center is more concrete than electronic capital flows.

At the same time this partial urbanization of major dynamics repositions the city itself as an object of study: what is it we are naming today when we use the construct of the city? The city has long been a debatable construct, whether in early writings (Castells 1977; Harvey 1982) or in very recent work

(Brenner 1998; Lloyd 2005; Paddison 2001; Drainville 2004; Satler 2006). Today we are seeing a partial unbundling of national space and the traditional hierarchies of scale centered on the national, with the city nested somewhere between the local and the region. This unbundling, even if partial, makes conceptualizing the city as nested in such hierarchies problematic. Major cities have historically been nodes where a variety of processes intersect in particularly pronounced concentrations. In the context of globalization many of these processes are operating at a global scale that cuts across historical borders, with the added complexities that brings with it.

Cities emerge as one territorial or scalar moment in a transurban dynamic.[1] The city here is not a bounded unit but a complex structure that can articulate a variety of cross-boundary processes and reconstitute them as a partly urban condition (Sassen 2001). Furthermore, this type of city cannot be located simply in a scalar hierarchy that puts it below the national, regional, and global. It is one of the spaces *of* the global, and it engages the global directly, often bypassing the national. Some cities may have had this capacity long before the current era, but today these conditions have been multiplied and amplified to the point where they can be read as contributing to a qualitatively different urban era.

Social theorists (for example, Giddens 1990; Taylor 1996; Brenner 1998, 2004; Beck 2006; Robinson 2004) have examined the "embedded statism" that has marked the social sciences generally and has become one obstacle to a theorization of the global through some of these issues. At the heart of embedded statism is the explicit or implicit assumption that the nation-state is the container of social processes. To this I add two features already discussed in Chapter Three: the implied correspondence of national territory with the national and the associated implication that the national and the nonnational are mutually exclusive conditions. These various assumptions work well for many of the subjects studied in the social sciences. But they are not helpful in elucidating a growing number of situations when it comes to globalization and a variety of transnational processes now being studied by social scientists. Nor are they helpful for developing the requisite research techniques. Furthermore, as argued in Chapter Three, although they describe conditions that have held for a long time—throughout much of the history of the modern state since World War I and in some cases for even longer—we are now seeing their partial unbundling. This partial unbundling of the national has significant implications for our analysis and theorization of major social transformations, such as globalization, and the possibility of focusing on the city to get at some of the critical empirical features of these major transformations. And it has significant implications for the city as an object of study.

Pivoting theorization and research on the city is one way of cutting across embedded statism and recovering the rescaling of spatial hierarchies that is under way. Interest in the city as a site for research on major contemporary dynamics is evident in numerous disciplines, each with its own analytic tools. The traditional tools of sociology and social theory, including urban sociology, can accommodate only some aspects of these trends. The exception is an early generation (for example, Castells 1989; Rodriguez and Feagin 1986; Gottdiener 1985; Timberlake 1985; Chase-Dunn 1984; King 1990; Zukin 1991;

Sassen-Koob 1982, 1984—to cite but a few) of what is today a small but rapidly growing sociological scholarship that has explicitly sought to theorize these new conditions and specify them empirically. Traditionally other branches of sociology have used the urban moment to construct their object of research even when it is nonurban. This is especially so because cities are also sites where major trends interact with one another in distinct, often complex manners in a way they do not in most other settings. Today all of this holds also for studying the global in its urban localizations.[2]

Besides the challenge of overcoming embedded statism, there is the challenge of recovering place in the context of globalization, telecommunications, and the proliferation of transnational and translocal dynamics. It is perhaps one of the ironies at the start of a new century that some of the old questions of the early Chicago school of urban sociology should resurface as promising and strategic to an understanding of certain critical issues today. One might ask whether the methods of those scholars (Park and Burgess, 1925; Suttles 1968; see also Duncan 1959) might be of particular use in recovering the category of place at a time when dominant forces such as globalization and telecommunications seem to signal that place and the details of the local no longer matter. Robert Park and the Chicago school conceived of "natural areas" as geographic areas determined by unplanned subcultural forces. This was an urban sociology that used fieldwork within a framework of human ecology and contributed many rich studies mapping detailed distributions and assuming functional complementarity among the diverse "natural areas" these sociologists identified in Chicago.[3]

Yet the old categories are not enough.[4] Some of the major conditions in cities today, including the urban moment of nonurban dynamics, challenge mainstream forms of theorization and urban empirical analysis. Fieldwork is a necessary step in capturing many of the new aspects of the urban condition, including those having to do with the major trends this chapter focuses on. But assuming complementarity or functionalism brings us back to the notion of the city as a bounded space rather than one site, albeit a strategic one, where multiple transboundary processes intersect and produce distinct sociospatial formations. Recovering place can be met only partially using the research techniques of the old Chicago school of urban sociology (see, for example, the debate in Dear et al. 2002; Soja 2000; Dear 2002; see also David A. Smith 1995). I do think we need to return to some of the depth of engagement with urban areas that the Chicago school achieved and the effort to produce detailed mappings. The type of ethnographies done by Duneier (1999), Talmadge Wright (1997), Lloyd 2005, Klinenberg 2002, Small 2004, and Burawoy et al. (2000) and the type of spatial analysis developed by Sampson and Raudenbush (2004) are excellent examples, as they use many of the same techniques yet work within a different set of framing assumptions.

But that is only part of the challenge of recovering place. Recovering place means recovering the multiplicity of presences in this landscape. The large city of today has emerged as a strategic site for a range of new types of operations—political, economic, "cultural," and subjective (Elijah Anderson 1990; Lloyd 2005; Abu-Lughod 1994; Miles 2003; Yuval-Davis 1999; Clark and Hoffmann-Matinot 1998; Nashashibi

2007; Allen, Massey, and Pryke 1999; Fincher and Jacobs 1998; Krause and Petro 2003; Bartlett 2007; Hagedorn 2006). It is one of the nexuses where new claims materialize and assume concrete forms. The loss of power at the national level produces the possibility for new forms of power and politics at the subnational level. Furthermore, insofar as the national as container of social process and power is cracked (for example, Taylor 1995; Sachar 1990; Garcia 2002; Parsa and Keivani 2002), it opens up possibilities for a geography of politics that links subnational spaces across borders. Cities are foremost in this new geography. One question the new geographies engender is whether we are seeing the formation of a new type of transnational politics that localizes in these cities.

Immigration, for instance, is one major process through which a new transnational political economy is being constituted, both at the macro level of global labor markets and at the micro level of translocal household survival strategies. It is still largely embedded in major cities insofar as most immigrants, certainly in the developed world, whether in the United States, Japan, or western Europe, are concentrated in major cities (Castles and Miller 2003; Bhachu 1985; Iredale et al. 2002; Tsuda 1998), although moving to smaller cities and suburbs is a second major pattern (Light 2006; Buntin, n.d.). For some scholars (Castles and Miller 2003; Sassen 1998, pt. 1; Ehrenreich and Hochschild 2003; Skeldon 1997; Samers 2002), immigration is one of the constitutive processes of globalization today, even though it is not recognized or represented as such in mainstream accounts of the global economy. The city is one of the key sites for the empirical study of these transnational flows and household strategies.

Global capital and the new immigrant workforce are two major instances of transnationalized actors with features that constitute each as a somewhat unitary actor overriding borders, but often in contestation with each other inside cities (Sassen 1998, chap. 1; Ehrenreich and Hochschild 2003; see also, for example, Bonilla et al. 1998; Cordero-Guzman, Smith, and Grosfoguel 2001). Researching and theorizing these issues require approaches that diverge from those of the more traditional studies of political elites, local party politics, neighborhood associations, immigrant communities, and others, through which the political landscape of cities and metropolitan regions has traditionally been conceptualized in sociology.

Place and Production in the Global Economy

Globalization can be deconstructed in terms of the strategic sites where global processes and the links that bind them materialize, as was already indicated in Chapters Two and Three. Among these sites are export-processing zones, offshore banking centers, and on a far more complex level, global cities. These sites produce specific geographies of globalization and underline the extent to which these do not encompass the entire world.[5] They are, furthermore, changing geographies that have been transformed over the last few centuries and over the last few decades.[6] Most recently these changing geographies have come to include electronic space.

The overall geography of globalization contains dynamics of spatial dispersal and centralization, the second only recently recognized (e.g., Friedmann 1986; Sassen 1984).[7] The evidence shows that under specific conditions the massive spatial dispersal of economic activities at the metropolitan, national, and global levels we associate with globalization has actually contributed to new forms of territorial centralization of top-level management and control operations (Sassen 1991, 2001). The spatial dispersal of economic activity made possible by telematics contributes to an expansion of territorially centralized functions if this dispersal is to take place under the continuing concentration in corporate control, ownership, and profit appropriation that characterizes the current economic system.[8] National and global markets, as well as globally integrated organizations, require central places where the work of globalization gets done.[9] Elsewhere (Sassen 2006a, chaps. 5 and 7) I have developed a thesis about finance today as being increasingly transaction-intensive and hence as raising the importance of financial centers because they contain the capabilities for managing this transactivity precisely at a time when the centers assume whole new features, given digitization. Furthermore, information industries require a vast physical infrastructure containing strategic nodes with a hyperconcentration of facilities; we need to distinguish between the capacity for global transmission and communications and the material conditions that make this capacity possible. Also, the most advanced information industries have a production process that is at least partially bound to place because of the combination of resources that process requires even when the outputs are hypermobile. Finally, the vast new economic topography that is being implemented through electronic space is one moment, one fragment, of an even vaster space or economic chain in good part embedded in nonelectronic spaces. There is no fully dematerialized firm or industry. Even the most advanced information industries, such as finance, are only partially installed in electronic space. And so are industries that produce digital products, such as software design. The growing digitization of economic activities has not eliminated the need for major international business and financial centers, or for Silicon Valleys, and all the material resources they concentrate, from state-of-the-art telematics infrastructure to brain talent (Castells 1989; Graham and Marvin 1996; Sassen 1984; 2006a, chaps. 5, 7, and 8).

In order to recover the infrastructure of activities, firms, and jobs that is necessary to run the advanced corporate economy, including its globalized sectors, in my research I have conceptualized cities as production sites for the leading information industries of our time.[10] These industries are typically conceptualized in terms of the hypermobility of their outputs and the high levels of expertise of their professionals rather than in terms of the production process involved and the requisite infrastructure of facilities and nonexpert jobs that are also part of these industries. A detailed analysis of service-based urban economies shows that there is a considerable articulation of firms, sectors, and workers that may appear to have little connection to an urban economy dominated by finance and specialized services but in fact fulfill a series of functions that are an integral part of that economy. They do so, however, under conditions of sharp social, earning, and often racial or ethnic segmentation (Sassen 2001, chaps. 8 and 9). In the day-to-day work of the leading complex of services dominated by finance, a great many of the jobs are low paying and manual, many of them held by women and immigrants. Although these types of jobs and workers are never represented as part of the global economy, they are in fact part of the infrastructure of the jobs involved in running and implementing the global economic system, including such an advanced form as international finance.[11] The top end of the corporate economy—the corporate towers that project engineering expertise, precision, *techne*—is far easier to mark as necessary for an advanced economic system than are truckers and other industrial service workers, even though those workers are a necessary ingredient.[12] We see here a dynamic of valorization at work that has sharply increased the distance between the devalorized and the valorized—indeed, the overvalorized—sectors of the economy.

For me as a sociologist, addressing these issues has meant working in several systems of representation and constructing spaces of intersection. There are analytic moments when two systems of representation intersect. Such moments are easily experienced as spaces of silence, of absence. One challenge is to see what happens in those spaces or what operations—of analysis, power, or meaning—take place there. One version of these spaces of intersection is what I have called analytic borderlands (Sassen 1998, chap. 1; 2006a, chap. 8). Why borderlands? Because they are spaces that are constituted in terms of discontinuities—discontinuities are here given a terrain rather than reduced to a dividing line. Much of my work on economic globalization and cities has focused on these discontinuities and has sought to reconstitute them analytically as borderlands rather than dividing lines. This perspective produces a terrain within which these discontinuities can be reconstituted in terms of economic operations whose properties are not merely a function of the spaces on each side (that is, a reduction to the condition of dividing line) but also, and most centrally, are a function of the discontinuity itself, the argument being that discontinuities are an integral part, a component, of the economic system.

A NEW GEOGRAPHY OF CENTERS AND MARGINS

The ascendancy of information industries and the growth of a global economy, two inextricably linked conditions, have contributed to a new geography of centrality and marginality. This geography partially reproduces existing inequalities but is also the outcome of a dynamic specific to current forms of economic growth. It assumes many forms and operates in many arenas, from the distribution of telecommunications facilities to the structure of both the economy and employment. Global cities accumulate immense concentrations of economic power, whereas cities that were once major manufacturing centers suffer inordinate declines; downtowns and business centers in metropolitan areas receive massive investments in real estate and telecommunications while low-income urban and metropolitan areas are starved for resources; highly educated workers in the corporate sector see their income rise to unusually high levels while low- or medium-skilled workers see theirs sink. Financial services produce superprofits while industrial services barely survive.[13]

The most powerful of the new geographies of centrality at the global level bind the major international financial and business centers: New York, London, Tokyo, Paris, Frankfurt, Zürich, Amsterdam, Los Angeles, Toronto, Sydney, and Hong Kong, among others. But this geography now also includes cities such as Bangkok, Taipei, São Paulo, and Mexico City. The intensity of transactions among these cities, particularly in the financial markets, trade in services, and investment, has increased sharply, and so have the orders of magnitude involved (for example, Sassen 2006b, chap. 2; Taylor 2004).[14] At the same time there has been a sharpening inequality in the concentration of strategic resources and activities in each of these cities compared with that of other cities in the same countries.[15] Alongside these new global and regional networks of cities is a vast territory that has become increasingly peripheral and increasingly excluded from the major economic processes that are seen as fueling economic growth in the global economy. Formerly important manufacturing centers and port cities have lost functions and are in decline, not only in the less-developed countries but also in the most advanced economies. Similarly, in the valuation of labor inputs, the overvalorization of specialized services and professional workers has marked many of the "other" types of economic activities and workers as unnecessary or irrelevant to an advanced economy.

There are other forms of this segmented marking of what is and what is not an instance of the new global economy. For example, the mainstream account of globalization recognizes that there is an international professional class of workers and highly internationalized business environments due to the presence of foreign firms and personnel. What has not been recognized is the possibility that we are seeing an internationalized labor market for low-wage manual and service workers or that there is an internationalized business environment in many immigrant communities. These processes continue to be couched in terms of immigration, a narrative rooted in an earlier historical period. This suggests that there are instances of the global or the transnational that have not been recognized as such or are contested. Among them is the question of immigration, as well as the multiplicity of work environments it contributes to large cities, often subsumed under the notions of the ethnic economy and the informal economy. Much of what we still narrate in the language of immigration and ethnicity, I would argue, is actually a series of processes having to do with, first, the globalization of economic activity, cultural activity, and identity formation and, second, the increasingly marked racialization of labor-market segmentation. Thus those components of the production process in the advanced global information economy taking place in immigrant work environments are components not recognized as part of that global information economy. Immigration and ethnicity are constituted as otherness. Understanding them as a set of processes whereby global elements are localized, international labor markets are constituted, and cultures from all over the world are de- and reterritorialized, puts them right there at the center, along with the internationalization of capital, as a fundamental aspect of globalization (see Chapter Five).

How have these new processes of valorization and devalorization and the inequalities they produce come about? This is the subject addressed in the next section.

Elements of a New Sociospatial Order

The implantation of global processes in major cities has meant that the internationalized sector of the urban economy has expanded sharply and has imposed a new set of criteria for valuing or pricing various economic activities and outcomes. This trend has had devastating effects on large sectors of the urban economy. It is not simply a quantitative transformation; we see here the elements of a new economic regime and its sociospatial expressions. This regime assumes distinct forms in the spatial organization of the urban economy, the structures for social reproduction, and the organization of the labor process. In these trends towards multiple forms of polarization lie conditions for the creation of employment-centered urban poverty and marginality and for new class formations.

The ascendancy of the specialized-services-led economy, particularly the new finance and corporate services complex, engenders what may be regarded as a new economic regime because although this sector may account for only a fraction of the economy of a city, it imposes itself on that larger economy. One of these pressures is toward polarization, as is the case with the possibility for superprofits in finance or in high-end real-estate development, which contributes to the devalorization of manufacturing, low-value-added services, and mid-income housing construction, insofar as these sectors cannot generate superprofits. The superprofit-making capacity of many of the leading industries is embedded in a complex combination of new trends: technologies that make possible the hypermobility of capital at a global scale and the deregulation of multiple markets that allows for implementing that hypermobility; financial inventions such as securitization, which liquefies hitherto illiquid capital and allows it to circulate and hence make additional profits. The increasing complexity and specialization of the corporate services involved have contributed to their valorization, as illustrated in the unusually high salary increases beginning in the 1980s for top-level professionals. Globalization further adds to the complexity of these services, their strategic character, and their glamour, and therewith to their overvalorization.

The presence of a critical mass of firms with extremely high profit-making capabilities contributes to the bidding up of the prices of commercial space, industrial services, and other business needs, thereby making the survival of firms with moderate profit-making capabilities increasingly precarious. And whereas these firms are essential to the operation of the urban economy and the daily needs of a city, their economic viability is threatened in a situation in which finance and specialized services can earn superprofits. High prices and high profit levels in the internationalized sector and its ancillary businesses, such as top-of-the-line restaurants and hotels, make it increasingly difficult for other sectors to compete for space and investments. Many of those other sectors have experienced considerable downgrading and/or displacement—for example, modest neighborhood shops being replaced by upscale boutiques and restaurants catering to the new high-income urban elite.

Inequality in the profit-making capabilities of different sectors of the economy has always existed. But what we see happening today takes place on another order of magnitude and is engendering massive distortions in the operations of various markets, including housing and labor. For example, the income polarization among firms and among households contributes, in my reading (Sassen 2001, chap. 9), to the informalization of a growing array of economic activities in advanced urban economies. When firms with low or modest profit-making capacities experience an ongoing, if not increasing, demand for their goods and services from households and firms in a city in which a significant sector of the economy makes superprofits, they often cannot compete even though there is an effective demand for what they produce. Operating informally is often one of the few ways in which such firms can survive—for example, by using space not zoned for commercial or manufacturing uses, such as a basement in a residential area, or space that is not up to code in terms of health, fire, and other workplace standards. Similarly, new firms in low-profit industries entering a strong market for their goods and services may be able to do so only informally. Another option for firms with limited profit-making capabilities is to subcontract part of their work to informal operations.[16] The recomposition of the sources of growth and profit making entailed by these transformations also contributes to a reorga-nization of some components of social reproduction or consumption. The rapid growth of industries with strong concentrations of high- and low-income jobs has assumed distinct forms in the consumption structure, which in turn has a feedback effect on the organization of work and the types of jobs being created. The expansion of the high-income workforce in conjunction with the emergence of new cultural forms has led to a process of high-income gentrification that rests, in the last analysis, on the availability of a vast supply of low-wage workers. In turn, the consumption needs of the low-income population in large cities are partially met by manufacturing and retail establishments which are small, rely on family labor, and often fail to meet minimum safety and health standards. Cheap, locally produced sweatshop garments, for example, can compete with low-cost Asian imports. A growing range of products and services, from low-cost furniture made in basements to "gypsy cabs" and family day care, is available to meet the demand for the growing low-income population. In short, while the middle strata still constitute the majority, the conditions that contributed to their expansion and politico-economic power in the postwar decades—the centrality of mass production and mass consumption in economic growth and profit realization—have been displaced by new sources of growth. This replacement is at its sharpest in global cities.

We can think of these development as constituting new geographies of centrality that cut across the old divide between poor and rich countries, and as constituting new geographies of marginality that have become increasingly evident not only in the less developed world but also within highly developed countries. In major cities in both the developed and the developing world we see a new geography of centers and margins that not only contributes to strengthening existing inequalities but also sets in motion a series of new dynamics of inequality. The new types of informalization evident in global cities are one such new dynamic (Venkatesh 2006; Buechler 2007). We can conceptualize informalization in advanced urban economies today as the systemic equivalent of what we call deregulation at the top of the economy (see Sassen 1998, chap. 8). Both the deregulation of a growing number of leading information industries and the informalization of a growing number of sectors with low profit-making capacities can be conceptualized as adjustments under conditions in which new economic developments and old regulations enter in growing tension.[17] "Regulatory fractures" is one concept I have used to capture this condition and not reduce it to notions of crime and violation.

The Localizations of the Global

Economic globalization, then, needs to be understood in its multiple localizations rather than only in terms of the broad, overarching macro-level processes that dominate the mainstream account. Furthermore, we need to see that some localizations do not generally get coded as part of the global economy. Here I want to focus on both recognized and on overlooked localizations of the global. The global city is one strategic instantiation of multiple localizations. Many of these localizations are embedded in the demographic transition evident in cities, where a majority of the resident workers are immigrants and/or women, often women of color. These cities are seeing an expansion of low-wage jobs that do not fit the master images of globalization yet are part of it. The fact that these jobs are largely held by immigrants, minoritized citizens, and disadvantaged women adds to their invisibility and contributes to the devalorization of this type of worker and work culture, and to the "legitimacy" of that devalorization.

This devaluing of workers in growth sectors is a rupture of the traditional dynamic whereby membership in leading economic sectors contributes to the empowerment of workers, a process long evident in Western industrialized economies. Women and immigrants come to replace the Fordist family-wage category of women and children (Sassen 1998, chap. 5; Ehrenreich and Hochschild 2003; Parreñas 2002).[18] Economic restructuring in global cities, one of the localizations of global dynamics, has generated a large growth in the demand for low-wage workers and for jobs that offer few possibilities of advancement. Women and immigrants emerge as the labor supply that facilitates the imposition of low-wages and powerlessness under conditions of high demand for those workers and the location of those jobs in high-growth sectors. It breaks the historic nexus that would have led to empowering workers and legitimates the break culturally. This is occurring amid an explosion in the wealth and power concentrated in global cities—that is, under conditions in which there is also a visible expansion in high-income jobs.

Another localization of this devaluing, one rarely associated with globalization, is informalization as discussed earlier. It reintroduces the community and the household as important economic spaces in global cities. In this setting informalization is the low-cost—and often feminized—equivalent of deregulation at the top of the system. As with deregulation (for example, financial deregulation), informalization introduces flexibility, reduces the "burdens" of regulation, and lowers costs—in this case, the costs of labor and workplace standards in particular. Informalization in major cities of highly developed countries (whether New York, London, Paris, or Berlin) can be seen as the downgrading of a variety of activities for which there is an effective demand. Informalization also brings with it a devaluing and enormous competition among poor workers, given low entry costs and few alternative forms of employment. Going informal is one way of producing and distributing goods and services at a lower cost and with greater flexibility. Immigrants and women, both important actors in the new informal economies of global cities, absorb the costs of informalization (see Sassen 1998, chap. 8; Buechler 2007).

The reconfiguration of economic spaces associated with globalization in major cities has had differential effects on women and men, male and female work cultures, and male- and female-centered forms of power and empowerment. The restructuring of the labor market brings with it a shift of labor-market functions to the household or the community. Women and households emerge as sites that should be part of the theorization of the particular social forms produced by these economic dynamics. In contrast, Fordism and mass production generally moved paid work away from women and households. Notwithstanding their many negative features, these transformations contain possibilities, even if limited, for the autonomy and empowerment of women. For instance, we might ask whether the growth of informalization in advanced urban economies reconfigures some economic relationships between men and women. With informalization the neighborhood and the household reemerge as sites for economic activity. This condition has its own dynamic possibilities for women. Economic downgrading through informalization creates "opportunities" for low-income female entrepreneurs and workers and therewith reconfigures some of the work and household hierarchies that women find themselves in, particularly for immigrant women from countries with rather traditional male-centered cultures. There is a large literature showing that immigrant women's paid work and their improved access to other public realms affect their gender relations (Fernandez-Kelly and Shefner 2005; Kofman et al. 2000; Ribas-Mateos 2005).

Immigrant women gain greater relative personal autonomy and independence while men lose ground. They gain more control over budgeting and other domestic decisions and greater leverage in requesting that men help with domestic chores. Besides the relatively greater empowerment of women in the household associated with waged employment, there is a second important outcome: their greater participation in the public sphere and their possible emergence as public actors. They are the ones in the family who access public services. This gives them a chance to become incorporated into the mainstream society and be the ones who mediate between the household and the state. There are two public arenas in which immigrant women are active: institutions for public and private assistance and the immigrant or ethnic community (Chinchilla and Hamilton 2001). For example, Hondagneu-Sotelo (1994) found that immigrant women come to assume more active public and social roles, further reinforcing their status in the household and the settlement process. Women are more active than men in community building and community activism, and they are positioned differently from men with regard to the broader economy and the state (Moghadan 2005). They are most likely the ones who deal with the legal vulnerability of the family in the process of seeking public and social services. This greater participation by women suggests the possibility that they may emerge as more forceful and visible actors. There is, to some extent, a joining of two dynamics in the condition of these segments of the low-income female workforce in global cities. On the one hand they are constituted as an invisible and disempowered class of workers in the service of the strategic sectors of the global economy (Ehrenreich and Hochschild 2003). This invisibility keeps them from emerging as whatever would be the contemporary equivalent of the "labor aristocracy" of earlier forms of economic organization, in which a low-wage worker's position in leading sectors had the effect of empowering that worker (it allowed for the possibility of unionizing). On the other hand the access to (albeit low) wages and salaries, the growing feminization of the job supply, and the growing feminization of business opportunities as a consequence of informalization alter the gender hierarchies in which women find themselves (Buechler 2007).[19]

It is likely that some women benefit more than others from these circumstances; we need more research to establish the impact of class, education, and income on these gendered outcomes (see, for example, Chesney-Lind and Hagedorn 1999).

THE GLOBAL CITY: A NEXUS FOR NEW POLITICO-ECONOMIC ALIGNMENTS

What makes the processes described above strategic, even though they involve powerless and often invisible workers, is that these global cities are also the strategic sites for the valorization of the new forms of global corporate capital, as described in the first section of this chapter. Typically the analysis of the globalization of the economy privileges the reconstitution of capital as an internationalized presence; it emphasizes the vanguard character of this reconstitution. At the same time it remains absolutely silent about another crucial element of transnationalization, one that some, like me, see as the counterpart of capital: the transnationalization of labor beyond top-level professionals. We are still using the language of immigration to describe low-wage transnational workers.[20] That analysis also overlooks the transnationalization in the formation of identities and loyalties among various population segments that explicitly reject the imagined community of the nation.

With this rejection come new solidarities and notions of membership. Major cities have emerged as strategic sites for both the transnationalization of labor and the formation of transnational identities. In this regard, they form a site for new types of politics, including new kinds of transnational politics.

Cities are the terrain on which people from many countries are most likely to meet and a multiplicity of cultures can come together. The international character of major cities lies not only in their telecommunications infrastructure and international firms; it lies also in the many cultural environments in which their workers exist. One can no longer think of centers of international business and finance simply in terms of their corporate towers and their corporate culture. The large Western city of today concentrates diversity. Its spaces are inscribed with the dominant corporate culture but also with a multiplicity of other cultures and identities. The slippage is evident: the dominant culture can encompass only part of the city.[21] And while corporate power inscribes these cultures and identities with "otherness," thereby devaluing them, they are present everywhere. For example, through immigration a proliferation of originally highly localized cultures has become a presence in many large cities. An immense array of cultures from around the world, each rooted in a particular country or village, is now reterritorialized in a few places, such as New York, Los Angeles, Paris, London, Amsterdam, and most recently, Tokyo.[22] Today's global cities are in part the spaces of postcolonialism and indeed contain conditions for the formation of a postcolonialist discourse (see, for example, Stuart Hall 1991; King 1990; Ribas-Mateos 2005; Tsuda 1999).[23]

Immigration and ethnicity are too often constituted as otherness. Understanding them as a set of processes whereby global elements are localized, international labor markets are constituted, and cultures from all over the world are deterritorialized, puts them right there at centerstage, along with the internationalization of capital, as a fundamental aspect of globalization today. Furthermore, this way of narrating the migration events of the postwar era captures the ongoing weight of colonialism and postcolonial forms of empire on major processes of globalization today, specifically those binding emigration and immigration countries (see Chapter Five). While the specific genesis and content of their responsibility will vary from case to case and period to period, none of the major immigration countries are innocent bystanders: their past as colonial powers in many of today's emigration countries lives on (Sassen 1988, 1999c). The centrality of global cities in immigration, including their role as a postcolonial frontier, engenders a transnational economic and political opening in the formation of new claims by immigrants and minoritized citizens (Hamilton and Chinchilla 2001; Farrer 2007; Stasiulis and Yuval-Davis 1995). Global cities have emerged as a site for claims by both global capital, which uses the city as an "organizational commodity," and disadvantaged sectors of the urban population, which are frequently as internationalized a presence in large cities as capital.

I see this as a type of political opening that contains unifying capacities across national boundaries and sharpening conflicts within those boundaries. Global capital and the new immigrant workforce are two major transnational categories, each with unifying properties internally and in contestation with each other in global cities. The leading sectors of corporate capital are now global in both their organization and their operations. And many of the disadvantaged workers in global cities are women, immigrants, and people of color, groups with a mostly troubled relation to the national state (Chatterjee 1993, chaps. 1, 6, and 7; Crenshaw et al. 1996; Geddes 2003; Schiffauer et al. 2006). The global city is a strategic site for their economic and political operations.

The linking of people to territory as constituted in global cities is less likely to be intermediated by the national state or the "national culture" than in other types of locations, such as suburbs or small towns. In global cities, the loosening of identities from their traditional sources, notably the nation or the village (Yaeger 1996; Nashashibi 2007), can engender new notions of community of membership and entitlement. Yet another way of thinking about the political implications of this strategic transnational space is the notion of the formation of new claims on that space. Economic globalization has partially shaped the formation of new claims, and thereby new entitlements, a process that is much clearer in the case of foreign firms than that of immigrants.[24]

Foreign firms and international businesspeople are among the new "city users" (Martinotti 1993) that have profoundly marked the urban landscape. Perhaps at the other extreme are those who use urban political violence to make their claims on the city, claims that lack the de facto legitimacy enjoyed by international businesspeople (Body-Gendrot 1999; Hagedorn 2006). These are claims made by actors struggling for recognition, entitlement, and their rights to the city.[25] There is something to be captured here: a distinction between powerlessness and the condition of being an actor or political subject even though one lacks power. I use the term *presence* to name this condition. In the context of a strategic space such as the global city, the types of disadvantaged people described here are not simply marginal; they acquire presence in a broader political process that escapes the boundaries of the formal polity. This presence signals the possibility of a politics. What that politics will be depends on the specific projects and practices of various communities (Drainville 2004; Bartlett 2007). Insofar as the sense of membership of these communities is not subsumed under the national, it may well signal the possibility of a transnational politics centered in concrete localities.

Conclusion

Large cities around the world are the terrain on which a multiplicity of globalization processes assume concrete, localized forms. These forms are in good part what globalization is about. If we consider further that a growing share of disadvantaged populations—immigrants in Europe and the United States, African Americans and Latinos in the United States, rural migrants in Asia, masses of shanty dwellers in the megacities of the developing world—are concentrated in large cities, then we can see that cities have become strategic spaces where a series of conflicts and contradictions take place. We can then think of cities also as one of the sites where the contradictions of the globalization of capital can play out. On the one hand large cities concentrate a disproportionate share of corporate power and are one of the key sites for the overvalorization of the corporate economy; on the other hand they concentrate a disproportionate share of the disadvantaged and are one of the key sites for their devalorization. This joint presence happens in a context where, first, the transnationalization of economies has grown sharply and cities have become increasingly strategic for global capital and, second, marginalized people have found their voice and are making their own claims on the city. This joint presence is further brought into focus by the sharpening of the distance between the two.

The enormity of the urban experience, the overwhelming presence of massive architectures and dense infrastructures, as well as the irresistible utility logics that organize much of the investments in today's cities, have produced displacement and estrangement among many individuals and whole communities. Such conditions unsettle older notions and experiences of the city generally and public space in particular. While the monumentalized public spaces of European cities remain vibrant sites for rituals and routines, for demonstrations and festivals, increasingly the overall sense is of a shift from civic to politicized urban space, with fragmentations along multiple differences.

The space constituted by the worldwide grid of global cities, a space with new economic and political potentialities, is perhaps one of the most strategic spaces for the formation of new types of politics, identities, and communities, including transnational ones. This is a space that is place-centered in that it is embedded in particular and strategic sites, and transterritorial in that it connects sites that are not geographically proximate yet are intensely connected to one another. It is not only the transmigration of capital that takes place on this global grid but also that of people, both rich (such as the new transnational professional workforce) and poor (most migrant workers), and it is a space for the transmigration of cultural forms, or the reterritorialization of "local" subcultures. An important question is whether it is also a space for a new politics, one going beyond the politics of culture and identity, though at least in part likely to be embedded in them. The analysis presented in this chapter suggests that it is.

The centrality of place in a context of global processes engenders a transnational economic and political opening in the formation of new claims and hence in the constitution of entitlements—notably, rights to place—and, ultimately in the constitution of new forms of "citizenship" and the diversifying of citizenship practices. The global city has emerged as a site for new claims: by global capital and the new city users, and by disadvantaged sectors of the urban population, frequently as internationalized a presence in large cities as the former. The denationalizing of urban space and the formation of new claims centered in transnational actors and involving contestation constitute the global city as a frontier zone for a new type of engagement.

Chapter Five
THE MAKING OF INTERNATIONAL MIGRATIONS

AS WITH THE STATE AND THE CITY, incorporating international migrations into a sociology of globalization entails engaging a vast scholarship that is not particularly focused on globalization.[1] Furthermore, it entails contesting a very different type of scholarship, as yet minor but growing fast, that seems to assume that we have immigrations because of globalization, an assumption it arrives at not through knowledge about migrations but by projecting standard globalization notions onto migration. While the first scholarship is a critical source of data and research techniques that need to be incorporated into sociological studies of globalization, the second is extremely problematic and to be avoided.

Cross-border migrations existed long before the current phase of globalization. Thus the task is to understand in what ways and under what conditions today's many migrations are or are not shaped by, grounded in, or merely inflected by globalization. The rich migration scholarship shows us, for instance, that transnational networks between sending and receiving countries were already part of many migration flows centuries ago. The content and modes of communications and transactions in the past may have differed sharply from today's, but the actual social fact was present in the past. Similarly, the scholarship finds that many features of past migrations, such as chain migration and family reunion, are present today.

Those facts raise several questions when it comes to migrations and globalization: In what ways might international migrations be part of globalization today, and might they be one of the constitutive processes? Furthermore, can an analysis of international migration illuminate and produce knowledge about globalization? Obversely, can an analysis of globalization illuminate and produce knowledge about international migration? For instance, might immigration research allow us to get at microstructures of globality, as indicated in the preceding chapter with the discussion of immigrant women in the global city? The presence of diverse immigrant communities brings postcolonial history out of the global South and into our cities and metropolitan areas. On the other hand, sociological research on globalization may give us details about various bridging dynamics as diverse as imaginaries shaped by the global entertainment industry or by work in offshore factories that make potential emigrants feel connected to the country they are aiming to go to. Such research can help establish whether and how globalization shortens the material and subjective distance between country of origin and country of destination.

Going Beyond Push-Pull Explanations

Economic and demographic analyses tend to explain the formation of international migrations in terms of push-pull factors. Among the leading push factors are poverty and unemployment, whereas leading pull factors are the possibilities of employment and better pay. In this sense, push-pull factors tend to refer to systemic conditions in a whole area or country. Given this scope, the presence of such push-pull factors should, strictly speaking, lead to massive out-migrations. But the evidence overwhelmingly shows that they do not. Thus push-pull factors may explain why some people move, but they cannot explain why a majority of people in similar conditions do not move. There are clearly additional variables at work. What sociology and anthropology can bring to an explanation of migration is a focus on those additional, perhaps less systemic variables, such as recruitment by employers or a household's decision that one of its members should emigrate. Push conditions, notably poverty, do matter, but the question should be: When does poverty *become* a push factor?

A focus on individuals is not sufficient either. Individuals may experience their migration as the outcome of a personal decision, but in large-scale migrations the option to migrate is itself socially produced. This fact is easily lost in much immigration analysis because immigration flows tend to share many characteristics: many immigrants do indeed come from less developed areas or countries and have low or medium levels of education and income, factors that have led to the notion that poverty and unemployment in general are what propel emigration. Yet many countries with extreme poverty and high unemployment lack any significant emigration history, and in others emigration is a recent event no matter how long-standing the poverty. It takes a number of other conditions to turn poverty into a push factor, and even then only a small minority of poor and middle-class people will likely attempt emigration. Emigration is not an undifferentiated escape from poverty and unemployment to prosperity.

The rationality of emigration is far more complex than push-pull explanations allow for. On the one hand subjective issues come into play. Critical is that many people have shown themselves willing to take undesirable jobs, including jobs below their educational and social stratum in their home country, and to live in extreme discomfort and under conditions they might not accept in their home country. There is, then, a subjectivity of the first-generation immigrant that needs to be factored in as one of the variables. On the other hand the bridging effects of globalization produce both material conditions and novel types of imaginaries that make emigration an option where not too long ago it was not.

Each country is unique, and each migration flow is produced by specific conditions in time and place (Appleyard 1999; Okuda 2000; Castles and Miller 2003; Robin Cohen 1995). But if we are to understand the possible effects of larger conditions, such as economic and cultural globalization, on the formation and reproduction of migration flows, we need to abstract from these particularities so as to examine more general tendencies. The emphasis should be on the specificity and complexity of migrations, as distinct from more general and simplified accounts. This emphasis entails assembling the variables that contribute to an explanation of the features of specific migration flows rather than generalizing for all times and places or particularizing every migration history. For instance, one condition that we now understand as significant is that constituted by former colonial bonds. Such bonds are shared by diverse countries and their particular migrations. Thus in Europe a majority of Algerian emigrants are in France, and a majority of subcontinental Indian emigrants are in the United King-

dom. More controversial, economic dominance and the formation of transnational spaces for economic activity associated
with the presence of U.S. firms overseas (Sassen 1988) are beginning to be recognized as factors explaining some of the migration patterns in the United States from countries as diverse
as Mexico or the Philippines. Similarly, U.S. direct or indirect
overseas military activity in Vietnam and El Salvador is clearly
a factor that conditioned some of the flows from those countries
into the United States in, respectively, the 1970s–1980s and
the 1980s–1990s (Portes and Rumbaut 2006).

Today the sharp growth in the organized export of workers,
both legal and illegal, adds another dynamic to the older, long-
standing ones. Organized exports can create whole new ways of
linking emigration and immigration countries, beyond old
colonial or new global economic links. Yet these new developments are also often linked to broader contextual conditions.
Thus older internal or regional trafficking networks are now
scaling up and becoming global; in that sense they are both
new and old. The formation of global systems has aided the upward scaling of what were often far more localized networks. It
has also induced the formation of new types of trafficking and
new flows, often as a response to the devastating effects of the
globalizing of the economies of poor countries or the development of massive tourism complexes in the global South.

Among the factors that may transform a general condition
of poverty and unemployment into a push for migration, we
can see several patterns (see explanations for different condi-
tionings in Battistella and Assis 1998; Wallace and Stola 2001;
Douglas S. Massey et al. 1993; Castles and Miller 2003; Parnreiter 1995; Papademetriou and Martin 1991). First, most mi-

grations have been *initiated* by direct recruitment by firms, governments, labor contractors, or traffickers. This pattern holds to a variable extent for different parts of the world and different historical periods. But once an immigrant community exists, the operation of the immigrant network tends to replace outside recruitment, and chain migration tends to set in. Second, recruitment by firms and governments typically takes place in countries with which there are preexisting linkages— colonial, neocolonial, military, or, increasingly, as part of economic globalization. Third, economic globalization has further strengthened the interdependence of a growing number of countries. It also may have contributed to the creation of new push factors in countries with already high levels of government debt by sharpening the debt and its negative impact on overall economic conditions through the imposition of structural adjustment programs. Fourth, there has been a significant increase in the organized export of workers beginning in the 1990s, particularly in the illegal international trade of migrants. (For sources on all four trends see Castles and Miller 2003; Portes and Rumbaut 2006; Cohen 1995; Battistella and Assis 1998.)

Three major trends detected in the issues discussed thus far may begin to articulate international migrations with critical global conditions. They are, first, the geoeconomics of international migrations, which explains the considerable degree of patterning evident in the migrations and provides the crucial context within which to understand the dynamic whereby an overall condition of poverty, unemployment, or underemployment can become activated as a migration push factor; second, the contemporary formation of mechanisms binding emigra-

tion and immigration countries, particularly mechanisms arising from economic globalization; and third, the organized legal
and illegal export of workers. I focus on these trends in the rest
of this chapter (see Sassen 1988, 1999c for sources).

THE GEOECONOMICS OF MIGRATION

It is important to note that some form of organized recruitment by employers or governments on behalf of employers often lies at the source of *new* immigration flows today, as it did
in the 1800s. But who recruits whom tends to be shaped by
prior politico-economic bonds—for example, colonialism or
current foreign investment and other cross-border operations
by firms in the context of economic globalization, as well as
today's multiplying global imaginaries. Eventually most migration flows gain a certain autonomy from the organized
recruitment mechanisms.

The large mass migrations of the 1800s emerged both as
part of and contributed to the formation of a transatlantic economic system binding several nation-states through economic
transactions and wars, particularly war-induced flows of people.
This transatlantic economy was at the core of the development
of the United States. Massive flows of capital, goods, and workers and specific structures produced this transatlantic system.
Before the nineteenth century, labor movements across the Atlantic had been largely forced—notably in the form of slavery
and mostly from colonized African and Asian territories. To
take another example, the migrations to England in the 1950s
originated in former British territories. And the migrations of
the 1960s and 1970s into western Europe occurred in a context
of direct recruitment and European regional dominance over

the Mediterranean and some eastern European countries. In brief, receiving countries have typically been participants in the processes leading to the formation of international migration.

The renewal of mass immigration to the United States in the 1960s, after five decades of little or no immigration, took place in a context of expanded U.S. economic and military activity in Asia and the Caribbean basin. The United States is at the heart of an international system of investment and production that binds these various regions together. In the 1960s and 1970s, the United States played a crucial role in the development of a world economic system; it passed legislation and promoted international agreements aimed at opening its own and other countries' economies to the flow of capital, goods, services, and information. This central military, political, and economic role contributed both to the creation of conditions that mobilized people in migrations, whether local or international, and to the formation of links with the United States that subsequently served as often-unintended bridges for international migration. (This bridging effect was most probably strengthened by the cold war context and the active ideological selling of the advantages of open democratic societies.) My, albeit controversial, interpretation is that these patterns show that measures commonly thought to deter emigration—foreign investment and the promotion of export-oriented growth in developing countries—seem to have had precisely the opposite effect, at least in the short and middle run (Sassen 1988, 1999c). Among the leading exporters of immigrants to the United States in the 1970s and 1980s were several of the newly industrialized countries of southern and Southeast Asia, whose extremely high growth rates are generally recognized as initially a result of foreign direct investment in export manufacturing. A parallel analysis of the "development" effect of the North American Free Trade Agreement (NAFTA) on Mexican emigration to the United States predicts ongoing emigration and eventual stabilization only thirty years after NAFTA's implementation (for example, Martin 1993, 2002).

The specific forms of internationalization of capital in the postwar period have contributed to the mobilization of migration streams and to the building of bridges between countries of origin and the United States. Long before the current phase of globalization, beginning in the 1960s, the implantation of Western development strategies was a factor generating emigration. The consequences of such development strategies led to the replacement of smallholder agriculture with export-oriented commercial agriculture, the Westernization of education systems, and other such outcomes. All of those outcomes in turn contributed to the mobilization of migration streams—regional, national, and transnational (Portes and Walton 1981; Safa 1995; Campos and Bonilla 1982; Bonilla et al. 1998; Portes and Bach 1985; Basch et al. 1994).

At the same time, the administrative commercial and developmental networks of the former European empires and the newer forms that those networks assumed under the Pax Americana and with the establishment of global systems (international direct foreign investment, export-processing zones, wars for democracy) have created bridges not only for the flow of capital, information, and high-level personnel from the center to the periphery but also for the flow of migrants. Stuart Hall (1991) describes the postwar influx of people from the British

Commonwealth into Great Britain and notes that a sense of England and Englishness was so pervasive in his native Jamaica as to make Jamaicans feel that London was the capital they were all headed to sooner or later. This narration of the migrations of the postwar era captures the ongoing weight of colonialism and postcolonial forms of empire on major processes of globalization today and, specifically, on those binding emigration and immigration countries. The major immigration countries are not passive bystanders; the specific genesis and content of their responsibility will vary from case to case and period to period.

On a more conceptual level one could generalize these tendencies and posit that immigration flows take place within systems and that these systems can be specified in a variety of ways (see, for example, Bustamante and Martinez 1979; Morokvasic 1984; Sassen 1988, 1999c; Bonilla et al. 1998; Potts 1990; King 2001; Ricca 1990). The economic specification developed here is but one of several possibilities. In other cases the system within which immigration takes place might be specified in political or ethnic terms. One could ask, for example, if there are systemic links underlying the current central and eastern European migrations to Germany and Austria (Sassen 1999c). Thus before World War II both Berlin and Vienna were major receivers of large migrations from a vast eastern region (Fassmann and Muenz 1994). Furthermore, those practices produced and reproduced migration systems as such. Finally, the aggressive cold war campaign showing the West as a place where economic well-being is the norm and well-paying jobs are easy to get had the effect of inducing westward migration; a more accurate portrayal of conditions in the West might have deterred potential migrants beyond those who were absolutely convinced and can be seen as constituting a pent-up demand—in other words, beyond those who would have migrated at all costs. These historical and current conditions contain elements for specifying the systems within which the current central and eastern European migrations to Germany and Austria take place.

The fact that there is a geoeconomics of migration is suggested by major immigration patterns. If immigration were simply a matter of policy and the will to enforce controls, then many of the current unauthorized flows should not exist (Massey 2005; Cornelius, Martin, and Hollifield 2003). In the case of the United States, the major reform passed in 1965 had an immense effect because it came at a time when the United States had a far-flung network of production sites and military operations in what eventually became emigration countries. There was not only a pent-up demand for emigration but also a broad network of links between those countries and the United States. That the new law alone was not enough to bring about the new immigration to the United States is also suggested by the fact that the new law, which was based on family reunion, was expected largely to induce the immigration of relatives of those already in the country—that is, mostly Europeans. Instead, the vast majority of immigrants came from the Caribbean basin and several Asian countries. This unexpected outcome points to the limits of policy in engendering or stopping migrations (Portes and Rumbaut 2006; Briggs 1992).

This geoeconomics of migration is brought to the fore by familiar patterns in Europe. For instance, in the United Kingdom 60 percent of the foreign residents are from Asian or

African countries that are former dominions or colonies. Until recently European immigration was rather low, with almost 75 percent from Ireland, also once a colonized territory. While the United Kingdom has few immigrants from Turkey and Yugoslavia, which provide the largest share to Germany, it has almost all of Europe's immigrants from the Indian subcontinent and from the English Caribbean. Continuing along these lines, in the first ten years after World War II the 8 million displaced ethnic Germans who resettled in Germany constituted the vast majority of "immigrants" to that country. Another major group was made up of the 3 million Germans who came from the German Democratic Republic before the Berlin Wall was erected in 1961. Almost all ethnic Germans went to Germany, and those who did not went overseas. These patterns of concentration have continued. By the 1990s, 86 percent of Greek immigrants in Europe were in Germany, as were 80 percent of Turkish immigrants and 76 percent of Yugoslavs before partition. Eventually Germany expanded its labor-recruitment, or sourcing, area to include Portugal, Algeria, Morocco, and Tunisia, even though the vast majority of immigrants from those countries reside in France. In brief, what we see in the case of Germany is initially a large migration rooted in a long history of domination over the eastern region and then an immigration originating in less developed countries following a by-now-classical dynamic of labor recruitment by the immigration country, thereby building a linkage that shapes particular countries as labor-exporting. Both the Netherlands and Belgium have received a significant number of immigrants from their former colonial empires and from countries such as Italy, Morocco, and Turkey that were marked as labor-exporting countries. Switzerland similarly received workers from traditionally labor-exporting countries: Italy, Spain, Portugal, Yugoslavia, and Turkey. All three labor-importing countries originally organized the recruitment of those workers, until eventually a somewhat autonomous set of flows was in place. Until recently, Sweden received 93 percent of Finnish immigrants in Europe. Also in Sweden, as in the other countries, there was a large expansion in the 1960s of the recruitment area to include workers from the traditionally labor-exporting countries of the Mediterranean. As a given labor-migration flow ages, it tends to become more diversified in terms of destination. This tendency suggests that a measure of autonomy from older colonial and neocolonial bonds sets in.

Patterning remains a feature even in today's European Union where residents have the right to cross-border mobility. EU figures for both the pre- and post-enlargement period show little cross-country migration among EU residents, going from 5 percent in 2003 to 5.5 percent in 2005 (Eurostat 2006); that 5 percent amounts to 25 million non-nationals (residents who are not citizens of the country where they live) living in the EU25. One would have expected far higher incidence of mobility given considerable variation in earnings levels across member states already before, and certainly after the 2004 enlargement of the Union which brought in poorer countries.

BUILDING BRIDGES

We can identify three major patterns among the variety of economic conditions that contribute to migration links between sending and receiving countries: links brought about by economic globalization, links specifically developed to recruit workers, and the legal and illegal organized export of workers. In this section I discuss the first two, in the next section I discuss the third.

Economic Links

Links created by economic internationalization range from the offshoring of production and the establishment of export-oriented agriculture through foreign investment to the weight of multinationals in the consumer markets of labor-exporting countries. For instance, the development of commercial agriculture and export-oriented standardized manufacturing has dislocated traditional economies and eliminated survival opportunities for small producers, who have been forced to become wage laborers. This transition has in turn contributed to the mobilization of displaced smallholders and crafts-based producers in labor migrations, migrations that initially may be internal but eventually can become international. There are numerous examples of this dynamic launching new cross-border migrations. Mahler (1995) found that Salvadoran immigrants in the United States often had prior experience as migrant workers on coffee plantations. Fernandez-Kelly (1982) found that some of the internal migrants in the northern industrialization zone of Mexico eventually immigrated to the United States. Campos and Bonilla (1982) found that the U.S.-sponsored Bootstraps Operation in Puerto Rico had a similar effect in promoting immigration to the United States.

Another type of economic link results from the large-scale development of manufacturing operations in low-wage countries by firms from highly developed countries. The aim here has been, and continues to be, to lower the cost of the production of goods meant for, and reexported to, markets in the home country. This offshoring creates a number of objective and subjective links between the highly developed countries and the low-wage countries. Two migration-inducing conditions are at work here. One is that the better-situated workers may gain access to the contacts for migration, and the second is that the most disadvantaged workers are often "used up" after a few years and then need to find new ways of surviving and helping their families, which may in turn lead to out-migration. Disadvantaged workers are partially in an extended or deterritorialized *local* labor market that connects the two countries involved (see Sassen 1988, 1995, for a full development of these issues). The growing use of offshore production to lower costs also contributes to the creation of conditions in the highly developed countries that may lead to the demand for and recruitment of low-wage immigrant workers, given the growing pressure among firms and countries to lower costs to remain competitive. The internationalization of both manufacturing production and agriculture has contributed to the weakening of unions and has generally led to the search for low-wage workers inside the developed countries.

The case of Japan is of interest here because it allows us to capture the intersection of economic internationalization and immigration in its inception, and to do so in a country whose history, culture, and to a lesser extent, economic organization are radically different from those of other advanced economies. Japan's lack of an immigration history in the high-growth postwar decades—though it had one in the 1800s—provides us with a sharp view of how an immigration can start where there was none before. Furthermore, it started in the 1980s, the start of the current global age. Though its advent was much later than that of most other advanced economies, Japan now has a growing workforce of unauthorized immigrants in low-wage, unskilled jobs, which Japanese workers reject (Tsuzuki 2000; Mori 1997). Why did immigration not occur during the period of extremely rapid economic growth, during the 1950s and 1960s, when Japan experienced very sharp labor shortages. The answer lies partially in the fact that in the 1980s Japan became a major presence in a regional Asian economic system: it became the leading investor, foreign-aid donor, and exporter of consumer goods (including cultural products). In the 1980s, Japanese firms began to set up a large number of manufacturing operations outside Japan, with a heavy concentration in other Asian countries. This expansion has created legal and illegal networks linking those countries and Japan, and made them into exporters of immigrants to Japan (Morita and Sassen 1994). In its period of rapid growth, Japan lacked the links with potential immigrant-exporting countries that could have facilitated the formation of international migration flows. As Japan internationalized its economy and became a key investor in South and Southeast Asia, it created—wittingly or not—a transnational space for the circulation of its goods, capital, and culture, which in turn created conditions for the circulation of people. A key factor was recruitment by organized crime syndicates and by the government (Sassen 2001, chaps. 8 and 9). We may be seeing the early stages of an international labor market, a market that both labor contractors and unauthorized immigrants can "step into." This space now includes professionals as well (Farrer 2007). The Japanese government also initiated the recruitment of Japanese descendants in Brazil and Peru, adjusting its immigration law to do so. These emergent immigrant communities have now entered the stage of chain migration (Tsuda 1999; Tsuzuki 2000).

Another type of link is shaped by the growing Westernization of advanced education systems (Portes and Walton 1981), which facilitates the movement of highly educated workers into the developed Western countries. This is a process that has been happening for many decades and is usually referred to as the brain drain. Today it assumes specific forms, given the growing interdependence among countries and the formation of global markets and global firms. That is, we are seeing the formation of an increasingly complex and flexible transnational labor market for high-level professionals in advanced corporate services that links a growing number of highly developed and developing countries (Sassen 2001; 2006a, chap. 6; see also Skeldon 1997), including through virtual migration (Aneesh 2006). This development is also occurring in the high-tech sector, where the firms of the highly developed countries are explicitly recruiting computer and software experts, especially from India. More generally we can capture these and other such dynamics in the strong trend for bimodal immigration in terms of education levels, with concentrations of low-wage, poorly educated workers and concentrations of highly educated workers.

Recruitment and Ethnic Networks

The second type of migration link includes a variety of mechanisms for the organized or informal recruitment of workers. This recruitment can operate through governments in the framework of a government-supported initiative by employers, it can operate directly through employers by illegally smuggling workers, or it can operate through kinship and family networks. Some of these mechanisms can also function as more generalized migration channels. Ethnic links established between communities of origin and communities of destination, typically via the formation of transnational households or broader kinship structures, emerge as crucial once a flow has been formed and serve to ensure its reproduction over time (Levitt 2001; Grasmuck and Pessar 1991; Basch, Schiller, and Blanc 1994; Wong 1996; Wallace and Stola 2001; White 1999; Farrer 2007). These recruitment and ethnic links tend to operate within the broader transnational spaces constituted by neocolonial processes and/or economic internationalization.

A key factor in the operation of ethnic and recruitment networks is the existence of an effective demand for immigrant workers in the receiving countries. The effective labor-market absorption of workers coming from different cultures with mostly lower levels of development arose as, and remains, an issue in the context of advanced service economies. Immigrants have a long history of getting hired to do low-wage jobs that require little education and are often situated in the least advanced sectors. Much analysis of postindustrial society and advanced economies generally posits a massive growth in the need for highly educated workers and little need for the types of jobs that a majority of immigrants have tended to hold. It suggests sharply reduced employment opportunities for workers with low levels of education in general and for immigrants in particular. Yet detailed empirical studies of major cities in highly developed countries show an ongoing demand for immigrant workers and a significant supply of old and new jobs requiring little education and paying low wages (Munger 2002; Harris 1995; Parrenas 2001, 2005). One current controversial issue is whether this job supply is merely or largely a residual partly inflated by the large supply of low-wage workers or mostly part of the reconfiguration of the job supply and employment relations that are in fact a feature of advanced service economies—that is, a systemic development that is an integral part of such economies. There are no precise measures, and a focus on the jobs by themselves will hardly illuminate the issue. The jobs pay low wages, require little education, are undesirable, with no advancement opportunities and often few if any fringe benefits. There are clearly some aspects of the growth dynamics in advanced service economies that are creating at least part of this job supply (Sassen 2001, chaps. 8 and 9; Munger 2002; Roulleau-Berger 2003), which is a crucial cog in the sets of links used and developed by co-ethnics and recruiters.

One condition in the reproduction of these links is that over the last few decades and, in some cases, over the last century, some countries have become marked as labor exporters. In many ways the labor-exporting country is put in a subordinate position and is continually represented in the media and in political discourse as a labor-exporting country. This was also the case in the last century, when some labor-exporting areas existed in conditions of economic subordination and often quasi-political subordination as well. The former Polish territories partitioned off to Germany constituted such a region, and they generated a significant migration of "ethnic" Poles to western Germany and beyond. It is also the case of the Irish in England.

And it is the case of Italy, which reproduced itself as a supplier of labor to the rest of Europe for over a century.

It does seem—and the history of economic development supports this assertion—that once an area becomes a significant emigration region, it does not easily catch up in terms of development with those areas that emerge as labor-importers. Precisely because the importers have high, or at least relatively high, rates of growth, a cumulative causation effect sets in, which amounts to an accumulation of advantage. Whether immigration contributes to the process of cumulative causation is a complex issue, though much scholarship shows that immigration countries have gained multiple benefits from access to immigrant labor in particular periods of high economic growth (Portes and Rumbaut 2006; Castles and Miller 2003). Furthermore, whether emigration contributes to the negative cumulative causation evident in exporting countries is also a complex matter. The evidence shows that individual households and localities may benefit but national economies do not. History suggests that the accumulation of advantage evident in receiving countries has tended to elude labor-exporting areas because they cannot catch up with, or are structurally excluded from, the actual spatialization of growth, precisely because it is characterized by uneven development. Italy and Ireland for two centuries were labor exporters, a fact that did not turn out to be a macroeconomic advantage. Their current economic dynamism and labor immigration have little to do with their history as emigration countries. Specific economic processes took hold, promoted by specific agents (Ireland's national state and Northern Italy's enterprises) and rapidly expanded each country's economy.

In brief, analytically we could argue that as today's labor-importing countries grew richer and more developed, they kept expanding their zones of recruitment or influence, covering a growing number of countries and including a variety of emigration-immigration dynamics, some rooted in past imperial conditions, others in the newer development asymmetries that underlie much migration today. There is a dynamic of inequality within which labor migrations are embedded that keeps on marking regions as labor exporting or labor importing, though a given country may switch categories, as is the case with Ireland and Italy today.

The Organized Export of Workers

The 1990s saw a sharp growth in the export of workers, both legal and illegal. This growth in exports is not simply the other side of the active recruitment of immigrants described above. It has its own specific features, consisting of operations for profit-making and for enhancing government revenue through the export of workers. In terms of economic conditioning, a crucial matter for research and explanation is what systemic links, if any, exist between the growth of the organized export of workers for private profit or government revenue enhancement, on the one hand, and major economic conditions in poor developing countries, on the other hand. Among these conditions are an increase in unemployment, the closure of a large number of typically small and medium-size enterprises oriented to national rather than export markets, and a large, often increasing government debt. While these economies are frequently grouped under the label of developing, they are in some cases struggling, stagnant, or even shrinking. (For the sake of brevity, we use *developing* here as shorthand for this variety of situations.) The evidence for these conditions is incomplete and partial, yet there is a growing consensus among experts that they are expanding and, furthermore, that women are often a majority of both the legal and illegal exported workers (IOM 2006; World Bank 2006).

The various types of exports of workers have strengthened at a time when major dynamics linked to economic globalization have had significant effects on developing economies. These economies have had to implement a bundle of new policies and accommodate new conditions associated with globalization: structural adjustment programs, the opening up of their economies to foreign firms, the elimination of multiple state subsidies, and, it would seem almost inevitably, financial crises and the prevailing types of programmatic solutions put forth by the IMF. It is now clear that in most of the countries involved, these conditions have created enormous costs for certain sectors of the economy and the population and have not fundamentally reduced government debt. For instance, the debt burden has affected state spending composition. We see this in Zambia, Ghana, and Uganda in the 1990s, when the World Bank saw their governments as cooperative and responsible and as effective in implementing Structural Adjustment Programs (SAPs). Zambia paid US$1.3 billion in debt but only US$37 million for primary education; Ghana paid $375 million in debt service but only $75 million in social expenses; and Uganda paid nine dollars per capita on its debt and only one dollar for health care (Ismi, 1998).

Are there systemic links between these two sets of developments: the growth of organized exports of workers from certain developing economies and the rise in unemployment and debt in their economies? One way of articulating this issue in substantive terms is to posit the growing importance in all these countries of alternative ways of making a living, making a profit, and securing government revenue due to the shrinking opportunities for employment; the shrinking opportunities for more traditional forms of profit making as foreign firms enter an expanding range of economic sectors in these countries; growing pressures to develop export industries; and the decrease in government revenues, partly linked to these conditions and to the burden of debt servicing. Prostitution and labor migration are ways of making a living; the legal and illegal trafficking in workers, including workers for the sex industry, is growing in importance as a way of making a profit; and the remittances sent home by emigrants, as well as the revenues from the organized export of workers, are increasingly important sources of foreign currency for some governments. Women are by far the majority group in the illegal trafficking for the sex industry and in governments' organized export of workers (see Sassen 2000 for sources on these variables).

The organized export of workers, whether legal or illegal, is facilitated in part by the organizational and technical infrastructure of the global economy: the formation of global markets, the intensification of transnational and translocal networks, the development of communications technologies that easily escape conventional surveillance practices. The strengthening of global networks and, in some of these cases, the formation of new global networks are embedded or made possible by the existence of a global economic system and its associated development of various institutional supports for cross-border money flows and markets. Once there is an institutional infrastructure for globalization, processes that have basically operated at the national level can scale up to the global level even when doing so is not necessary for their operation. Operating globally in such cases contrasts with processes that are by their very features global, such as the network of financial centers underlying the formation of a global capital market.

Debt and debt-servicing problems have become a systemic feature of the developing world since the 1980s and are contributing to the expanded efforts to export workers both legally and illegally. A considerable body of research shows the detrimental effects of such debt on government programs for women and children, notably, programs for education and health care, which are clearly investments necessary to ensure a better future. Furthermore, the increased unemployment typically associated with the austerity and adjustment programs implemented by international agencies to address government debt has been found to have adverse effects on broad sectors of the population. Subsistence food production, informal work, emigration, prostitution—all have grown as survival options. Heavy government debt and high unemployment have brought with them the need to search for alternative sources of government revenue, and the shrinking of regular economic opportunities has brought with it a widened use of illegal profit making by enterprises and organizations. Generally, most countries that became deeply indebted in the 1980s have not been able to solve the problem. And in the 1990s we saw a new set of countries become deeply indebted. Over those two decades many innovations were launched, most importantly by the IMF and the World Bank through their structural adjustment programs and structural adjustment loans, respectively. The latter were tied to economic policy reform rather than the funding of a particular project. The purpose of such programs is to make states more "competitive," which typically means making sharp cuts in various social programs. (For evidence on these various trends, see Ward 1990; Beneria and Feldman 1992; Bradshaw et al. 1993; Cagatay and Ozler 1995; Pyle and Ward 2003; Buechler 2007.)

In the 1990s, thirty-three of the forty-one "heavily indebted poor countries" (HIPCs) paid $3 in debt-service payments to the highly developed countries for every $1 received in development assistance. Debt-service ratios to gross national product (GNP) in many of the HIPCs exceed sustainable limits (United Nations Conference on Trade and Development 1999). Those ratios are far more extreme than what were considered unmanageable levels in the Latin American debt crisis of the 1980s. Debt (including interest)-to-GNP ratios are especially high in Africa, where they stand at 123 percent, compared with 42 percent in Latin America and 28 percent in Asia. The IMF now asks HIPCs to pay 20 to 25 percent of their export earnings toward debt service. In contrast, in 1953 the Allies cancelled 80 percent of Germany's war debt and insisted on a debt service of only 3 to 5 percent of export earnings. The ratio was 8 percent for Central Europe after Communism. This debt burden inevitably has large repercussions for state-spending composition and thus for the population. By 2003 debt service as a share of exports ranged from extremely high levels for Zambia (29.6 percent) and Mauritania (27.7 percent), to significantly lowered levels compared with the 1990s for Uganda (down from 19.8 percent in 1995 to 7.1 percent in 2003) and Mozambique (down from 34.5 percent in 1995 to 6.9 percent in 2003) (World Bank 2005; UNDP 2005). And in 2006 the governments of the leading developed countries cancelled the debt of the eighteen poorest countries, recognizing they would never be able to pay their debts.

A body of research literature on the devastating impact of government debt focused on the implementation of a first generation of structural adjustment programs in several developing countries in the 1980s and on a second generation of such programs, one more directly linked to the implementation of the global economy, in the 1990s. This literature has documented the disproportionate burden that these programs have placed on the lower middle classes, the working poor, and most especially, women (for example, Ward 1990; Bose and Acosta-Belen 1995; Buechler 2007; Tinker 1990; Oxfam 1999; UNDP 2005). These conditions push households and individuals to accept or seek legal or illegal traffickers to take them to any job anywhere.

Yet even under these extreme conditions, in which traffickers often function as recruiters who may initiate the procedure, only a minority of people are emigrating. The participation of traffickers to some extent alters the type of patterning associated with the government and corporate recruitment discussed above, which tends to be embedded in older sets of links connecting the countries involved.

Remittances sent by immigrants represent a major source of foreign exchange reserves for the governments of many developing countries. While the flow of remittances may be minor compared with the massive daily capital flows in various financial markets, it is often very significant for developing or struggling economies. From 1998 to 2005, global remittances sent by immigrants to their home country rose from $70 billion to $230 billion (World Bank 2006). To understand the significance of that figure, it should be related to the GDP and foreign currency reserves in the specific countries involved. For instance, in the Philippines, a key exporter of migrants generally and of women for work in the entertainment industry of several countries, remittances have represented the third largest source of foreign exchange over the last several years. In Bangladesh, a country with a significant number of workers in the Middle East, Japan, and several European countries, remittances represent about one third of foreign exchange.

The illegal exportation of migrants is above all a profitable business for the traffickers, though it can also add to the flow of legal remittances. According to a United Nations report, criminal organizations in the 1990s generated an estimated $3.5 billion per year in profits from trafficking male and female migrants for work. By 2006, trafficking for the sex trades was estimated at US$19 billion by Interpol and US$27 billion by the International Labor Office (Leidholdt 2005:5). Once this trafficking was mostly the trade of petty criminals. Today it is an increasingly organized operation that functions at the global scale. The involvement of organized crime is a recent development in the case of migrant trafficking. There are also reports that organized crime groups are creating intercontinental strategic alliances through networks of co-ethnics throughout several countries; such alliances facilitate transportation, local contacts and distribution, and the provision of false documents.

Men and women are trafficked for work, with women at a

greater risk of being diverted to work in the sex trades. Some women know that they are being trafficked for prostitution, but for many the conditions of their recruitment and the extent of abuse and bondage become evident only after they arrive in the receiving country. The conditions of confinement are often extreme, akin to slavery, and so are the conditions of abuse, including rape and other forms of sexual violence, as well as physical punishment. Sex workers are severely underpaid, and their wages are often withheld.

The next two sections focus on two aspects of the organized exportation of workers: government exports and the illegal trafficking in women for the sex industry.

Government-Organized Exports

The exportation of workers is a means by which governments cope with unemployment and foreign debt. There are two ways in which governments have secured benefits through this strategy. One is highly formalized, and the other is simply a byproduct of the migration process itself. Among the strongest examples of the formalized mode are South Korea and the Philippines (Sassen 1988; Parreñas 2001) and now China. In the 1970s, South Korea promoted the export of workers as an integral part of its growing overseas construction industry, initially to the Middle Eastern members of the Organization of Petroleum Exporting Countries (OPEC) and then worldwide. This is the model pursued by China in its current African investments. When South Korea experienced its own economic boom, exports of workers fell and imports began (Seol and Skrentny 2003). In contrast, the Philippine government has expanded and diversified the export of its citizens to deal with unemployment and secure revenue.

The Filipino case illuminates a series of issues concerning a government's exportation of workers (Yamamoto 2006). The government has played an important role in the emigration of Filipino women to the United States, the Middle East, and Japan through the Philippines Overseas Employment Administration (POEA). Established in 1982, POEA organized and oversaw the export of nurses and maids to high-demand areas around the world. High foreign debt and high unemployment combined to make this policy attractive (Sassen 1988). Overseas Filipino workers have sent home almost $1 billion a year on average in the last few years. Labor-importing countries have welcomed this policy for their own reasons. Middle Eastern OPEC members saw the demand for domestic workers grow sharply after the 1973 oil boom. The United States, confronted with an acute shortage of nurses, a profession that demands years of training yet garners rather low wages and little recognition, passed the Immigration Nursing Relief Act in 1989, opposed by the American Nursing Association. About 80 percent of the nurses brought in under that act were from the Philippines. And in the 1980s, when its economy was booming, expendable income was rising, and labor shortages were intensifying, Japan passed legislation that permitted the entry of "entertainment workers," mostly from the Philippines. The government of the Philippines also passed regulations that permitted mail-order-bride agencies to recruit young Filipinas to marry foreign men as a matter of contractual agreement; this was an organized effort by the government. Among the major clients were the

United States and Japan. Japan's agricultural communities were a key destination for Filipina brides, given the enormous shortages of people, and especially young women, in the Japanese countryside when the economy was booming and the demand for labor in the large metropolitan areas was extremely high. Municipal governments made it a policy to accept Filipina brides. The largest number of Filipinas going through these government-promoted channels work overseas as maids, particularly in other Asian countries (Parreñas 2001, 2005; Chin 1997; Heyzer 1994). The second largest group, and the fastest growing, comprises entertainers, most of whom work in Japan (Sassen 2001, chap. 9; Yamamoto 2006).

The rapid increase in the number of Filipina migrants working as entertainers is largely due to the "entertainment brokers" in the Philippines, more than five hundred of them, who operate outside the state—even though the government may still benefit from the remittances sent home by these overseas workers. The brokers provide women for the sex industry in Japan, which is basically supported or controlled by organized gangs, rather than going through the government-controlled program for the entry of entertainers. The women are recruited for singing and entertaining, but frequently, perhaps mostly, they are forced into prostitution as well. They are recruited and brought into Japan through both formal legal channels and illegal ones. Either way they have little power to resist once they are in the system. And even though they are paid below minimum wage, they produce significant profits for the brokers and employers. There has recently been an enormous increase in the number of so-called entertainment businesses in Japan (Sassen 2001, chap. 9; Yamamoto 2006).

The government of the Philippines approved most mail-order-bride organizations until 1989. But under the government of Corazon Aquino, the stories of abuse by foreign husbands led to the banning of the business. Nevertheless, it is almost impossible to eliminate these organizations, and they continue to operate in violation of the law.

The Philippines is not the only country to have explored official strategies for the exportation of its workers, although it is perhaps the one with the most developed program. After its 1997–1998 financial crisis, Thailand started a campaign to promote emigration for work and recruitment of Thai workers by overseas firms. The government sought to export workers to the Middle East, the United States, Great Britain, Germany, Australia, and Greece. Sri Lanka's government has tried to export 200,000 workers in addition to the 1 million it already has overseas; Sri Lankan women remitted $880 million in 1998, mostly from their earnings as maids in the Middle East and Far East (Anonymous 1999). By the 1970s, Bangladesh had already organized extensive labor-exporting programs to OPEC members of the Middle East. These programs have continued and—along with individual migration to OPEC nations as well as various other countries, notably the United States and the United Kingdom—are a significant source of foreign exchange. Bangladesh's overseas workers remitted $1.4 billion a year in the late 1990s (David 1999).

Trafficking in Women
International trafficking in women for the sex industry has grown sharply over the last decade (Lin and Wijers 1997; Shannon 1999; Kyle and Koslowski 2001). The available evidence

suggests that it is highly profitable for those running the trade. The United Nations estimates that 4 million people were trafficked in 1998, producing a profit of $7 billion to criminal groups. Those funds include remittances from prostitutes' earnings and payments to organizers and facilitators.

It is estimated that in recent years several million women and girls have been trafficked within and outside Asia and the former Soviet Union, two major trafficking areas. Growth in those areas can be linked to women being pushed into poverty or sold to brokers due to the poverty of their households. High unemployment in the former Soviet republics has been a factor promoting growth of criminal gangs as well as the increase in trafficking in women. For instance, Ukrainian and Russian women, highly prized in the sex market, earn criminal gangs between $500 and $1,000 per woman delivered. The women can be expected to service on average fifteen clients a day and can be expected to make about $215,000 per month for a gang (International Organization for Migration 1996).

Such networks also facilitate the organized circulation of trafficked women among third-party countries. Thus traffickers may move women from Myanmar, Laos, Vietnam, and China to Thailand, whereas Thai women may have been moved to Japan and the United States. There are various reports on the particular cross-border movements in trafficking. Malay brokers sell Malay women into prostitution in Australia. Gangs have sold women from Albania and Kosovo into prostitution in London (Hamzic and Sheehan 1999). European teens from Paris and other cities have been sold to Arab and African customers (Shannon 1999). In the United States the police broke up an international Asian ring that imported women from China,

Thailand, Korea, Malaysia, and Vietnam (Booth 1999). The trafficked women were charged between $30,000 and $40,000 in contracts to be paid through their work in the sex or garment trade.

As tourism has grown sharply over the last decade and has become a major development strategy for cities, regions, and whole countries, the entertainment sector has experienced a parallel growth and is seen now as a key aspect of this development strategy. In many places the sex trade is part of the entertainment industry and has similarly grown. At some point it becomes clear that the sex trade itself can become a development strategy in areas with high unemployment, poverty, and a government desperate for revenue and foreign exchange reserves. When local manufacturing and agriculture can no longer function as sources of employment, profits, and government revenue, what was once a marginal source of earnings, profits, and revenue now becomes far more important. The increased importance of tourism in development generates multiplying tie-ins. For instance, when the IMF and the World Bank see tourism as a solution to some of the obstacles to growth in many poor countries and provide loans for its development, they may well be contributing also to the development of a broader institutional setting for the growth of the entertainment industry and, indirectly, the sex trade. This tie-in with development strategies is a signal that trafficking in women may well see a sharp expansion.

The entry of organized crime into the sex trades, the formation of cross-border ethnic networks, and the growing transnationalization in so many aspects of tourism suggest that we are likely to see further development of a global sex industry. This development could mean greater attempts to enter into more and more "markets" and a general expansion of the industry. Given the growing number of women with few if any employment options, the prospects are grim. Women in the sex industry become—in certain kinds of economies—a crucial link supporting the expansion of the entertainment industry, and through that they become a link to tourism as a development strategy, which in turn becomes a source of government revenue. These tie-ins are structural, not a function of conspiracies. Their weight in an economy will be increased by the absence or limitations of other sources for securing a livelihood, profits, and revenues for, respectively, workers, enterprises, and governments.

Conclusion

In this chapter I have sought to specify the ways in which international migration flows are conditioned by broader politico-economic dynamics, even though they cannot be fully explained without introducing more sociological variables. One of the major implications of this type of analysis is that we need to detect the shaping of a migration option and situate the decisions by individual migrants within these broader dynamics.

Three types of social conditions facilitate the decision to migrate and induce individuals to make that decision. A first set of broad structural conditions has to do with the types of links brought about by economic internationalization in its many instantiations: old colonial and more recent neocolonial forms and particular types of links brought about by current forms of economic globalization. A second set of conditions involves the direct recruitment of immigrant workers by employers, by governments on behalf of employers, or through the immigrant network. A third and final set of conditions involves the organized export and trafficking, increasingly illegal, of men, women, and children. These activities create whole new ways of linking labor-export and labor-importing countries, beyond the old colonial or the new global economic connections.

Such active links help make emigration an actual option, in turn helping individuals and households make the decision to emigrate. These active links derive their objective and subjective meaning in part from the existence of large systemic configurations that incorporate both the sending and the receiving areas. Each of these links lies at the intersection of formal systems and actual practices. It is at this point that current global and denationalizing dynamics become significant variables for the study and explanation of today's migration processes, even though they produce only a partial account of such processes. The research agenda that comes out of this calls for close examinations of the institutional insertions of the mix of processes that constitute what we have come to name "immigration." Understanding how today's phase differs from earlier immigration phases will require tracking the complex and often micro shifts that are taking place in immigration processes, in the ideological constructions of these processes, and in the subjective meaning of these processes for immigrants themselves.

Chapter Six
EMERGENT GLOBAL CLASSES

THE CONCEPT OF CLASS has a long and distinguished lineage in sociology. In this chapter the term is used to attempt a first aggregation of varieties of social groups that are beginning to cohere into recognizable global social forms. That is, I take liberties with the concept. Of interest to a sociology of globalization is that the formation of these classes points to dynamics that partially disaggregate the national from within. These classes take shape in specific institutional orders: the state apparatus, the economy, and society in the narrower sense of the term. Furthermore, this disaggregating weakens the grip that national politics, systems, and policy regimes have historically had on the particular groups comprised by these emergent classes. At the same time the particular features of these classes, especially their ambiguous position between the global and the national, point to their ongoing, even if partial, embeddedness in national domains. Hence, they are better described as partially denationalized classes, an interpretation that also contests the widespread notion that global classes are cosmopolitan because they are outside the reach of the national. Because the more common term in the scholarship is "global classes," I will use this designation here.

In the first section of this chapter, I examine what we can take from the existing scholarship in sociology, a discipline for which class has been a central category for analysis, in order to understand today's emergent global forms. In the ensuing sections, I examine class elements coalescing into three emergent social classes. I use the term *class* loosely here, more as a sensitizing concept that helps us keep the problematic alive and keeps us from reducing it to the notion of professionals who are also frequent travelers.

THE MEANING OF SOCIAL CLASS WHEN STRUCTURES CHANGE

At its broadest, the analysis in this chapter contests claims that class is declining in significance in advanced industrial societies. Some authors promoting that view (Clark and Lipset 1991; Pakulski and Waters 1996) have focused on questions of class *formation* and political organization. Others argue that transformations associated with postindustrialism or post-Fordism also signal the disintegration of class *structure* (for the distinction between formation and structure, see Erik Olin Wright 1985); this argument attributes much of the dynamics of class formation to authority relations embedded in the bureaucratic, vertically integrated firm. Perhaps the best analyses of class as seen through the lens of such authority relations without reducing it *to* those relations can be found in Edwards (1979) and Burawoy (1979). Edwards situates his analysis structurally, from the standpoint of the organization of class struggle on the workshop floor, whereas Burawoy analyzes class from the standpoint of the workers who confront the organizational structures in place. It can then be argued that the decline of such organizational structure reduces the dynamics of societal hierarchy (Piore and Sabel 1984; Amin 1994; but see Portes 2000 for a critique). These changes in the organization of work and the growing diversification in the content of occupations have contributed to a type of analysis that posits the emergence of structural conditions that move from class narrowly defined toward a looser condition that might be captured in terms of "postmodern lifestyles"—fragmented, identitarian, and basically not classlike—insofar as the deep foundational inequalities that continue to function fail to engender something akin to class consciousness (Harvey 1989; Stuart Hall 1988).

These arguments assume a particular definition of class, one grounded in domination. This Weberian understanding equates hierarchy with the exercise of power by organized actors; organizational hierarchy causes the centralization of valued resources in the hands of an elite few. However, a more Marxian understanding emphasizes the location of classes within the structural framework of a mode of production and the relational interdependencies of the various classes (Erik Olin Wright 1979, 1985). By that account, the changing organizational structure of corporate activity modifies the class formation, even as capitalist class structure remains in place. Hence, the observed decline of organizational hierarchy may affect conjunctural class situations, but the class structure itself can remain intact. Although Wright's emphasis on structure tends to sideline analysis of the concrete groups and actors who occupy the positions in a class structure, it provides a point of departure for theorizing the persistence of class throughout transformations within capitalism.

To theorize the actual and concrete processes out of which classes form, a method capable of grasping the subjective and objective dimensions of class structure simultaneously is required. To devise such a method, we must become more concrete and move from class formations to the practical situations that compose the class structure and the larger system. Following Bourdieu (1977), we might look at the actual manifestations of structure: how it constrains possibilities of collective action and defines a strategic space for actors. Grusky and Sorensen (1998; also Grusky, Weeden, and Sorensen 2000) go some distance in this direction by advocating that attention be paid to actual occupational groups and by arguing that this level of analysis best captures the actual behaviors, cultures, and practices of class actors.

However, their attention to the "disaggregated," or micro, level of class process comes at the expense of theorization about the macrostructures invoked by authors such as Wright and at the expense of how they emerge from these microinteractions and processes (Portes 2000). Structural constraints on group action are not defined exclusively by the relative power of different groups; they are defined as well by systemic necessities imposed by the valorization of capital (Postone 1993; Harvey 1982). Competition between groups takes place within a set of institutionalized rules (Fligstein 2001), which can be interpreted in terms of hegemonic determination by the dictates of capital and markets. While these "rules" objectively structure the actions of economic groups, their significance for class analysis resides on at least two other axes. First, as suggested by Bourdieu (1977) they define a strategic context for collective action. I would then extend this and posit that connection to functionally important positions within the global economic system can increase access to valuable resources and thereby can increase group power. Moreover, strategic competition results in the inhabitancy of a position within the class structure as defined by functional position within the process of valorization, thereby keeping a systemic referent. Second, these rules are not themselves absolute. By securing a functional position in the global economy, by bridging the global and the local, groups may imprint a degree of their particular practices and culture on the structure of the global economy as a whole; structure is thus mediated through practices and cultures (Dezalay and Garth 1995; Giddens 1984).

Hence denationalized classes must be analyzed both objectively and subjectively. An account that lays out the structural positions determined by the abstract logic of capital is insufficient. But so is one that is confined to the strategies and actions of particular groups, whether economic or social. A denationalized class emerges out of both kinds of processes as groups strategically attempt to secure the opportunities created by a functioning global system and are at the same time constrained by national systems (Sassen 2006a, chaps. 5 and 7).

Although still small, there is a body of scholarship that has examined the emergence of something akin to a global class. A first characteristic of this scholarship is its focus on a new stratum of transnational professionals and executives (Pijl 1998; Sklair 2001; Robinson 2004). But in terms of functional positions and the interests arising from these positions, I see at least two other global—or, partly, denationalized—classes. One of these arises from the proliferation of transnational networks of government officials; among these networks are those formed by experts on a variety of issues critical to a global corporate economy: judges having to negotiate a growing array of international rules and prohibitions that require some measure of cross-border standardization, immigration officials needing to coordinate border controls, police officials in charge of discovering financial flows supporting terrorism. The other is an emergent class of disadvantaged or resource-poor workers and activists, including key sectors of global civil society, diasporic networks, and transnational immigrant communities and households; there is a rapidly growing scholarship on some of these, but it has not dealt with the notion of an emergent global class.

A second characteristic of the existing scholarship on global classes is its prevalent tendency to equate the globalism of the transnational professional and executive class with cosmopolitanism. A more careful examination of that class raises some doubts about its cosmopolitanism. Doubts are also raised about the cosmopolitanism of the other two global classes I identify. All three of these classes evince forms of globality that, in my reading, are not cosmopolitan. Each of them remains embedded, in often unexpected ways, in thick localized environments: respectively, financial and business centers, national governments, and the localized microstructures of daily civic life and struggles. And each of these classes is guided by a single logic rather than the multiple logics at the heart of genuine cosmopolitanism: profits in the case of the new professional elites (no matter how cosmopolitan their tastes for, say, art and food), specific and narrow global governance issues in the case of government networks, and specific local struggles and conflicts, no matter how much they recur around the world, in the case of global civil society, diasporas, and immigrant networks.

The existence of global classes that are not necessarily cosmopolitan and remain partially embedded in localized environments leads me to posit that they are partially denationalized rather than global. Their ongoing embeddedness raises a host of issues. One is that insofar as these classes are part—indeed, constitutive parts—of current forms of inequality, they and the underlying socioeconomic structures may well be more subject to government policy and governance mechanisms than the imagery of globality typically allows for. The political options will be different from those involved in the case of genuinely cosmopolitan classes. At the same time, although not cosmopolitan, their incipient globality does make a difference. One can think about these classes as bridging the thick national environments within which most politics, economics, and civic life still functions and the global dynamics that are "denationalizing" particular components of those national settings.

The other issue concerns the variety of economic, political, and subjective structures underlying the formation of these global classes. Each of these classes entails global networks with varying degrees of formalization and institutionalization. Those global networks are not seamless, as is often thought. They are lumpy: they contain nodes (global cities, major supranational institutions, activists' targets), and it is in these nodes that much of the global action takes place. Furthermore, factors such as the global corporate economy and the international human rights regime also play critical roles in the proliferation of these global networks. Third, these and other globalizing dynamics have contributed to the weakening of the exclusive objective and subjective authority of national states over people, their imaginaries, and their sense of where they belong. This weakening facilitates the entry of nonstate actors into international domains once exclusive to national states. Economic, political, and civic processes once confined largely to the national sphere can now go global even when this process is only an imaginary, or subjective disposition, rather than a daily reality for many of the actors involved.

At this time it is only in particular domains that these globalizing processes generate actual new social forms. My research (2001; 2006a, chaps. 5 and 6) suggests that it is largely at the top and bottom of the social system that the national state has weakened its grip in shaping the experience of membership and identity. Vast middle strata—whether workers, firms, or places—have not been particularly affected by these processes of transformation. Similarly, most of the work of governments has not been affected either, even though there is a specific type of government official who is at the forefront in the work of developing the technical infrastructure for corporate globalization and key aspects of global governance.

Much of the classical sociological analysis of class formation has focused on the dialectic between state and class (Poulantzas 1973; Skocpol 1979; Skocpol 1985; Erik Olin Wright 1979). In large measure, the state enters these accounts as a primary focusing point for processes organizing social groups. These social groups are defined by a shared and objective economic interest, and they are organized as coherent collective actors capable of articulating and pursuing their interests both with and against other social groups. The Marxian variant emphasizes the translation of objective class structure, defined by position within a mode of production, into actual class struggles: in this process of class formation, political and ideological factors determine which objectively identified social classes become organized collective actors and which remain disorganized. The state as a central power plays a central role in the process (Erik Olin Wright 1979, 1985; Przeworski 1985; Piven and Cloward 1971). The Weberian version, in contrast, defines classes by shared "life chances" (Max Weber 1944, 181ff.) determined by market situation. Market situation is in turn influenced by the relative power of organized groups able to monopolize scarce resources and extract rents on that basis. Parkin (1979) emphasizes property and credentialism as primary mechanisms for securing this monopoly and highlights the role of the state in their enforcement (but see also Bok 1993).

, In each of these accounts the nation-state figures prominently because of its centrality in power struggles, however conceived. Holding a "monopoly of the legitimate use of physical force within a given territory" (Max Weber 1944, 78; see also Giddens 1987) and centralizing the repressive and ideological state apparatuses (Althusser 1971), the state functions as a crucial element of class domination and, thereby, as a crucial element of class organization within national political space. As the authority of the state is called on to organize non-national actors or to secure rights across borders (Sassen 1996, 2006a), however, the state affects class organization across multiple scales. Similarly, as transnational NGOs increasingly participate in the organization of social groups, the hegemony of the state over class organization is likewise challenged.

The class and state dialectic has become more complex than is represented in extant accounts of class formation, as classes and states engage simultaneously in national and non-national activities (Sassen 2006a, chaps. 5 and 6). Although the analytic emphasis on organization is not necessarily wedded to the geographic scale of the nation-state at the most general level, it is worth noting that research has tended to focus on the interrelationship of the nation-state and national classes—that is, on the struggle between ruled and ruling classes within a national space. Analysis of class formation in global context must undertake the difficult task of specifying the multiple organizational domains in which classes are formed, and of theorizing the resulting interpenetration of scales of power and its effect on the emergence of classes. Thus the emergent denationalized classes I focus on here are partial and specific outcomes. They are not necessarily new social forms as such; they can also arise from a subjective, self-reflexive repositioning of an old social practice or condition in a transnational framing. For instance, transnational immigrant households have long existed, but today they assume a new meaning, and the immigrants themselves know it and act on it. Similarly, an international class of powerful elites has long existed, but in today's context it carries novel implications. It is partly their objective systemic position and partly this subjective interpretation that give the new global classes their political import, as I argue in the conclusion of this chapter. In my reading, one of the crucial dynamics at work here is a changed attachment to the national as historically constructed—a process of incipient denationalization.

Transnational Elites

National attachments and identities are becoming weaker among global firms and at least some of their customers. This change is particularly strong in the West but may develop in other parts of the world as well. Deregulation and privatization have weakened the attachment to the *national* economy. Global financial products are accessible in national markets, and national investors can operate in global markets. For instance, foreign firms can now list directly in the major global stock exchanges and bypass their own country's exchange. And the major global exchanges are increasingly the object of attempted acquisitions by foreign exchanges; a good example is the New York Stock Exchange's attempted acquisition of Euronext (which comprises the stock exchanges of Amsterdam, Paris, Brussels and Lisbon). Another indicator of this trend is the fact that major firms set up key operations in one or another leading business center regardless of what country it is in. Thus to a much larger extent than in the past, the major U.S. and European investment banks have set up specialized offices in London to handle various aspects of their global business. Even French banks have set up some of their specialized global operations in London, an event inconceivable a decade ago and still not avowed in the national rhetoric. Japanese firms have also opted to set up in London for some of their financial operations aimed at the the rest of Europe. Finally, most major firms now have vast worldwide networks of affiliates and other types of collaborative arrangements with local firms. All these trends have begun to denationalize bits and pieces of the national economies involved, no matter the renationalizing of political discourse this can also bring about.

The proliferation of these worldwide activities and networks can be seen as a kind of operational infrastructure for corporate economic globalization. The existence and functioning of such globalization take vast numbers of professionals, managers, executives, and technical staff members. A good part of this high-level workforce is quite mobile and easily represented as a new transnational professional class. This class is not centrally defined by its "relationship to the means of production"; much like the "new middle class," or managerial stratum identified in postwar class research, this group is defined more by its control than by its ownership of the means of production (Berle and Means 1932; Dahrendorf 1959; Erik Olin Wright 1985). Whereas the older middle class was defined by its location within a vertically integrated bureaucracy (Whyte 1956; Erik Olin Wright [1985] provides a useful polemical review), the location of today's new professional class within a condition of bureaucratic disintegration suggests that its position within the economy has shifted. For starters, whereas earlier research focused on the social position of an integrated firm within a structure defined by other firms and banks (Zeitlin 1974; Mintz and Schwartz 1985; Mizruchi and Stearns 1994, 319–26), today the social connections of these professionals themselves has taken on increasing importance. This shift fundamentally alters the strategic field in which this emergent class finds itself: mobility is a function not only of service to a firm but also of maximizing social capital. The forms of institutional power identified in the older research (accruing especially to banks) has by no means disappeared. But professionals with highly developed network connections of their own provide valuable sources of information to firms and investors in complex environments and can extract rent on that basis.[1] Hence we might expect intergroup competition for the control of these information flows to acquire a renewed significance and to constitute a key point of the articulation of occupational groups with class structure. I would posit that under these conditions, membership in this class is akin to a positional good.

The basic agenda for this class remains profit-making, which today is contingently embedded in transnational work and networked organizational forms. Through this work, however, members of this class are also contributing to the instituting of cross-border transactions and standards. Furthermore, their work requires a physical infrastructure—the hyperspace of global business: state-of-the-art office buildings, residential districts, airports, and hotels. At its most developed, this is the worldwide network of about forty global cities that functions as an organizational infrastructure for the management side of the global corporate economy (see Chapters 2 and 4). This organizational infrastructure is critical for the aggregate of feature of this class I described above as akin to a positional good. The new transnational professional workforce both navigates through and contributes to the construction of this cross-border corporate economic space.

It is important to capture three sets of distinctions here. First, we must distinguish the driving force that feeds the emergence of this cross-border domain from the forces driving and constituting cosmopolitanism in the rich sense of the word. Although this new transnational professional class may open up to diverse cuisines and urban landscapes, the particular condition that constitutes it as a global class is a rather narrow utility logic: the drive for profits. In itself this is not a cosmopolitan drive, even though it may help global professionals become a little more worldly. Second, we must distinguish the systemic position of this class from that of a country's national business community even though particular individuals may circulate in both spheres. Through its work this new global class is shaping an increasingly significant change in its relation to the system of national states. Third, we must distinguish between the global circulation of this class and its work as partially embedded in national terrains—most conspicuously in the network of global cities. To be global and hypermobile, this class needs a state-of-the-art platform. From here, then, comes a particular type of engagement and a partial dependence on national states, a fact easily obscured by the language of the new cosmopolitanism and hypermobile capital.

One way of describing this process of producing such a platform is as a partial, often highly specialized denationalizing of particular institutional domains. Much of this was covered in Chapters 2, 3, and 4. Here I want to emphasize a feature not yet addressed: insofar as the global corporate economy is partly embedded in national territories it brings with it the need for top-level corporate workers to have rights of admission to the countries involved. National states have invented new types of visas and renovated old visas for global professionals. Insufficiently noted is the fact that all the major free trade agreements also provide such rights of access to professionals. The World Trade Organization (WTO) and the North America Free Trade Agreement (NAFTA), among others, give transnational professionals mobility rights. These rights constitute a new legal "infrastructure." Professionals in each of the specific sectors, which include finance, business services, and telecommunications, can reside in any signatory country for at least three years and enjoy various rights and protections. This runs in the face of the explicit position of free trade agreements that they do not deal with immigration. The mobility rights free-trade agreements grant professionals are buried under such headings as "the internationalization of trade and investment in business services." This language obscures the fact that these are mobility rights given to what are ultimately migrant workers.

This process of specialized and partial denationalization has been strengthened by state policy enabling privatization and foreign acquisition. In some ways one might say that the Asian financial crisis has functioned as a mechanism to denationalize, at least in part, national control over key sectors of economies that allowed the massive entry of foreign investment but never relinquished that national control.

The network of global cities produces what we can think of as a new subculture, a move from the "national" version of international activities to the "global" version. Both Europe's long-standing resistance to mergers and acquisitions, especially hostile takeovers, and East Asia's resistance to foreign ownership and control signal national business cultures that are somewhat incompatible with the new global economic culture. I would posit that global cities and various global business meetings (such as those held by the World Economic Forum (WEF) in Davos, Switzerland, and similar events contribute to the partial denationalization of corporate elites (as well as government elites). Whether this is good or bad is a separate issue; but it is, I would argue, one of the conditions for setting in place the systems and subcultures necessary for a global economic system. A key feature, then, of the new global class is its intermediate position between the national and the global.

Transnational Networks of Government Officials

Transgovernment networks have existed for a long time. But novel types of networks emerging in the 1980s and 1990s are clearly connected to today's corporate globalization and the globalizing of other government responsibilities and aims—for example, those regarding human rights, the environment, and now the struggle to contain terrorism. An older and common type of international government network is found in international organizations. There the key actors are government officials representing the pertinent national ministries or agencies. Transgovernment regulatory networks can be found among trade ministers who are a party to the General Agreement on Tariffs and Trade (GATT), financial ministers in the IMF, defense and foreign ministers in the North Atlantic Treaty Organization, central bankers in the Bank for International Settlements, and in various efforts within the OECD and the Council of the European Union. In one of the most exhaustive studies on the subject, Anne-Marie Slaughter (2004) finds that these are often enormously powerful networks of government officials in charge of critical work in the development of a global corporate economy. In some cases the secretariat of an international institution explicitly tries to form a network of officials from specific governments to act as a negotiating vanguard in developing new rules that are eventually to apply to all members; examples are the WTO's negotiations on behalf of TRIPS (trade-related aspects of intellectual property rights), negotiations for the governance of the Internet, and so on.

There are also government networks within the framework of executive agreements (Slaughter 2004) that function outside a formal international institution. Members operate within a framework agreed on at least by the heads of their respective governments. Pollack and Shaffer (2001) examined several such executive arrangements whereby US and European Commission presidents agreed to foster increased cooperation, including the Transatlantic Declaration of 1990, the New Transatlantic Agenda of 1995 (with a joint U.S.-E.U. action plan attached) and the Transatlantic Economic Partnership Agreement of 1998. They found that each of those meetings produced ad hoc meetings among lower-level officials, firms, and environmental and consumer activist groups focused on shared issues.

Finally, a very new development is the formation of informal networks operating outside intergovernment agreements—that is, outside treaties and executive agreements (Slaughter 2004). Among these are the Basel Committee, which is focused on financial governance; the international arbitration community; high-level members of the judiciary; and experts from the private and government sectors working on international standards. What these networks do is not legally binding on the members but often serves as the preparatory work for formal arrangements. The turbulence of financial markets and the market uncertainties confronting global firms have given such informal deliberations weight and strategic importance (Sassen 2006a, chap. 7). Most recently we have seen a proliferation of agreements between the regulatory agencies of two or more countries; there has been a far sharper growth in those agreements than in traditional treaty negotiations. These agreements can be instituted by the domestic regulators themselves and in this sense are an interesting instance of denationalized state work; they do not require approval by national leg-islators (Sassen 1996, chap. 1, and Sassen 2006a in general).

What is critical about these transgovernment networks as an emergent, partially denationalized class is the change brought about by globalization beginning in the 1980s, when a tipping point was reached (Sassen 2006a, chap. 4). This is no longer the post–World War II Bretton Woods decade of inter-government collaboration. The aim is not simply intergovern-ment or international communications and collaboration. It is, rather, a deregulatory project that aims at denationalizing those components of state work that are necessary for corporate glob-alization (or, in other settings, for implementing global treaties on the environment, human rights, and other noneconomic is-sues). In the early Bretton Woods period the project was one of global governance to protect national economies; by the 1980s, the goal was to open up national economies and create hos-pitable and institutionalized environments for global firms and markets (Chapters 2 and 3). This shift saw the proliferation of highly specialized transgovernment networks to institute com-patible competition policies, accounting standards, financial re-porting standards, and so on. The work of the pertinent, typically highly specialized government officials thus began to orient itself toward a global project. One consequence is an in-creased commonality among officials within each transnational network and a growing distance from colleagues in the national bureaucracies back home. In this sense, then, we can speak of an incipient global class that occupies that ambiguous position between the national and the global.

Much of the work of generating uniform cross-national standards and practices within the global economy can be seen in a purely functional relationship to the structures of capitalism. At least two possibilities suggest this type of analysis is limited. First, as I have already argued, we must consider the political strategies embodied in the adoption of neoliberal policies. The subjective meanings attached to economic situations and government actors' reasons for adopting neoliberal policies substantially affect the types of policies implemented (Babb and Fourcade-Gourinchas 2002). This suggests the second limitation of a purely structural perspective: if the strategies and interpretations of governing bodies affect the substance of government action, there is possibly a more generalized autonomy from the interests of the ruling class and the functional necessities of capital. We can ask whether the relationship between institutions of economic governance and the logic of capital is purely contingent. If it is, governance might be guided by alternative normative paradigms, provided adequate political organization and power exist. Or is there a structural and necessary relationship between economic governance and capitalist logic akin to the relationships identified by an earlier generation of scholars studying the advanced capitalist state (Offe 1984; Jessop 1982: chap. 3)? The conjunctural analyses of Skocpol's historical sociology (Skocpol, Evans, and Rueschemeyer 1985) may provide a better way of approaching this question. I ask, under what conditions—economic, social, political, ideological, and so on—will this emergent stratum of agents of economic governance act against the interests of either local or transnational ruling classes, against the interests of markets, or in opposition to the functional necessities of capitalism (see Buechler 2007 on municipal elites)? The shifting of governance functions to the institutional boundaries of the nation-state necessitates caution in the generalization of state-based historical research regarding the contemporary period. But it poses another set of questions as well. The relationship between the nation-state and national "ruling classes" remains undertheorized, as does the relationship of the transnational governing stratum to both national entities.

THE NEW GLOBAL CLASS OF THE DISADVANTAGED

We are seeing emerge a distinct global formation comprising a mix of individuals, population categories, and organizations. Notwithstanding sharp internal diversity and a preponderant lack of interaction, there are shared objective conditions and subjective dynamics in this formation. I posit that it cannot be thought of as equivalent to global civil society even though at specific times part of it is, and even though the imaginary of such a global civil society is a significant subjective condition shared by some of the people and projects involved. What is of particular interest to the concerns of this book is the fact that most of the people involved are quite immobile. They are not part of a traveling transnational class or the new global civil society of international elites. Yet they are either objectively or subjectively part of specific forms of globality.

One of my concerns in developing the category denationalization has been with the types of cross-border networks that resource-poor people and organizations can construct and join even if they are not mobile (Sassen 2006a, chap. 7). The key is that localized activist struggles can be global even if they are confined to local settings and their members lack the means or permissions to travel. We can think of these struggles as localizations of global civil society. Important spaces for such localizations are global cities, home to multiple diasporic and activist networks and organizations. The actors may include disadvantaged sectors: a variety of groupings and organizations that have limited resources, have no or little power, often lack proper documentation, are often invisible to national politics and national civil society, are unrecognized as politico-civic actors, or are unauthorized by the formal political system.

Cities, which are critical to global civil society, contain at least two key spaces. One is the concrete space for politico-civic activities (as distinct from the highly formalized space of national politics and national civil society). The other is the state-of-the-art environment constructed for the command functions and social reproduction of global corporate capital, which makes the increasingly elusive global corporate sector visible (Chapter 4). Critical also is the partly deterritorialized space of global electronic networks. Here the public-access Internet is enormously important. It allows easy low-cost communication, distribution, and crucially, the formation of electronic domains where multiple actors from many different localities can join in (Chapter 7).

Arising from these conditions, the following five issues can be identified. One issue concerns the forms of politico-civic engagement that are made possible for the disadvantaged in global cities; these are at least partially enabled by globalization and the human rights regime. A second issue is that the presence of immigrant communities produces specific transnational forms of engagement, including globalized diasporas. For instance, we see a growing number of immigrant networks concerned with specific struggles, such as exposing illegal trafficking groups and mail-order-bride organizations, which have the effect of partially turning these communities away from a one-to-one orientation to their home country and focusing them instead on other immigrant communities in the city or on co-nationals in other immigrant-receiving countries. A third issue involves the modes of engagement made possible in the global city between the disadvantaged and global corporate power—for instance, anti-gentrification struggles or organized opposition to the trend of transforming industrial districts into luxury office districts. A fourth issue is the extent to which access to the new media—specifically, the Internet—allows or induces various types of groups to transnationalize their efforts (for example, poor women's organizations, environment and human rights activists, and other such groups). Many of these groups have begun to connect with kindred groups in other countries, whereas before their efforts were purely local. The binding is through the shared objectives rather than travel and meetings. The fifth issue concerns the extent to which such multiple activities and engagements contribute to the denationalization of the global city and thereby enable more global forms of consciousness and membership or belonging even among the disadvantaged and immobile. All of these elements are part of the localized microstructures of global civil society.

The masses of people from all over the world who often encounter one another for the first time in the streets, workplaces, and neighborhoods of today's global cities produce a kind of transnationalism in situ. Those encounters may involve co-ethnics with high-level professional jobs—that is, a class encounter. We see an emergent recognition of globality, often shaped by the knowledge of recurrent struggles and inequities in city after city. This knowledge, enabled by both global media and the rapidly spreading use of the Internet among activists, functions as both fact and subjective formation. In my travels around the world, I have found that this subjective dimension increasingly enables the disadvantaged and the localized to recognize the presence of the global in these cities and their participation in it. Thus the global becomes visible, thereby producing an ambiguous position between the national and the global for mostly activist, disadvantaged, and localized actors.

CONCLUSION

The new global classes are probably best thought of as emergent social forces. Their points of insertion into our societies are today not primarily through long established institutional frameworks and the more typical political struggles, those enacted through party politics and union politics. But a key point of the analysis in this chapter is that even though global, they are to varying extents embedded in national settings and hence perhaps better conceived of as partially denationalized. This distinction is critical in considering their articulation with national class structure and whether they unsettle the latter.

A first issue, then, is the relationship between these classes and national settings. There are clearly significant differences when it comes to their insertion into national contexts. The new transnational professional class has far more exit options than do the other two. But as the analysis in this chapter seeks to show, this class is ultimately far more place bound than one might expect given the imagery about it. The reverse is the case with the amalgamated class of disadvantaged workers: here it becomes important to recognize that this class is far more embedded in what we might think of as the global workplace and transnational politics than the imagery associated with these workers would lead one to expect. Finally, the proliferation of networks of specialized government officials can be seen as building international social capital for the governments involved, but to extract the utility of this social capital will take building some bridges between international and national policy and politics on questions that have typically been thought of as national. That is, it will take recognizing that the global is partially constituted in national settings.

All three in their own distinctive ways have a strong insertion into territorially bounded contexts—global cities and national governments. One might say that each is an agent making the global partially endogenous to specific national settings. My assumption here, then, is that this analysis carries implications for both class analysis and national government policy. These implications are the opposite of what might be those associated with notions of free-floating cosmopolitan classes with no national attachments or needs.

A second issue concerns the relationship between the new global classes and domestic class structures. This relationship holds largely for the professionals and the disadvantaged working class. There is much to be said on this subject, but given space limitations, I will focus on two critical aspects. One is that these two global classes are part of a deep economic restructuring that has contributed to a growing demand for both high-level professionals and low-wage service and production workers. Nowhere does bimodal labor demand become clearer—both on the street and in statistical data sets—than in global cities. In this regard current forms of advanced economic globalization add to inequality and indeed produce new types of inequalities. One challenge for analysis is to recognize the interconnections of social forms and outcomes that we usually think of as unconnected. For instance, the state-of-the-art international financial centers in cities such as New York and London actually depend on a far broader range of workers and firms than is usually assumed: all kinds of low-wage service workers labor in these global workplaces. Public opinion and policy frameworks classify these low-wage workers as belonging to backward economic sectors. That is a mistake. A class analysis, as distinct from a stratification or occupational groups analysis, would be centered on systemic interconnections. But the standard containers for *national* class analysis (firms and nation-states) would need reworking.

The third critical aspect, relating to global classes and domestic class structures, is that the new segmentations get filtered through distinct political and policy cultures: a neoliberal policy culture that opens up a country to the upper-level professional circuits of global capital, on the one hand, and immigration policies that close a country to lower-level labor-market circuits, on the other hand. Filtering the novel processes through these policy frames, which in many ways are older, has the effect of obscuring precisely those features of globalization that this chapter seeks to illuminate: the greater-than-evident place boundedness of the new global professional classes and the greater-than-evident globality of the new disadvantaged workforce. These two unconnected policy frames basically contribute to obscure the fact that the new types of segmentation these two global classes introduce into the political and civic fabric of a society are part of advanced capitalism. Class analysis needs to factor in the structures of the latter, and the fact that today, more so than in the twentieth century, they function through multi-sited global geographies. Finally, it needs to factor in that the global class of low-wage workers is more global and hence more indicative of the future, rather than of a backward past, than is usually assumed.

Chapter Seven
LOCAL ACTORS IN GLOBAL POLITICS

GLOBALIZATION AND THE NEW ICTs have enabled a variety of local political actors to enter international arenas that were once exclusive to national states. Numerous types of claim making and oppositional politics articulate these developments. Going global has been facilitated and conditioned in part by the infrastructure of the global economy even as that infrastructure has often been the object of oppositional politics. Most important in my analysis, the possibility of global imaginaries has enabled even those who are geographically immobile to become involved in global politics (see also Chapter 6). In brief, NGOs and indigenous peoples, immigrants and refugees who become the subject of adjudication in human rights decisions, human rights and environmental activists, and many others are increasingly becoming actors in global politics.

That is, nonstate actors can enter and gain visibility in international forums or global politics as individuals and collectivities, emerging from the invisibility of aggregate membership in a nation-state that is exclusively represented by a sovereign. This new process can be interpreted in terms of an incipient unbundling of the exclusive authority over territory and people that has long been associated with the national state. The most strategic instantiation of this unbundling is probably the global city, which operates as a partially denationalized platform for global capital and is also emerging as a key site for the coming together of the most astounding mix of people from all over the world as discussed in Chapter 4. The growing intensity of transactions among major cities is creating a strategic cross-border geography that partially bypasses national states. The new network technologies further strengthen these transactions, whether they are electronic transfers of specialized services among firms or Internet-based communications among the members of globally dispersed diasporas and civil society organizations. The new ICTs, especially the public-access Internet, have actually strengthened this politics of places and have expanded the geography for civil society actors beyond the strategic networks of global cities to include often peripheral localities.

Together these various trends have enabled the shaping of a politics of places on global networks. This global politics of places also functions as a critical infrastructure for the embedding of global civil society. A key question organizing this chapter concerns the ways in which localized actors and struggles actually constitute these new types of global politics and subjectivities. The argument is that local actors, even when geographically immobile and resource-poor, can contribute to the formation of global domains or virtual public spheres, and thereby to a type of local political subjectivity that needs to be distinguished from what we would usually consider local. The new ICTs are important. But, as I will discuss, they are important given two conditions. One condition is the existence of social networks, and it is here that the cross-border geographies connecting places, especially global cities, can be critical in that they provide conducive environments for the growth of such social networks. The second condition, one often overlooked in the emerging scholarship on the subject, is the extensive organizing and development of adequate technical infrastructures and software necessary to enable disadvantaged actors to use the new ICTs. Civil society organizations and individuals have played crucial roles in the work of adapting global North technologies to global South conditions. The result has been that particular instantiations of the local can actually be constituted at multiple scales and can thereby be part of global formations that tend toward lateralized and horizontal networks. These differ from the vertical and hierarchical forms typical of major global actors, such as the IMF and the WTO. I examine these issues with a focus on various political practices and technologies, partly because they remain understudied and misunderstood in the social sciences. Such a focus also takes the analysis beyond the new geographies of centrality constructed through the network of the forty or so global cities in the world today examined in Chapters Two and Four. It accommodates the possibility that even rather peripheralized locations can become part of global networks.

These developments contribute to distinct kinds of political practices and subjectivities. The chapter examines two dynamics that come together in producing these new types of politics and subjectivities. One is the ascendance of subnational and transnational spaces and actors, examined in the first section. The other is that the new ICTs have enabled local actors to become part of global networks, the subject of the second and third sections. The concluding section examines the implications of these developments for political subjectivity.

MICROSPACES AND ACTORS IN GLOBAL CIVIL SOCIETY

Cities and the new strategic geographies that connect them and bypass national states can be seen as constituting part of the infrastructure of global domains, including global civil society. They do so from the ground up, through multiple microsites and microtransactions. Among the actors in this political landscape are a variety of organizations focused on transboundary issues, such as immigration, asylum, international women's agendas, and anti-globalization struggles. While these organizations are not necessarily urban in their orientation or genesis, they tend to converge in cities. The new network technologies, especially the Internet, ironically have strengthened the urban map of transboundary networks. It does not have to be that way, but at this time cities and the networks that bind them function as an anchor and an enabler of cross-border struggles. Global cities, then, are thick enabling environments for these types of activities even when the networks are not urban per se. In this regard, global cities help people experience themselves as part of global nonstate networks in their daily lives. They enact some version of the global in the microspaces of daily life rather than on some putative global stage.

A key nexus in this configuration is that the weakening of the exclusive formal authority of states over national territory facilitates the ascendance of sub- and transnational spaces and actors in politico-civic processes. These spaces and actors include those confined to the national domain, which can now become part of global networks; these are novel spaces that have evolved in the context of globalization and the new ICTs. As discussed in Chapter Two, the loss of power at the national level produces the possibility of new forms of power and politics at the subnational and supranational levels. The national as container of social process and power is cracked (Taylor 2000; Abu-Lughod 1999b). This cracked casing opens up a geography of politics and civics that links subnational spaces. Cities are foremost in this new geography. The density of political and civic cultures in large cities enables the localizing of global civil society in people's lives (see, for example, Bartlett 2007).

As discussed in the preceding chapters, the organizational side of the global economy materializes in a worldwide grid of strategic places, uppermost among which are major international business and financial centers. We can think of this global grid as constituting a new economic geography of centrality, one that cuts across both national boundaries and, increasingly, the old North-South divide. It has emerged as a transnational space for the formation of new claims by global capital. The question here is whether other types of actors are also enabled to make claims in this new transnational geography of centrality and, if they are, whether they are constituting alternative political geographies.

Economic globalization and telecommunications have contributed to the production of an urban space that pivots on deterritorialized cross-border networks and territorial locations with massive concentrations of resources. This is not a completely new feature. Over the centuries cities have been at the intersection of processes with supraurban and even intercontinental scaling. Ancient Athens and Rome, the cities of the Hanseatic League, Genoa, Venice, Baghdad, Cairo, Istanbul— all were at the crossroads of major dynamics in their time (Braudel 1984). What is different today is the coexistence of multiple networks and their intensity, complexity, and global span. Those features have served to increase the number of cities that are part of cross-border networks operating on often vast geographic scales. Under these conditions much of what we experience and represent as the local level turns out to be a microenvironment with global span.

The new urban spatiality thus produced is partial in a double sense: it accounts for only part of what happens in cities and what cities are about, and it inhabits only part of what we might think of as the space of the city, whether this is understood in terms of a city's administrative boundaries or in the sense of the public life of a city's people. It is, nonetheless, one way in which cities can become part of the living infrastructure of global civil society. But cities and their global networks also enable the operations of militant, criminal, and terrorist organizations. Globalization, telecommunications, and flexible loyalties and identities facilitate the formation of cross-border geographies for an increasing range of activities and communities of membership. The evidence that has emerged since the terrorist attacks of September 11, 2001, has made it clear that the global financial system also served the terrorists' purposes and that several major cities n Europe were key bases for Osama bin Laden's al Qaeda net work. Several other militant organizations have set up an international network of bases in various cities. For instance, London has been a key base for the international secretariat of Sri Lanka's Liberation Tigers of Tamil Eelam, and cities in France, Norway, Sweden, Canada, and the United States are home to their various centers of activity. In addition, al Qaeda is known to have established a support network in Great Britain, run from an office in London called the Advice and Reformation Committee, which was founded in July 1994 and has since been closed. (For more details, see the description of al Qaeda in Anheier, Glasius, and Kaldor 2002, chap. 1.)

We might conceive of these networked spaces as assemblages of networks/platforms, territorial insertions, multiple transactions, and diverse users in play. These conditions point to the enormous capabilities of these technologies, but also to their limitations. Such assemblages are not formal entities. It is in good part the social logics of users and actors that contribute to the outcomes. The mixing of these social logics with the technologies can, in principle, produce very diverse assemblages and projects. These will not inevitably globalize users and eliminate their articulation with particular localities, but they can make globality a working resource. Complex assemblages can capture global social and political capital, and they can "house" this capital. In that sense they are more than simply a political act. The space constituted by the worldwide grid of global cities can function as such an assemblage. One particular form of social and political capital it can capture for the disadvantaged or less powerful is a variety of types of transnationalisms and politics that deborder the nation-state.

People's Networks: Micropolitics for Global Civil Society

The cross-border network of global cities is a space in which we are seeing the formation of new types of global politics of place that contest corporate globalization, environmental and human rights abuses, and so on. The demonstrations by the "alter-globalization" movement signal the potential for developing a politics centered on places understood as locations on global networks. This is a place-specific politics with a global span. It is a type of political work deeply embedded in people's actions and activities but made possible in part by the existence of global digital links. These links are mostly organizations operating through networks of cities and involving informal political actors—that is, actors who are not necessarily engaging in politics as narrowly defined citizens, for whom voting is the most formalized type of citizen politics. Among the informal political actors are women who engage in political struggles in their condition as mothers, anti-globalization activists who go to a foreign country as tourists but to do citizen politics, and undocumented immigrants who join protests against police brutality.

These practices constitute a specific type of global politics, one that runs through localities and is not predicated on the existence of global institutions. The engagement can be with global institutions, such as the IMF or the WTO, or with local institutions, such as a particular government or local police force charged with human rights abuses. Theoretically this type of global politics illuminates the distinction between a global network and the actual transactions that constitute it: the global character of a network does not necessarily imply that its transactions are equally global or that they all have to happen at the global level. It shows the local to be multiscalar.

Computer-centered technologies have made a significant difference.[1] The public-access Internet matters not only because of low-cost connectivity and the possibility of effective use (via e-mail) even with low bandwidth availability, but also and most important because of some of its key features. Simultaneous decentralized access can give local actors a sense of participation in struggles that are not necessarily global but are globally distributed in that they recur in locality after locality. Thus the technology can also help in the formation of cross-border public spheres for these types of actors, and it can do so without needing to run through global institutions[2] and using forms of recognition that do not depend on much direct interaction or on joint action on the ground. Among the implications of these options are the possibility of forming global networks that bypass central authority and—what is especially significant for resource-poor organizations—the possibility that those who may never be able to travel can nonetheless be part of global struggles and global publics.

Such forms of recognition are not historically new. Yet there are two matters that signal the need for empirical and theoretical work on their ICT-enabled forms. One is that much of the conceptualization of the local in the social sciences has assumed geographic proximity, and thereby a sharply defined territorial boundedness and the associated implied closure. The other, partly a consequence of the first, is a strong tendency to conceive of the local as part of a hierarchy of nested scales, especially once there are national states. To a very large extent, these conceptualizations hold for most of the instantiations of the local today and, more specifically, for most of the actual practices and formations likely to constitute the local in most of the world. But there are also conditions today that contribute to the destabilization of these practices and formations and hence invite a reconceptualization of the local that can accommodate a set of instances that diverge from dominant patterns. Key among these current conditions are globalization

and/or globality as constitutive not only of cross-border institutional spaces but also of powerful imaginaries enabling aspi-
rations to transboundary political practice even when the actors
involved are immobile. For instance, women have become increasingly active in this world of cross-border efforts. This has
often meant the potential transformation of a whole range of
"local" conditions or domestic institutional domains—such
as the household, the community, or the neighborhood, where
women find themselves confined to domestic roles—into political spaces. Women can emerge as political and civic subjects
without having to step out of these domestic worlds (for example, Hamilton and Chinchilla 2001; Friedman 2005). From being lived or experienced as nonpolitical or domestic, these
places are transformed into microenvironments with a global
span (Naples and Desai 2002; Nash 2005). A community of
practice can emerge that creates multiple lateral, horizontal
communications, collaborations, solidarities, and supports.

The city is a far more concrete space for politics than the nation. It becomes a place where nonformal political actors can be
part of the political scene in a way that is more difficult,
though not impossible, at the national level (for example,
Williamson, Alperovitz, and Imbroscio 2002). Nationally, politics needs to run through existing formal systems, whether the
electoral system or the judiciary (taking state agencies to
court). To do this, one needs to be a citizen. Nonformal political actors are thereby more easily rendered invisible in the
space of national politics. The space of the city accommodates a
broad range of political activities—squatting, demonstrating
against police brutality, fighting for the rights of immigrants
and the homeless—and a broad range of issues—such as the

politics of culture and identity or gay and lesbian and queer politics. Much of this becomes visible on the street. Much of urban politics is concrete, enacted by people rather than dependent on massive media technologies. Street-level politics makes possible the formation of new types of political subjects that do not have to go through the formal political system.

It is in this sense that those who lack power and are "unauthorized"—that is, unauthorized immigrants, those who are disadvantaged, outsiders, and discriminated-against minorities—can gain *presence* in global cities, vis-à-vis power and one another (Sassen 2002b). A good example of this was the Europewide demonstrations of largely "Turkish" Kurds in response to the arrest of Abdullah Ocalan: suddenly they were on the map not only as an oppressed minority but also as a diaspora in their own right, distinct from the Turks. For me, this phenomenon signals the possibility of a new type of politics centered in new types of political actors. It is not simply a matter of having or not having power. Now there are new hybrid bases from which to act. A growing number of organizations are largely focused on a variety of grievances of powerless groups and individuals. Some are global and others national. Although powerless, these individuals and groups are acquiring a presence on a broader politico-civic stage.[3]

One of the characteristics of the type of organization discussed here is that it engages in "noncosmopolitan" forms of global politics. Partly enabled by the Internet, activists can develop global networks not only for circulating information (about environmental, housing, political, and other issues) but also for engaging in political work and executing strategies. Yet they remain grounded in specific issues and are often focused on their localities even as they operate as part of global networks. There are many examples of this new type of cross-border political work. For instance, SPARC (Society for the Promotion of Area Resource Centers), started by and focused on women, began as an effort to organize slum dwellers in Mumbai to obtain housing. Now it has a network of groups throughout Asia and in some cities in Latin America and Africa. The focus is local, and so are the participants and those whom they seek to reach, usually local governments. The various organizations making up the broader network do not necessarily gain power or material resources from global networking, but they gain strength for themselves and for their negotiations with the agencies to which they present their demands. This is one of the key forms of critical politics that the Internet can make possible: a politics of the local with a big difference in that the localities are connected with one another across a region, a country, or the world. Although the network is global, its constitutive events are local.

Using the New ICTs

Computer-centered interactive technologies have played an important role in the making of global settings and global imaginaries. These technologies facilitate multiscalar transactions and simultaneous interconnectivity. They can be used to further develop old strategies (for example, Tsaliki 2002; Lannon 2002) and to develop new ways of organizing, notably, electronic activism (Monberg 1998; Bousquet and Wills 2003; Denning 2001; Peter J. Smith 2001; Yang 2003). Non-Web-based Internet media are the main type of ICT used for organizing. E-mail is perhaps the most widely used medium, partly because organizations in the global South often have narrow bandwidth and slow connections, making the Web a far less usable and effective option. To achieve the forms of globality that concern me in this chapter, it is important that there be a recognition of these constraints among major transnational organizations dealing with the global South: for instance, this means making text-only databases, with no visuals or hypertext markup language, no spreadsheets, and none of the other facilities that demand considerable bandwidth and fast connections (for example, Pace and Panganiban 2002, 113; on workspaces generally, see Bach and Stark 2005; Sack 2005).[4]

As has been widely recognized by now, new ICTs do not simply replace existing media techniques. (For a variety of issues, see Woolgar 2002; Thrift 2005; Lievrouw and Livingstone 2002; Elmer 2004; Coleman 2004). The evidence is far from systematic, and the object of study is continuously undergoing change. But we can identify two basic patterns. On the one hand there might be no genuine need for these particular technologies given the nature of the organizing effort, or the technologies might be underutilized (for studies of particular organizations, see Tsaliki [2002], Cederman and Kraus [2005].[5] For instance, a survey of local and grassroots human rights NGOs in several regions of the world found that the Internet makes the exchange of information easier and is helpful in developing other kinds of collaboration, but it does not help to launch joint projects (Lannon 2002, 33). On the other hand, there are highly creative ways of using the new ICTs, along with older media, that recognize the needs of particular communities (Dean et al. 2006). A good example is using the Internet to send audio files that can be broadcast over loudspeakers to groups who lack access to the Internet or are illiterate. The M. S. Swaminathan Research Foundation in southern India has supported this type of strategy by setting up Village Knowledge Centers catering to populations that although mostly illiterate, know exactly what type of information they need or want. When we consider mixed uses, it becomes clear that the Internet can often fulfill highly creative functions when used with other technologies, whether old or new. Thus Amnesty International's International Secretariat has set up an infrastructure to collect electronic news feeds via satellite, which it then processes and redistributes to its staff workstations (Lebert 2003).

But there is also evidence that use of these technologies has led to the formation of new types of organizations and activism, especially with some of the more recent inventions such as peer-to-peer and wiki technologies. For instance, Yang (2003) found that what were originally exclusively online discussions among groups and individuals in China concerned with the environment evolved into active NGOs. Furthermore, one result of this genesis is that their membership is national, distributed among different parts of the country. The variety of online activism examined by Denning (1999) involved largely new types. To mention what is perhaps one of the most widely known cases of how the Internet made a strategic difference, the Zapatista movement became two organizational efforts, one a local rebellion in Mexico, the other a transnational civil society movement. The civil society movement involved the participation of multiple NGOs concerned with peace, trade, human rights, and other struggles for social justice. It worked through both the Internet and conventional media (Cleaver 1998; Arquilla and Ronfeld 2001) to put pressure on the Mexican government. What is important is that it shaped a new concept for civil organizing: multiple rhizomatically connected autonomous groups (Cleaver 1998; but see Bennett 2003).

What is far less known is that the local rebellion of the Zapatistas operated basically without e-mail infrastructure (Cleaver 1998). Subcommandante Marcos was not on e-mail, let alone able to join collaborative workspaces on the Web. Messages had to be hand-carried across military lines to be put on the Internet; furthermore, not all the solidarity networks themselves had e-mail, and local communities sympathetic to the struggle often had problems with Internet access (Mills 2002, 83). Yet Internet-based media did contribute to the movement enormously, in good part because of preexisting social networks (in this regard see also Garcia 2002). Among the electronic networks involved, LaNeta played a crucial role in globalizing the struggle. LaNeta is a civil society network established with support of a San Francisco–based NGO, the Institute for Global Communications (IGC). In 1993 LaNeta became a member of the Association for Progressive Communications (APC) and began to function as a key connection between civil society organizations in and outside Mexico. In this regard, it is interesting to note that a local movement made LaNeta into a transnational information hub.

There is little doubt that the gathering, storage, and dissemination of information are crucial functions for these kinds of organizations (Carrie A. Meyer 1997; Tuijl and Jordan 1999; Bach and Stark 2005; but see also Bowker and Starr 1999). Human rights, large development, and environmental organizations are at this point the leaders in the effort to build online databases and archives. (See, for example, the Web sites of Human Rights Internet, Greenpeace, and Oxfam International).[6] Oxfam has also set up knowledge centers on its Web site—specialized collections devoted to particular issues, such as the land rights in Africa—and a related resources bank (Warkentin 2001, 136). Specialized campaigns such as those opposing the WTO; advocating banning land mines, or canceling the debt of hyperindebted poor countries (the Jubilee 2000 campaign), have also been effective at building online databases, and developing tools for using ICTs (Donk et al. 2005).

Software can also be designed to address specific needs of organizations or campaigns. For example, HR Information and Documentation Systems International (HURIDOCS), a transnational network of human rights organizations, aims at improving access to, and dissemination and use of, human rights information. It runs a program to develop tools, standards, and techniques for documenting violations. The evidence on NGO use of Internet media also shows the importance of institutional mechanisms and the use of appropriate software. Amnesty International has set up an institutional mechanism to help victims of human rights abuses use the Internet to contact transnational organizations for help: its Urgent Action Network is a worldwide e-mail alerting system with seventy-five networks of letter-writing members who respond to urgent cases by immediately sending e-mail messages to key and pertinent entities.[7]

The Forging of New Political Subjects: The Multiscalar Politics of Local Actors

The technical and political resources discussed so far facilitate a new type of cross-border politics, one centered in multiple localities yet intensely connected digitally (Mills 2002; Kuntze, Rottmann, and Symons 2002; Whittell 2001). Adams (1996), among others, shows us how telecommunications create new links across space that underline the importance of networks of relations and partly bypass older hierarchies of scale. Activists can develop networks for circulating place-based information— about local environmental, housing, and political conditions— that can become part of the political work and strategies addressing a global condition—the environment, growing worldwide poverty and unemployment, the lack of accountability among multinationals, and so on. The issue here is not so much the possibility of such political practices: they have long existed even though with other media and other velocities. The issue is rather one of orders of magnitude, scope, and simultaneity: the technologies, the institutions, and the imaginaries that mark the current global digital context inscribe local political practice with new meanings and new potentialities.[8]

There are many examples that illustrate the fact of new possibilities and potentials for action. Besides some of the cases already discussed, there is the vastly expanded repertory of actions that can be taken when electronic activism is also an option. The New Tactics in Human Rights project of the Center for Victims of Torture has compiled a workbook containing 120 anti-torture tactics, including exclusively online forms of action.[9] The Web site of the New York–based Electronic Disturbance Theater, a group of cyberactivists and artists, contains detailed information about electronic repertories for action.[10] The International Campaign to Ban Landmines, officially launched in 1992 by six NGOs in the United States, France, the United Kingdom, and Germany, evolved into a coalition of over 1,000 NGOs in 60 countries. It succeeded when 130 countries signed the Mine Ban Treaty in 1997 (Williams and Goose 1998). The campaign used both traditional techniques and ICTs. Internet-based media provided mass distribution more effectively and more cheaply than telephone and fax (Matthew J. O. Scott 2001; Rutherford 2002). Jubilee 2000 used the Internet to great effect: its Web site brought together all the information on debt and campaign work considered necessary for the effort, and information was distributed via Majordomo list management, databases, and e-mail address books.[11] Generally speaking, preexisting online communications networks are important for e-mail alerts aimed at rapid mobilization. Distributed access is crucial: once an alert enters the network from no matter what point of access, it spreads quickly through the network. Amnesty's Urgent Action Network is such a system. However, anonymous Web sites are also part of such communication networks. An example is s11.org, a Web site that can be used for worldwide mobilizations insofar as it is part of multiple online communications networks. The Melbourne mobilization against the September 2000 Asia Pacific Economic Summit of the WEF brought activist groups from around Australia together on this site to coordinate their actions, which succeeded in paralyzing a good part of the gathering, a first in the history of the WEF meetings (Redden 2001). There are by now several much-studied mobilizations that were organized online; the protest of the WTO in Seattle in 1999 and the anti-Nike campaign are two of the best known (see generally Khagram et al. 2002; Donk et al. 2005).[12]

An important feature of this type of multiscalar politics of the local is that it is not confined to moving through a set of nested scales from the local to the national to the international but can directly access other local actors whether in the same country or across borders. One Internet-based technology that reflects this possibility of escaping nested hierarchies of scale is the online workspace, often used for Internet-based collaboration. Such a space can constitute a community of practice (Sharp 1997) or a knowledge network (Creech and Willard 2001). An example of an online workspace is the Sustainable Development Communications Network, also described as a knowledge space (Kuntze, Rottmann, and Symons 2002), set up by a group of civil society organizations in 1998; it is a virtual, open, and collaborative organization aiming at engaging in joint communications activities to inform broader audiences about sustainable development and build members' capacities to use ICT effectively. Its trilingual SD Gateway, which integrates and showcases members' communication efforts, contains links to thousands of member-contributed documents, a job bank, and mailing lists on sustainable development. It is one of several NGOs whose aim is to promote civil society collaboration through ICTs; among others are the APC, OneWorld.net, and Bellanet.

This possibility of exiting or avoiding hierarchies of scale does not preclude the fact that powerful actors can use the existence of different jurisdictional scales to their advantage (Morrill 1999) and that local resistance is constrained by how the state deploys scaling through jurisdictional, administrative, and regulatory orders (Judd 1998). On the contrary, it might well be that the conditions analyzed by Morrill and Judd, among others, force the issue, so to speak. Why work through the power relations that are shaped into state-centered hierarchies of scale? Why not jump ship if that is an option? This combination of conditions and options is well illustrated by research showing how the power of national governments can subvert the legal claims of first-nation people (Howitt 1998; Silvern 1999), which has in turn increasingly led those people to seek direct representation in international forums, bypassing the national state.[13] In this sense, then, my effort here is to recover a particular type of multiscalar context, one characterized by direct local-global transactions or by a multiplication of local transactions as part of global networks. Neither type is marked by nested scalings.

There are many examples of such types of cross-border political work. We can distinguish two forms of it, each capturing a specific type of scalar interaction. In one the scale of struggle remains the locality, and the object is to engage local actors—for example, a local housing or environmental agency—but with the knowledge and explicit or tacit invocation of multiple localities around the world engaged in similar localized struggles with similar local actors. It is this combination of multiplication and self-reflexivity that contributes to the constitution of a global condition from these localized practices and rhetorics. It means, in a sense, taking Kevin Cox's notion of scaled "spaces of engagement" constitutive of local politics and situating it in a specific type of context, not necessarily the one Cox himself might have had in mind. Beyond the fact of relations between scales as being crucial to local politics, it is perhaps the social and political construction itself of scale as social action (Howitt 1993; Swyngedouw 1997; Brenner 1998) that needs emphasizing.[14] Finally, and crucial to my analysis (Sassen 2006a, chap. 7), is the actual thick and particularized content of the struggle or dynamic that gets instantiated.

The other form of multiscalar interaction is one in which localized struggles are aimed at engaging global actors—for example, the WTO, the IMF, and multinational firms—either at the global scale or in multiple localities.[15] A significant feature of this organizational form is the possibility of expanded decentralization and simultaneous integration. It parallels the analysis of the growth of global finance in Chapter 4—the articulation of the capital market with a growing network of financial centers. That the former relies on public access networks and the second on private dedicated networks does not alter this organizational outcome and its threshold effects: the possibility of constituting transboundary publics rather than merely global communications and information searches. Insofar as the network technologies strengthen and create new types of cross-border activities among nonstate actors, they enable a distinct and only partly digital condition variously referred to as global civil society, global publics, and commons. From struggles for human rights and the environment to workers' strikes and AIDS campaigns against the large pharmaceutical firms, the Internet has emerged as a powerful medium through which non-elites can create the equivalent of insider groups at scales going from the local to the global.[16] The possibility of doing so transnationally at a time when a growing set of issues are seen as escaping the bounds of nation states makes this even more significant.

Yet another key scalar element here is that digital networks can be used by political activists to strengthen local transactions. Digital networks, primed to span the world, can actually serve to intensify transactions among residents of a city or region; it can serve to make them aware of neighboring communities and help them gain an understanding of local issues that resonate positively or negatively with communities that are there in the same city rather than at the other end of the world (Riemens and Lovink 2002). Recovering the way the new digital technology can serve to support local initiatives and alliances inside a locality is conceptually important given the almost exclusive emphasis in the representation of these technologies on their global scope and deployment.[17]

Coming back to Howitt's (1993) point about constructing the geographic scales at which social action can occur, let me suggest that cyberspace, like the city, can be a more concrete space for social struggles than that of the national political system. It becomes a place where nonformal political actors can take part in politics in a way that is much more difficult in national institutional channels. Cyberspace can accommodate a broad range of social struggles and facilitate the emergence of new types of political subjects that do not have to go through the formal political system. Individuals and groups that historically have been excluded from formal political systems and whose struggles can be enacted in part outside those systems can find in cyberspace an enabling environment for their emergence as nonformal political actors, and for their struggles.

The mix of focused activism and local or global networks represented by the organizations described in this chapter creates conditions for the emergence of at least partly transnational identities. The possibility of identifying with larger communities of practice or membership can bring about the partial unmooring of identities referred to in the first section.

Although this identification does not necessarily neutralize attachments to a country or a national cause, it does shift the attachment to include translocal communities of practice and/or membership. This shift is a crucial building block for a global politics of localized actors—that is, a politics that can incorporate the micropractices and microobjectives of people's daily lives as well as their political passions. The possibility of thinner transnational identities emerging as a consequence of this thickness of micropolitics raises interesting theoretical questions. And it matters for strengthening global politics, even as the risk of nationalisms and fundamentalism is clearly present in these dynamics as well.

The types of political practice discussed here do not form the cosmopolitan route to the global.[18] They are global through the knowing multiplication of local practices. These are types of sociability and struggle deeply embedded in people's actions and activities. They are also forms of institution-building work with a global scope that can come from localities and networks of localities with limited resources and from informal social actors. They do not have to become cosmopolitan in this process; they may well remain domestic and particularistic in their orientation and remain engaged with their households and local community struggles, yet they are participating in emergent global politics.

Chapter Eight
EMERGENT GLOBAL FORMATIONS
AND RESEARCH AGENDAS

THE SUBJECT OF THIS BOOK is history in the making. The effort in each chapter was to detect shapes and construct objects of study around what is ultimately a roving animal moving with increasing vigor and velocity. In this chapter, I want to explore what we might think of as extreme instances of emergent global formations that capture some of the trends discussed thus far.

If there is one theme that captures aspects of all I have discussed, it is the notion of borders. Thus the first section of this chapter disaggregates the institution of the border into its multiple components in order to capture the often-sharp repositioning and redeployment of some of those components. Acute and perhaps extreme novel types of borderings are microenvironments with global span (see Chapter 7), the subject of the second section. Such environments might consist of a household or a firm oriented toward global networks and technologically enabled to reach them. The whole question of context and surroundings as part of the locality is profoundly unsettled in this case. I conclude with the elements for a sociology of digital space. The focus is on electronic interactive domains—including formations as diverse as markets and activist networks—and the socialities they are constituting. Much social science concerns the technology and the social psychology of these domains, but their sociology remains under-theorized. This chapter is, then, a series of partial excavations into emergent global formations.

From National Borders to Embedded Borderings

The globalization of a broad range of processes is producing ruptures in the mosaic of border regimes and contributing to the formation of new types of borderings.[1] These ruptures and borderings are beginning to alter the meaning of what we think of as borders. They also help make legible the features and conditionalities of what has been the dominant border regime, associated with the nation-state, which though still the prevalent border regime of our times is now less so than it was even fifteen years ago. Such transformations are helping us understand the extent to which the historiography and geography covering the geopolitics of the last two centuries have largely been produced from the perspective of the nation-state, producing a kind of methodological nationalism (e.g., Beck 2006; Giddens 1987). Nation-state capture in these modes of analysis has had the effect of simplifying the question of the border: the border to a large extent has been reduced to a geographic event and the immediate institutional apparatus through which it was controlled, protected, and generally governed. What globalization brings to this condition is the actual and heuristic disaggregating of "the border"; from being typically represented as a unitary condition in policy discourse, now its multiple components are becoming legible. Thus, the opening up of borders to flows of capital and services has functioned alongside the ongoing and indeed increasing border closure when it comes to low-wage immigration. Furthermore, I will argue that such ruptures and new borders allow us to see that the border extends far beyond the geographic line of internationally recognized treaties and its directly linked institutions such as consulates and airport immigration controls: borders are constituted through many more institutions and have more locations than standard representations suggest.

Here I begin by mapping the complexities of borders and the multiple institutions and locations that constitute them; I then move on to examine novel types of bordering that arise from current global dynamics. I conclude with a discussion of the implications of these transformations for exclusive state authority, a foundational issue for the category of "the border" as historically constructed and theoretically represented over the last two centuries.

Disaggregating the Border

The multiple regimes that constitute the border as an institution can be grouped on the one hand into a formalized apparatus that is part of the interstate system and on the other into an as yet far less formalized array of novel types of borderings lying largely outside the framing of the interstate system. The first component has at its core the body of regulations covering a variety of international flows, flows of different types of commodities, capital, people, services, and information. No matter their variety, these multiple regimes tend to cohere around the state's unilateral authority to define and enforce regulations and the state's obligation to respect and uphold the regulations emerging from the international treaty system or bilateral arrangements. The second component, the new type of bordering dynamics arising outside the framing of the interstate system, does not necessarily entail a self-evident crossing of borders; it includes a range of dynamics arising from specific contemporary developments, notably emergent systems of global law and a growing range of globally networked interactive digital domains.

Systems of global law are not centered in state law—that is, they are to be distinguished from both national and international law. And global interactive digital domains are mostly informal and hence outside the existing treaty system; they are often ensconced in subnational localities that are part of cross-border networks. The formation of these distinct systems of global law and globally networked interactive domains entails a multiplication of bordered spaces. But the national notion of borders as delimiting two sovereign territorial states is not quite in play. Global bordering operates at a transnational, supranational, or subnational scale. And although the spaces may cross national borders, they are not necessarily part of the new open-border regimes that are state centered, such as those, for instance, of the global trading and financial systems. Insofar as these are global bordered domains, they entail a novel instance of the notion of borders.

In the following discussion, I briefly examine some key analytic distinctions we might use to disaggregate state-centered border regimes and locate a given site in a global web of bordered spaces.

State-Centered Border Regimes: Locating the Border

Today's multiple border regimes have varied contents and locations. For instance, cross-border flows of capital require a sequence of interventions that differs in character from that for goods and has very different institutional and geographic locations. The actual geographic border crossing is part of the cross-border flow of goods but not part of the flow of capital, unless cash is being transported. Each border-control intervention can be conceived of as one point in a chain of locations. In the case of traded goods, an intervention might involve a pre-border inspection or certification site. In the case of capital flows, the chain of locations will involve banks, stock markets, and electronic networks. The geographic borderline is but one point in the chain; institutional points of border-control intervention can form long chains inside a country.

We might capture the notion of multiple locations by imagining that the sites for the enforcement of border regimes range from banks to bodies. When a bank executes the most elementary money transfer to another country, the bank is one site for border-regime enforcement. A certified good represents a case in which the object itself crossing the border is one of the sites for enforcement: the emblematic case is a certified agricultural product, but it also encompasses the case of the tourist carrying a tourist visa and the immigrant carrying the requisite immigration certification. Indeed, in the case of immigration, it is the body of the immigrant that is both the carrier of much of the regime and the crucial site for enforcement, and in the case of an unauthorized immigrant, it is, again, the immigrant's body that is the carrier of the violation of the law—and the carrier of the corresponding punishment (detention or expulsion).

A direct effect of globalization, especially corporate economic globalization, has been the creation of increasing divergence among different border regimes. Thus the lifting of border controls on a growing variety of capital, services, and information flows has taken place even as other border regimes maintain closure and even as impediments to cross-border flows are made stronger, as is the case for the migration of low-wage workers. We are also seeing the construction of specific "borderings" to contain and govern emerging, often strategic or specialized flows that cut across traditional national borders, as is the case, for instance, with the new regimes of NAFTA and the GATTS for the cross-border circulation of high-level professionals. Where in the past those professionals may have been part of a country's general immigration regime, now we have an increasing divergence between that regime and the specialized regime governing professionals.[2]

Positioning a Site in a Global Web of Borders

If I am to consider what might be involved, for example, in locating an economic site in a global web of "borders," a first step in my research practice is to conceive of the global economy as constituted through a set of specialized or partial circuits and multiple, often overlapping space economies. The question then becomes how a given area is articulated with various circuits and space economies.

The articulation of a site with global circuits can be direct or indirect and part of long chains or short chains. An instance of a direct articulation is a site located on a specialized global circuit, as might be the case with export forestry, a mine, offshore manufacturing, or offshore banking. An instance of an indirect articulation is a site located on national economic circuits—for example, a site for the production of processed consumer goods marketed by major distributors, with export occurring through multiple complex national and foreign urban markets. The chains of transactions involving these types of products are likely to be shorter in the case of extractive industries than in the case of manufactures, especially if consumer goods, where export-import handlers and multiple distributors are likely to be part of the chain.

As for the second element, the space economies involved, a first critical issue is that a given site can be constituted through one or more such economies. A forestry site or an agricultural site is likely to be constituted through fewer space economies than a financial center or a manufacturing complex. A second critical issue is that none, only one, or several of the space economies of a given site might be global. It seems to me crucial to disaggregate a site along these lines and not reify it as simply "rural." For instance, the space economy of even a sparsely populated area, such as a forestry site, can be far more complex than common sense might suggest even if it is located on only one global circuit, as in the case of an international logging company that has contracted to purchase all the wood produced on a site. The multinational's acquisition of the wood demands that it satisfy a great mix of requirements typically executed via specialized corporate services, notably accounting and law and probably financing, which in turn are subject to national regulations. We might say, then, that the forestry site is actually constituted through several, or at the least two, space economies: logging and specialized corporate services. But it is likely part of a third space economy, that of global financial markets; for instance, if the logging company is part of a stock exchange listing, it may well have "liquefied" the logs by converting them to financial futures that can circulate in the global capital market.[3] This insertion in global financial markets is to be distinguished from the financing of the actual work—of logging; rather, it has to do with the ability of global finance to liquefy even the most immobile material good, such as real estate, so that it may circulate as a profit-making financial instrument in the global capital market, in addition to providing the profit-making potential of the material good itself.

There is a kind of analytics that bridges the particularity of state-centered border regimes and the empirical work of locating a site that is part of a global web of such regimes. It is an analytics that aims at disaggregating the border function into the character, locations, and sites for enforcement of a given border regime. The effect is to make legible the multiple territorial, spatial, and institutional dimensions of "the border." These novel types of bordering dynamics intersect with the sovereign state and destabilize the meaning of conventional borders, the subject I turn to next.

Disembedding the Border from Its National Encasements

A critical and growing component of the broader field of forces within which states operate today is the proliferation of specialized types of private authority. These include the expansion of older systems, such as commercial arbitration, into new economic sectors, as well as new forms of private authority that are highly specialized and oriented toward specific economic sectors, such as the system of rules governing the international operations of large construction and engineering firms. The proliferation of self-regulatory regimes is especially evident in sectors dominated by a limited number of very large firms.

One outcome of key aspects of these trends is the emergence of a strategic field of operations that represents a partial disembedding of specific bordering operations from the institutions of the nation-state. It is a fairly rarefied field of cross-border transactions aimed at addressing the new conditions produced and demanded by economic globalization. The transactions are strategic, cut across borders, and entail specific interactions among private actors and, sometimes, government agencies or officials. They do not entail the state as such, as in the case of international treaties, but consist of the operations and aims of private actors—in this case mostly firms and markets globalizing their operations. These transactions also concern the standards and regulations imposed on firms and markets operating globally; in so doing, they push toward cross-national convergence of national regulations and laws pertinent to corporate globalization.

There are two distinct features about this field of transactions that lead me to posit that we can conceive of it as a disembedded space in the process of being structured. One feature is that while the actors involved operate in familiar settings—the state and interstate system in the case of officials and agencies of governments, and the supranational system and the "private sector" in the case of nonstate economic actors—they are actually constituting a distinct space that assembles bits of national territory, authority, and rights into new types of specialized and typically highly particularized fields. These fields cannot be confined to the institutional world of the interstate nor national system. The other feature is the proliferation of rules that begin to get assembled into partial specialized systems of law. Here we enter a new domain of private authorities—fragmented, specialized, increasingly formalized, but not subject to national law per se. One implication of this proliferation of specialized, mostly private or supranational systems of law is the destabilizing of conventional understandings of national borders (see, for instance, Chen 2005).

Over the last two decades we have seen a multiplication of cross-border systems of rule that evince varying degrees of autonomy from national law. At one end are systems clearly centered in what is emerging as a transnational public domain, and at the other are systems that are completely autonomous and largely private. Some scholars (for example, Teubner 2004) see in this development an emergent global law. We might conceive of it as a type of law that is disembedded from national law systems. At the heart of the notion of global law, as distinct from international law, lies the possibility of a law that is not centered in national law and that goes beyond the project of harmonizing the different national laws. Such harmonizing is central to much of the supranational system developed to address economic globalization, environmental issues, and human rights. These highly differentiated systems of rules, some connected to the supranational system though not centered in national law, and others private, amount to the elements for a global law.

There is no full agreement as to the existence of an entity such as global law. For instance, Dezalay and Garth (1995) note that the "international" is itself constituted largely out of a competition among national approaches. Thus the international emerges as a site for regulatory competition among essentially national approaches, whatever the issue—environmental protection, competition policy, or human rights (Charny 1991; Trachtman 1993; Carbonneau 2004).[4] But there is an emergent scholarship (Fischer-Lescano and Teubner 2004) that finds the beginnings of global law centered in the development of autonomous, typically highly specialized, and hence partial regimes. The Project on International Courts and Tribunals has identified about 125 international institutions in which independent authorities reach final legal decisions.[5] These range from institutions in the public domain, such as human rights courts, to those in the private sector. They function through courts, quasi courts, and other mechanisms for settling disputes, such as international commercial arbitration. They include the international maritime court, various tribunals for reparations, international criminal courts, hybrid instances of international-national tribunals, judicial bodies for trade and investment, regional human rights tribunals, and convention-derived institutions, as well as other regional courts, such as the Court of Justice of the European Communities, the European Free Trade Association Court, and the Court of Justice of the Benelux Economic Union. The number of private systems has grown sharply in the last decade. These new regimes go beyond existing international law. They also go beyond new types of law that require states to institute particular regulations inside their national legal systems, an example of which is the law that emerges from the WTO's negotiations on behalf of TRIPS and involves the community of member states. Most prominently, Teubner sees a multiplication of sectoral regimes that overlies national legal systems. The outcome is a foundational transformation of the criteria for differentiating law—not the law of nations nor the distinction between private and public but the recognition of multiple specialized segmented processes of juridification, which today are largely private: "Societal fragmentation impacts upon law in a manner such that the political regulation of differentiated societal spheres requires the parceling out of issue-specific policy-arenas, which, for their part, juridify themselves" (Teubner 2004). From this perspective, global law is segmented into transnational legal regimes, which define the "external reach of their jurisdiction along issue-specific rather than territorial lines, and which claim a global validity for themselves."

To take a concrete case, a type of private authority that illustrates some—though by no means all—of these issues can be seen in the so-called *lex constructionis*, a combination of rules and standard contracts for cross-border construction projects. This case combines the notion of an autonomous global system of rules internal to an economic sector with the fact of a few large firms having disproportionate control over that sector, thereby facilitating the making of such private systems of rules. The international construction sector is dominated by a small number of well-organized private associations: the International Federation of Consulting Engineers (FIDIC), the European Construction Industry Federation (FIEC), the Institution of Civil Engineers (ICE), the Engineering Advancement Association of Japan (ENAA), and the American Institute of Architects (AIA). In addition, the World Bank, the United Nations Commission on International Trade Law (UNCITRAL), the International Institute for the Unification of Private Law (UNIDROIT), and certain international law firms contribute to developing legal norms for how the sector is meant to function. Because of the nature of large construction and engineering projects, this case also illuminates the ways in which having an autonomous system of rules and the type of power that large global firms have does not mean that those firms can escape all outside constraints. Thus the firms increasingly "need" to address environmental protection. The way they do so in the *lex constructionis* is also emblematic of what other such autonomously governed sectors do: it is largely a strategy of deference that aims at externalizing the responsibility for regulating the environmental issues arising from large-scale construction projects. The externalizing is to the "extracontractual" realm of the law of the host state, using "compliance" provisions that are today part of the standard contract.

These and other such transnational institutions and regimes do signal a shift in authority from the public to the private when it comes to governing the global economy. Along with other such institutions, they have emerged as important governance mechanisms whose authority is not centered in the state even when they need to engage the state. Each is a bordered system, a key conditionality for its effectiveness and validity. But the bordering capability is not part of national state borders.

In sum, we are seeing the formation of global, only partly territorial borderings that incorporate what were once protections encased in geographically grounded border regimes. Insofar as the state has historically developed the administrative and legal instruments to encase its territory, it also has the capability to change that encasement—for instance, to deregulate its borders and open itself up to foreign firms and investment. Such changes in turn open up national territory to allow for the insertion of a growing number of novel bordered spaces and regimes and thereby raise a question about how bordering, historically represented largely as the protection of the perimeter of national territory, functions *inside* the nation-state.

Rethinking Context: Sited Materialities with Global Span

A second type of emergent formation is the localized microenvironment inserted in global networked operations. While I will focus here largely on economic formations, the logic of the argument I develop holds for a broad range of such microenvironments, notably those examined in Chapter Seven.

There is a specific kind of materiality underlying the leading economic sectors of our era, notwithstanding the fact that they take place partly in electronic space. As discussed in Chapters Four and Six, even the most digitized and globalized sector, notably global finance, hits the ground at some point in its operations. And when it does, it does so in vast concentrations of very material structures. There are three issues about locality and context that are illuminated by this configuration. These are issues that elaborate on some of the dynamics presented throughout the book but from a far more detailed and specific angle: the notion that a growing number of activities are increasingly taking place in both digital and nondigital spaces. Using the particular type of subeconomy touched on in Chapter Four in the discussion of global cities is one way to get at the three issues that concern me here: the growing importance of networked formats to handle economic transactions; the point of intersection between the physical and digital spaces within which a firm or, more generally, this subeconomy operates; and the consequences of these features for the notion of context. The characteristics of the networked subeconomy (partly deeply centered in particular sites, partly deterritorialized and operating on a global digital span) would seem to unbundle established concepts of context. These concepts emphasize connection to physical surroundings through a series of variables—social, visual, operational, or rhetorical.

A Networked Subeconomy

The subeconomy in question is internally networked, partly digital, and largely oriented toward global-markets while operating out of multiple but specific sites around the world. For the most part this sector consists of a large number of relatively small, highly specialized firms. Even if some of the financial services firms can mobilize enormous amounts of capital and control vast quantities of assets, especially given recent mergers, they are small firms in terms of employment and the actual physical space they occupy compared, for example, with the large manufacturing firms. They are human-capital intensive. Another key characteristic of this subeconomy is that specialized services firms need and benefit from proximity to kindred specialized firms—those providing financial services, legal services, accounting, economic forecasting, credit ratings, complex and specialized financial software design, public relations, and other types of expertise in a broad range of fields. This bundle of networked activities is also at the core of the global city's economic function, discussed in Chapter Four.

Physical proximity has clearly emerged as an advantage insofar as time is of the essence and the complexity is such that direct transactions are often more efficient and cheaper than telecommunications. Even with enormous bandwidth, tele-communications does not allow for a full array of acts of communication; it does not allow for the shorthand ways in which enormous amounts of information can be exchanged when people are in one another's presence. Despite this physical proximity, the actual operational context of these firms is not confined to their immediate surrounding environments. They are linked in various ways to other producer service firms in other cities across the world. Consequently, this networked sector has global scope.

Another confounding factor for conventional ideas of context is that these firms operate in part in digital space.[6] Their activities inhabit both physical spaces and digital spaces. They need material and digital structures built with specific requirements to accommodate the fact that their activities are simultaneously deterritorialized and deeply territorialized. Because these activities span the globe yet are highly concentrated in specific places, they produce a strategic geography that cuts across borders and spaces yet installs itself in specific cities. In their aggregate these factors contribute to increasingly dense interurban networks.

The Intersection between Actual and Digital Space

There is a new topography of economic activity, sharply evident in this subeconomy but also present more generally, including in domains other than the economy. This topography weaves in and out of actual and digital space. Today there is still no fully virtualized firm or economic sector. Even finance, the most digitized and globalized of all activities, has a topography that weaves in and out of actual and digital space.[7] To varying degrees, depending on the firm or the sector, a firm's tasks are now distributed across these two kinds of spaces. More generally, these conditions are reshaping the organization of economic space (Graham 2004; Rutherford 2004; Allen, Massey, and Pryke 1999; Taylor 2004). This reshaping ranges from the spatial virtualization of a growing number of economic activities to the reconfiguration of the geography of the built environment *for* economic activity. Whether in electronic space or in the geography of the built environment, the reshaping involves organizational and structural changes (for example, Ernst 2005; Burdett 2006). The actual configurations are subject to considerable transformation as tasks are computerized or standardized, markets are further globalized, and so on.

One question here is whether the point of intersection between the two kinds of spaces in a firm's work and, more generally, any type of activity that inhabits these two spaces, is worth thinking about, theorizing, or exploring. This intersection is typically assumed to be a mere line that divides two mutually exclusive zones. Here my concern is understanding this point of intersection not as a line that separates two mutually exclusive entities but as a border *zone* with its own particular features—an "analytic borderland" that demands its own empirical specification and theorization and contains its own possibilities for shaping practices and organizational forms (Sassen 2006a, chap. 8). The space of the computer screen, which one might posit is one version of the intersection, will not do or is at most a partial enactment of this intersection. The question of this intersection, then, is one I have found to be more complex and more worthy of theorization than is suggested by its common representation as an interface. This is a subject I elaborate on later in this chapter (see also Sassen 2006a, chap. 7; Latham and Sassen 2005, chap. 1).

Shifting Meanings of Contextuality

A networked subeconomy that operates partially in physical space and partially in digital space cannot be easily contextualized in terms of its surroundings. Nor can the individual firms operating in this subeconomy. A firm's orientation is simultaneously toward itself and the global. The intensity of its internal transactions is such that it overrides all considerations of the broader locality or region within which it exists. The connections with other areas and sectors in the "context" that surrounds such subeconomies are unclear, a subject for further empirical research. The immediate physical surrounding of the financial or business district may be changed to conform to what is today a much-in-vogue "contextual" architecture and urban design aimed at visually connecting the business district to its immediate surroundings. Yet this would be a way of veiling, or hiding, the fact that the immediate surroundings are actually not a "context" for this networked subeconomy.

Spatial discontinuities are not new. But they take on specific forms and contents across space and time. Thus we need to research their current forms and contents. What, then, is the "context" here? The new networked subeconomy inhabits only a fraction of its "local" setting, and its boundaries are not those of the city or the "neighborhood" in which it is partially located. Its boundaries are determined by the spaces occupied by the vast concentration of very material resources it needs when it operates at both the local and the global scales. For instance, the financial districts in most global cities have infrastructures for digital networks that are confined to those districts: they do not spread across the larger city, but they do span the globe and connect those districts with one another. This separateness allows for continuous upgrading in the infrastructure for connectivity in the district without the added costs of upgrading even the immediate surroundings. The "interlocutor" for this subeconomy is not its immediate surroundings, the context, but the other major business centers around the world, which together constitute a strategic geography that cuts across borders. Further, these subeconomies are embedded in a range of other kinds of spaces in the cities where they are located. The new low-wage serving classes discussed in Chapter Four are one key example. (See Chapter Four for more cases.)

It is not clear what this simultaneous embeddedness in physical sites and tearing away from the immediate context (which comes to be replaced by the global) mean theoretically, empirically, and operationally. The strategic operation for such a subeconomy is not the search for a connection with the "surroundings." It is, rather, accessing the strategic cross-border geography constituted through multiple such specialized districts. Context here no longer refers simply to the immediate surroundings. The strategic global geography constituted through the expanding network of global cities becomes the main, if not the dominant, context for these subeconomies. In the case of these economies, we can see that the old hierarchies of scale typically shaped by some elementary criterion of size—local, regional, national, or international—no longer hold (see Chapter Two). Going to the next scale in terms of size is no longer the way the world economy is accessed. Even a very small firm can interact directly with other very small firms across the globe. In this sense, we see the forming of a geography that explodes the boundaries of contextuality, locality, and traditional hierarchies of scale.

A SOCIOLOGY OF GLOBAL DIGITAL SPACES?

Inextricably linked to the question of globalization is that of the creation of global digital spaces as both infrastructure (for global electronic markets, for the outsourcing of work, and so on) and a form of the social (Internet-based e-mail and chat groups). Exploring these global digital spaces requires a specific conceptual architecture. At the most general level, I want to emphasize the importance of analytic operations that allow us to capture the complex articulations between the computer capabilities involved and the spaces, both immediate and networked, within which they are deployed or used. A second set of analytic operations concerns the mediating practices and cultures that organize the relationship between these technologies and users in order to understand more precisely the social logics at work. Until quite recently there was no critical elaboration of these mediations because it was assumed that questions of access, competence, and interface design fully captured mediating experience. A third set of analytic operations is aimed at recognizing questions of scaling, an area in which these particular technologies have evinced enormous transformative and constitutive capabilities. In the social sciences scale has largely been conceived of as a given, not as socially constituted (see the discussion in Chapters One and Two). In this regard, therefore, it has not been a critical category. The new technologies have brought scale to the fore precisely through their destabilization of existing hierarchies of scale and notions of nested hierarchies. Thereby they have contributed to the launching of a new heuristic, which interestingly also resonates with developments in the natural sciences, where questions of scaling have surfaced in novel ways, particularly in fields relating to ecology. The next three subsections develop these issues very briefly.

Imbrications of the Digital and the Social

The scholarship on the relationship between the digital and the social tends to be characterized by either technological determinism or indeterminacy. In the first case, the technology is the independent variable which functions as a sort of black box that remains unexamined. In the second, the technology becomes performative when part of a social ecology. Using the term *imbrication* is a way of specifying an interaction that is not characterized by either technological determinism or the hybridity of indeterminacy. The digital and the social can shape and condition each other, but each is and remains specific and distinct. And such interactions can occur in often short or long chains, where one social outcome contributes to a new technical element, which in turn contributes a new social element, and so on. Throughout these interactions the specificity is maintained even as each, the digital and the social, is in turn transformed. In this sense the process can be described as one of imbrications. Thus I use the term *imbrication* to capture this simultaneous interdependence and specificity of both the digital and the nondigital. They work on each other, but they do not become hybrids in this process. Each maintains its distinct irreducible character (Sassen 2006a, chap. 7).

As a first approximation we can identify three features of this process of imbrication. To illustrate, we can use one of the key capabilities of these technologies, that of increasing the mobility of capital and thereby changing the relationship between mobile firms and territorial nation-states. Central to the increased mobility of capital is the "dematerialization" brought about by the digitization of much economic activity. Digitization increases mobility, including of what we have customarily thought of as immobile or barely mobile. Once digitized, an economic activity or good gains the potential for hypermobility—instantaneous circulation through digital networks with global span. Both mobility and digitization are usually seen as mere effects or at best functions of the new technologies. Such conceptions erase the fact that achieving this outcome requires multiple conditions, including such diverse ones as infrastructure for connectivity and legal changes permitting cross-border circulation (Chapters 3 and 4). Thus, hypermobility is produced; it is not merely a function of the technology.

Once we recognize that the hypermobility of the instrument had to be *produced*, we introduce nondigital variables in our analysis of the digital. The first feature, then, is that the production of both capital mobility and "dematerialization" takes capital fixity—state-of-the-art built environments, a talented professional workforce on the ground at least some of the time, legal systems, computer hardware, and conventional infrastructure, from highways to airports and railways. These are all partially place-bound conditions. Such an interpretation carries implications for theory and practice. For instance, simply having access to these technologies does not necessarily alter the position of resource-poor countries or organizations in an international system with enormous inequality in resources.[8]

The second feature that needs to be recovered here is that the capital fixity needed for hypermobility and dematerialization is itself transformed in this process. The real estate industry illustrates some of these issues. Financial services firms have invented instruments that liquefy real estate,[9] thereby facilitating investment in and circulation of these instruments in global markets. Yet part of what constitutes real estate remains very physical. At the same time, however, that which remains physical has been transformed by the fact that it is represented by highly liquid instruments that can circulate in global markets. One way of capturing the difference would be to call it a form of extreme landlord absenteeism. It may look the same, it may involve the same bricks and mortar, it may be new or old, but it is a transformed entity.

As in the example of real estate, the nature of place boundedness here differs from what it may have been one hundred years ago, when it was far more likely to be a form of immobility. Today it is a place boundedness that is in turn inflected or inscribed by the hypermobility of some of its components, products, and outcomes. Both capital fixity and mobility are now partially located in a temporal frame where speed is ascendant and consequential. Thus, this moment of capital fixity cannot be fully captured through a description confined to its material and locational traits.

The third feature in this process of imbrication can be captured through the notion of the social logics organizing the process. Many of the digital components of financial markets are inflected by the agendas that drive global finance, and these agendas are not technological per se. Different users of the same technical properties can produce outcomes that differ from those of finance. Much of our interacting in digital space would lack any meaning or referents if we were to exclude the nondigital world. It is deeply inflected by the cultures, the material practices, the legal systems, the imaginaries, that take place outside digital space. It is necessary, then, to distinguish between the digital technologies as such and the digital formations they make possible. The interactive digital spaces of concern here are not exclusively technical conditions that stand outside the social. They are embedded in the larger societal, cultural, subjective, economic, and imaginary structurations of lived experience and the systems within which we exist and operate (Latham and Sassen, 2005).

In this regard, then, digitization is multivalent. It brings with it an amplification of both mobile and fixed capacities. It inscribes, but is also inscribed by, the nondigital. The specific content, implications, and consequences of each of these variants are empirical questions, objects for study. So what is conditioning the outcome when digital technologies are at work, and what is conditioned by the outcome? We have difficulty capturing this multivalence through our conventional categories, which tend to dualize and posit mutual exclusivity: if it is immobile, it *is* immobile, and if it is mobile, it *is* mobile (a type of endogeneity problem). Using the example of real estate signals that the partial representation of real estate through liquid financial instruments produces a complex imbrication of the material and the digitized moments of that which we continue to call real estate. And so does the partial endogeneity of physical infrastructure in electronic financial markets.

Mediating Practices and Cultures

One consequence of the above dynamic is that the articulations between digital space and users—whether social, political, or economic actors—are constituted in terms of mediating cultures and/or practices. These articulations result in part from the values, cultures, power systems, and institutional orders within which users are embedded. Use is not simply a question of access and understanding how to use the hardware and the software (see, for example, Dean et al. 2006).

There is a strong tendency in the literature to assume use to be an unmediated event and hence to make it unproblematic (once access and competence are given). When it comes to questions of access, however, there is in fact much more of a critical literature. But recognition of a mediating culture has been confined, at best, to that of the techie. This techie culture has become naturalized rather than recognized as one particular type of mediating culture. Beyond this thick computer-centered use culture, there is a tendency to flatten the practices of users to questions of competence and utility.

From the perspective of the social sciences, use of the technology should be problematized rather than simply seen as shaped by technical requirements and the necessary knowledge for use, which is the perspective of the computer scientist and the engineer who designed it. For instance, in his research on use of the Internet by different types of Arab groups in the Middle East, Jon W. Anderson (2003) found that the young "Westernized" Arabs in his study made the same use of the Internet as many youths in the United States did: cruising, chat clubs, and shopping. In contrast, scholars of the Koran, the most traditional group in his study, made far more sophisticated use of the technology as they hyperlinked their way through the text and prior text annotations. The premium on interpretation and annotation gave these scholars of the text a complex mediating culture that allowed them to use the technology (no matter how "traditional" the activity) far more intensely. These mediating cultures also can produce a subject and a subjectivity that become part of the mediation. For instance, in Open Source networks much meaning is derived from the fact that practitioners contest a dominant economic-legal system centered in protections of private property (Weber 2005). Participants become active subjects in a process that extends beyond their individual work and produces a culture.

There are multiple ways in which to conceptualize the articulations between digital space and users. Theoretically it is important to move beyond issues of access. This articulation is socially mediated (see Moghadan 2005). There are, moreover, multiple ways of examining the various social mediations organizing use. Among others, these can conceivably range from small-scale ethnographies to macrolevel surveys, and include descriptive studies, highly theorized accounts, a focus on ideational forms, studies of structural conditions. Through these theoretical and methodological approaches, we can gain insights into the diversity of cultures mediating use.

Scaling: Transformative and Constitutive Capabilities of Digital Technologies

Narrowing the discussion of scaling to the formation of transboundary domains (for example, transnational civil society, transnational corporate networks, and regional integration), we can identify four types of scaling dynamics in the constitution of global digital formations. These four dynamics are not mutually exclusive, as is evident from the examination in Chapter 3 of one of the most globalized and advanced instances of a digital formation: electronic financial markets. A first scaling dynamic is the formation of global domains that function at the self-evidently global scale—for example, some types of very-large-scale Internet-based conversations (see, for example, Sack 2005) or global digitized outsourcing (Aneesh 2006).

The second scaling dynamic can be found in the local practices and conditions that become directly articulated with global dynamics. In this case local elements no longer have to move through the traditional hierarchy of jurisdictions. Electronic financial markets can again be used as an illustration. The starting point is floor- or screen-based trading in exchanges and firms that are part of a worldwide network of financial centers. These localized transactions link up directly to a global electronic market. What begins as local gets rescaled at the global level.

The third scaling dynamic results from the fact that interconnectivity and decentralized simultaneous access multiply the cross-border connections among various localities. This action produces a very particular type of global formation, as we saw in the preceding section and in Chapter 7. It is a kind of distributed outcome in that it arises out of the multiplication of lateral and horizontal transactions or in the recurrence of a process across local sites without the aggregation that leads to an actual globally scaled digital formation, as is the case with electronic markets. Instances are Open Source software development, certain types of early-conflict warning systems, and worldwide activist networks (see, for example, Weber 2005; Alker 2005; Sassen 2005).

A fourth scaling dynamic results from the fact that global formations can actually be partially embedded in subnational sites and move between these differently scaled practices and organizational forms in a continuous two-way flow. For instance, the global electronic financial market is constituted through both electronic markets with global span and locally embedded conditions—that is, financial centers and all they entail, from infrastructure to systems of trust. This formation is also illustrated in the case of the global communication systems of multinational corporations (see Ernst 2005).

The new digital technologies have not caused these developments, but they have facilitated and shaped them in variable yet specific ways. The overall effect is similar to the reconceptualization of the meaning of context discussed earlier. When internetworked, the meaning of each of the local and the global is repositioned because each can be multiscalar. Part of the work of constructing electronic communications structures and interactive domains as objects for sociological study is to locate them against the scalar complexity that the new technologies have made possible rather than taking scales as givens and self-contained.

NOTES

CHAPTER 2   ELEMENTS FOR A SOCIOLOGY OF GLOBALIZATION

1. Diverging somewhat from what has emerged as the main proposition in globalization research—growing interdependence—I argue that the critical context against which we need to understand globalization is the way in which the national has been constructed over the last century or more, depending on the country. From here, then, comes my emphasis on denationalization: for global firms and markets or global subjectivities and human rights to exist, some components of the national need to become denationalized (Sassen 2006a). Such focus allows us to capture the enormous variability across countries regarding the incorporation of, or resistance to, globalization; these processes are partly shaped by the specifics of each country, whether formal and de jure or informal and de facto. At the same time this type of approach avoids the trap of comparative studies (which put countries on parallel tracks and tend to standardize in order to compare) because it starts from the insight that the conditionalities of a global system are multisited and hence need to be met in part through specific structurations in multiple countries

2. The best source on intercity flows and locations is http://www.1boro.ac.uk/gawc, the ongoing website of GaWC (Globalization and World Cities).

3. There are many cases that do correspond to this view. For instance, illegal traffickers of people who used to operate regionally now can go global because of the infrastructure for communications and money transfers brought about by globalization. (For a development of this particular argument, see Sassen, 2000).

4. In my early research on the global city, I began to understand some of these questions of reified scales. Much of the literature on global and world cities has a critical appraisal of questions of scaling, but with important exceptions (Taylor 1995; Brenner 1998) this appraisal tends to be embryonic, undertheorized, and not quite explicated. On the other hand, the scholarship on "glocalization" recognizes and theorizes questions of scale but often remains attached to a notion of nested scalings (for example, Swyngedouw 1997). I find that among the literatures in geography that come closest in their conceptualization to what I develop in this book, albeit focused on very different issues, are those on first-nation-peoples' claims to sovereignty (for example, Howitt 1993; Silvern 1999; Notzke

1995). Clearly there is a particularly illuminating positioning of the issues in this case because from the outset there is a) the coexistence of two exclusive claims over a single territory, and b) the endogeneity of both types of claims—that of the modern sovereign and that of the indigenous nation. What matters to this discussion can be rephrased as the coexistence of the claim of the historical sovereign and the claim of the global as endogenized in the transformed denationalized sovereign. (For a full development of this somewhat abstract statement, see Sassen 2006a). This is a very particular usage of scale, one in which the analytics of scale are drenched, so to speak, in specific and thick conditions and struggles (see Amin 2002 for a treatment of scale along these lines).

5. Several of the dynamics that come together in the model of the global city were explored by scholars with other objectives in mind Among them are Castells (1983), Walton (1982), Kratke (1991), Doreen B. Massey (1984), Harvey (1973, 1989), and Häusserman and Siebel (1987). Other scholars have pursued deeply related aspects from a variety of angles—for example, Robert Cohen (1981), Thrift and Leyshon (1994), Santos, Aparecida de Souza, and Silveira (1994), Lo and Yeung (1996), and Komlosy et al. (1997) For one of the best reviews of some of the critical urban questions and models and the associated sources, see Paddison (2001, introduction).

6. Here Arrighi's (1994) analysis is of interest in that it posits the recurrence of certain organizational patterns in different phases of the capitalist world economy, but at progressively higher orders of complexity and expanded scope, and timed to follow or precede particular configurations of the world economy. In this framing we can say that world cities have existed for centuries, whereas the global city is a far more specific concept in that it seeks to capture the present configuration and incorporates the enormous complexities of current techno-economic systems.

7. In developing this hypothesis, I was responding to the very common notion that it is the number of headquarters that determines whether a city is global. Empirically it may still be the case in many countries that the leading business center is also the place with the leading concentration of headquarters. But this may well be because there is an absence of alternative locational options. In countries with a well-developed infrastructure outside the leading business center, however, there are likely to be multiple locational options for such headquarters.

8. Even as I confine this discussion to what are described as states effectively functioning under the rule of law, we must allow for considerable differences in the powers of these states. As has been said many times, the government of the United States can aim at imposing conditions on the global markets and participating states, whereas the government of Argentina, for instance, cannot—though Datz (2007) shows they have some powers.

9. I use this term to distinguish this type of production from that involved in making "law" or "jurisprudence" (Sassen 1996, chap. 1).

10. This dominance assumes many forms and does not affect only poorer and weaker countries. France, for instance, ranks among the top providers of information services and industrial engineering services in Europe and has a strong, though not outstanding, position in financial and insurance services. But it has found itself at an increasing disadvantage in legal and accounting services because Anglo-American law and standards dominate in international transactions. Anglo-American firms with offices in Paris service the legal needs of firms, whether French or foreign, operating out of France. Similarly, Anglo-American law is increasingly dominant in international commercial arbitration, an institution grounded in Continental, particularly French and Swiss, traditions of jurisprudence

11. Although it is well-known, it is worth remembering that this guarantee of the rights of capital is embedded in a certain type of state, a certain conception of the rights of capital, and a certain type of international legal regime: the states of the most developed and most powerful countries in the world, in Western notions of contract and property rights, and in new legal regimes aimed at furthering economic globalization, as in the efforts to get countries to support copyright law.

12. While we take this autonomy for granted in the United States or in most countries of the European Union (though not all! Thus France's central bank, before the formation of the European Central Bank, was not considered fully independent from the executive branch of government), in many countries the executive branch of government or the local oligarchy has long had undue influence on the central banks—incidentally, not necessarily always to the disadvantage of the disadvantaged.

13. In terms of research and theorization this is a vast, uncharted terrain: it entails examining how that production takes place and gets legitimated. The process signals the possibility of cross-national variations (which would then need to be established, measured, and interpreted).

14. When I first developed the construct denationalization in the 1995 Leonard Hastings Schoff Memorial Lectures (Sassen 1996), I intended it to denote a specific dynamic I did *not* intend it as some general notion that can be used interchangeably with *postnational, global*, or other such terms. In this regard, see the debate in Bosniak et al. (2000).

15. See Dezalay and Garth (1996) on international commercial arbitration, Aman 1998, Cutler, Haufler, and Porter (1999) and Rodney Bruce Hall and Thomas J. Biersteker (2002) on private authority.

16. See, for example, the argument by Arrighi (1994); see also the debate in Davis (1999, pt. 4).

17. There are parallels here with a totally different sphere of state activity and transnational processes: the role of national courts in implementing instruments of the interna-

tional human rights regime, and, in several new national constitutions, the incorporation of provisions that limit the national state's presumption to represent its entire people in international forums (Sassen 1996, chap. 3).

Chapter 3   The State Confronts the Global Economy and Digital Networks

1. Two very different bodies of scholarship that develop lines of analysis helpful in capturing some of these conditions are represented by the work of Rosenau, particularly his examination of the domestic "frontier" within the national state (1997), and by the work of Walker (1993) in problematizing the distinction of inside/outside in IR theory.

2. Elsewhere (Sassen 2006a, chaps. 6 and 8) I examine how these dynamics also position citizens (still largely confined to national state institutions for the full execution of their rights) vis-à-vis these types of global struggles. My argument is that state participation creates an enabling environment not only for global corporate capital but also for those seeking to subject that capital to greater accountability and public scrutiny. But unlike what has happened with global corporate capital, the necessary legal and administrative instruments and regimes have not been developed. The trade-offs and the resources that can be mobilized are quite different in the case of citizens seeking to globalize their capacities for governing compared with the trade-offs for global capital seeking to form regimes that enable and protect it

3. For a detailed examination of these two aspects, see Sassen (2001, chaps. 4, 5, and 7).

4. This process of corporate integration should not be confused with vertical integration as conventionally defined. See as well Gereffi (1995) on commodity chains and Porter (1990) on value-added chains, two constructs that also illustrate the difference between corporate integration at a world scale and vertical integration as conventionally defined.

5. A central proposition here (and also Chapter Four) is that we cannot take the existence of a global economic system as a given but, rather, need to examine the particular ways in which the conditions for economic globalization are produced. This requires examining not only communications capacities and the power of multinationals but also the infrastructure of facilities and the work processes necessary for the implementation of global economic systems, including the production of those inputs that constitute the capability for global control and the diverse jobs involved in this production. The recovery of place and production also implies that global processes can be studied in great empirical detail.

6. Affiliates are but one form of overseas operation and hence their number underrepresents the dispersal of a firm's operations. There are today multiple forms, ranging from new temporary partnerships to older types involving subcontracting and contracting.

7. This index is an average based on ratios of the share that foreign sales, assets, and employment represent in a firm's total of each. If we consider the world's top 100 transnational corporations for 1997, some of which have changed names, the European Union has 48 and the United States has 28; many of the remaining are Japanese. Thus together the European Union and the United States accounted for over two thirds of the world's 100 largest transnationals. Just five countries (the United States, the United Kingdom, France, Germany, and Japan) together accounted for three quarters of those 100 firms in 1997; that has been roughly the case since 1990. The average transnationality index for the European Union is 56.7 percent, compared with 38.5 percent for the United States (but 79.2 percent for Canada). Most of the U.S. and E.U. transnational corporations in this top-100 list have very high levels of foreign assets as a percentage of their total assets: for instance, 51 percent for IBM, 55 percent for the Volkswagen Group; 91 percent for Nestlé, 96 percent for Asea Brown Boveri, 62 percent for Elf Aquitaine, 91 percent for Bayer, 79 percent for Hoechst, 77 percent for Philips Electronics, 43 percent for Siemens, 45 percent for Renault, 98 percent for Seagram, 67 percent for Rhône-Poulenc, 59 percent for BMW, 69 percent for Ferruzzi/Montedison, 97 percent for Thomson, 85 percent for Michelin, 71 percent for Ericsson, 58 percent for Exxon, 85 percent for Unilever, 55 percent for MacDonald's, 68 percent for Coca-Cola, and so on. Foreign employment as a share of total employment is often even higher (see Organization for Economic Cooperation and Development 2000 for the full listing).

8. Two major developments that can alter some of the features of the present configuration are the growth of the Eurozone and the growth of electronic trading. First, the creation of an enormous consolidated capital market in the Eurozone raises serious questions about the feasibility of maintaining the current pattern with as many international financial centers as there are member countries and in some countries several such centers. Some capital markets may lose top international functions and get repositioned in complex and hierarchical divisions of labor. Secondly, electronic trading is leading to a distinct shift toward strategic alliances among major financial centers, which in turn is producing a cross-border digital market embedded in a set of specific city-based financial markets. I have examined this at greater length in Sassen (2001, chaps. 4, 5, and 7, 2006a, chaps 5 and 7).

9. Hence, for Arrighi the geography of power in the contemporary cycle of accumulation is marked by a situation unique within the history of capitalism: military hegemony and financial hegemony are not exercised by the same state. Rather, they are held respectively by the United States (strong militarily but deeply indebted) and financially rich East Asia. While Arrighi sees a unique situation within the contemporary world system, the spatiality of the world system itself has remained relatively unmodified Power remains distributed among core and peripheral regions, not among points in a global network. The primary difference is that the world is now multipolar instead of unipolar, for the main military power has become inefficient relative to the main financial power.

10. It is quite possible that globalization may have the effect of blurring the boundaries between these two regulatory worlds.

11. I am trying to distinguish these current forms from older notions of the state as a tool for capital, such as comprador bourgeoisies, or neocolonialism. Furthermore, there are important parallels in this research with scholarship focused on the work of the state in producing the distinction between private and public law (see Cutler 2002) and with scholarship on the work of the state in setting up the various legal and administrative frameworks that gave the modern state its shape (see for example, Novak 1996, Clemens 1997, for a review of the case of the United States)

12. I use the term *convergence* for expediency. In the larger project, I posit that conceptualizing these outcomes as convergence is actually problematic and often incorrect. Rather than a dynamic whereby individual states wind up converging, what is at work is a global dynamic that gets filtered through the specifics of each "participating" state. Hence what is of central concern is not so much the outcome—convergence—as the work of producing the outcome.

13. I examine these two issues in greater detail elsewhere (Sassen 2006a, chaps. 8 and 9).

14. This section consists of the revised text of the Keck Lecture, delivered at Amherst College, Amherst, Mass., on February 13, 2000, and is based on a larger project (Sassen 2006a).

15. What constitutes the Internet is continuously changing (World Information Order 2002; Dean et al. 2006). Some years ago it could still be described as a network of computer networks using a common communications protocol (Internet protocol) Today networks using other communications protocols are also connected to other networks via gateways. Furthermore, the Internet is not constituted only by computers connected to other computers; point-of-sale terminals, cameras, robots, telescopes, cellular phones, TV sets, and an assortment of other hardware components are also connected to the Internet.

16. Federal Networking Council, "FNC Resolution. Definition of 'Internet,' " National Coordinating Office for Networking and Information Research and Development, http://www.nitrd.gov/fnc/Internet_res.html.

17. The U.S. government's power to engage in multiple forms of surveillance, including surveillance of corporations in countries run by governments that are strong and long-term allies, was illustrated by the U.S. government's alleged use of its Echelon surveillance system to spy on European corporations (World Information Network 2002, chap. 6).

18. Lessig (1999) labels the architecture of the Internet "code," by which he means the software and hardware that constitute it and determine how people interact or exist in its space.

19. Elsewhere I have made a similar argument using the notion of the emergence of cybersegmentations (see Sassen 1999b).

20. This centrally managed function of the Internet involves the control and assignment of the numbers that computers need to locate an address. It therefore can instruct all the top "root servers" of the Net—the computers that execute address inquiries—so that they will accept those instructions. This function is clearly a power of sorts. As is well-known, the particular function of assigning addresses is crucial and was for many years under the informal control of one particular scientist, who named this function the Internet Assigned Numbers Authority. More generally, the scientists who labored to make the Net workable and had to reach many agreements on a broad range of technical matters, have long been a sort of informal central authority. In most other cultural settings they probably would have become a formal, recognizable body—with, one might add, considerable power. There is an interesting sociology here.

21. There are also more specific issues that may affect the regulation of particular forms of digital activity through a focus on infrastructure. Different types of infrastructure exist for different types of digital activities—for instance, those for financial markets and those for consumer wireless phones. The regulatory potential of such diverse infrastructures also varies.

22 With the growth of business interest in the Internet in the mid-1990s, the de facto authority of the pioneers and their logic for assigning addresses began to be criticized. To cite a familiar case, firms found that their names had already been assigned to other parties and that there was little they could do about it; the idea of brand names and intellectual property rights to a name was not part of the early Internet culture.

23. Since October 2000, the board of ICANN has been the final decision-making authority on standards. But a complex and changing web of organizations is actually involved in various aspects of the operation of the Internet. The Internet Society and its subsidiary organizations—the Internet Architecture Board, the Internet Engineering Steering Group, the Internet Engineering Task Force, and the Internet Research Task Force—are responsible for the development of communications and operational standards and protocols that allow users to communicate with one another on the Net. The Internet Societal Task Force is responsible for naming Internet policy issues. The copyright on the protocols is held by the Internet Society. Other organizations, such as the World Wide Web Consortium, specialize in the development of standards for certain services of the Net.

24. The U.S. government's "Framework for Global Electronic Commerce," an early blueprint for Internet governance, argued that because of the Internet's global reach and evolving technology, regulation should be kept to a minimum. It also suggested that in the few areas in which rules are needed, such as privacy and taxation, policy should be made by

quasi-governmental bodies such as the World Intellectual Property Organization (WIPO) or the Organisation for Economic Co-operation and Development. One of the issues with this type of proposal is the absence of transparency and the problems that brings with it. These problems became evident in one of the first big Net policy dilemmas: cybersquatting (private speculators' seizing valuable corporate brand names on the Internet and selling them, at an enormous price, to the firms those names belonged to). Net addresses are important for establishing an identity online. So companies want to establish a rule that they are entitled to any domain names using their trademarks. But the Net is used for more purposes than e-commerce, so consumer advocates say this rule would unfairly restrict the rights of schools, museums, political parties, and other noncommercial Net users. In the deliberations that have taken place at WIPO, however, in meetings usually held behind doors, it is mostly the large firms who are participating. This course of events privatizes the effort to design regulations for the Net.

25. See, for example, Lovink and Schultz (1997) for summaries of the debates.

26. The distinctions noted here partly follow Pare's classification and research on the subject (2003, chap. 3). See also Drake and Williams 2006; Mueller 2004.

27. Pare (2003) calls for and develops another kind of approach in the study of these questions of governance and coordination. He argues that an emphasis on end results and optimal governance strategies, which is typical of the work of the authors briefly discussed here, produces analytic blind spots. A crucial issue is the need to understand the dynamic relationship between the institutional forms delivering technology and the network structures that emerge over time. See also Lessig (1999), Mueller 2004,.and Latham and Sassen (2005).

28. Retail investment and stock trading use the Internet. So does direct online investment, which is mostly retail and represents a minor share of the overall global financial market. Even factoring in its expected tripling in value over the next three or four years will not give it the type of power characterizing the wholesale global financial market I am discussing here.

29. For instance, after Mexico's financial crisis and before the first signs of a crisis in Asia, the leading financial services firms negotiated a large number of very innovative deals that contributed to the further expansion of volume in the financial markets and to the incorporation of new sources of profit, thereby ensuring liquidity even in a situation of at least partial crisis. Typically, these deals involved novel concepts of how to sell debt and what to consider a salable debt—they made acceptable what had been unacceptable.

30. The foreign exchange market was the first one to globalize, in the mid-1970s. Today it is the biggest and in many ways the only truly global market. It has gone from a daily turnover rate of about $15 billion in the 1970s to $60 billion in the early 1980s and an es-

timated $1.3 trillion in 1999 and in 2004. In contrast, the total foreign currency reserves of the rich industrial countries at the end of the 1990s amounted to about $1 trillion.

31. For extensive evidence on the issues discussed in this section, see Sassen (2001, chaps. 3, 4, and 7). For a different perspective on some of the issues concerning global finance, see also Datz 2007, Garrett (1998), and Eichengreen (2003)

32. According to some estimates, we have reached only the midpoint of a fifty-year process in terms of the full integration of these markets. Given the growth dynamics made possible by digitization, this estimate signals that financial markets could expand even further in relation to the size of other components, such as direct investment and trade

33. I try to capture this normative transformation in the notion of the privatizing of certain capacities for making norms that in the recent history of states under the rule of law were in the public domain. (I am not concerned here with cases such as the Catholic Church, which has long had what could be described as private norm-making capacities but is of course a non-state institution, or is meant to be.) Today, what are actually elements of a private logic emerge as public norms even though they represent particular rather than public interests. This is not a new occurrence in itself for national states under the rule of law; what is perhaps different is the extent to which the interests involved are global (for a fuller discussion, see Sassen 2006a, chap. 5)

34. A particular feature that matters for my current research on denationalization is the fact that many states—or, more precisely, specific agencies and departments within states—have participated in the formation and implementation of these conditions and rules.

35 Since the Southeast Asian financial crisis, there has been a revision of some of the specifics of these standards. For instance, exchange-rate parity is now posited in less strict terms. The crisis in Argentina that began in December 2001 has raised further questions about aspects of IMF conditionality. But neither crisis has eliminated that conditionality.

36. For instance, the growth of electronic trading and electronic network alliances among major financial centers is allowing us to see the particular way in which digitized markets are partially embedded in these vast concentrations of material resources and human talent represented by financial centers (see Sassen 2001, chaps 4, 5, and 7, 2006a, chap. 5).

Chapter 4   The Global City: Recovering Place and Social Practices

1 I have theorized this in terms of the network of global cities, where those cities are partly a function of that network. For example, the growth of the financial centers in New York and London is fed by what flows through the worldwide network of financial centers,

given deregulation of national economies. The cities at the top of this global hierarchy concentrate the capacities to maximize their capturing of the proceeds, so to speak.

2. Several disciplines have made significant contributions. Among these are anthropology (Bestor 2001; Low 1999), economic geography (for example, Knox and Taylor 1995; Short and Kim 1999), and cultural studies (for example, Palumbo-Liu 1999; Krause and Petro 2003; Bridge and Watson 2000). All have developed an extensive urban scholarship; most recently, economists (for example, Glaeser and Gottlieb 2006; Fujita et al. 2004) are beginning to address the urban and regional economy in ways that differ from an older tradition of urban economics, one that had lost much of its vigor and persuasiveness.

3. We can see these results in early works such as Paul G. Cressey's *Taxi-Dance Hall* and (1932) Harvey Warren Zorbaugh's *Gold Coast and the Slum* (1929) and later for example, in Suttles (1968).

4. Globalization, the rise of the new information technologies, the intensifying of transnational and translocal dynamics, and the strengthening presence and voice of specific types of sociocultural diversity—all of these are on the cutting edge of actual change that social theory needs to factor in to a far greater extent than it has. At the same time it is important to emphasize that these trends do not encompass the majority of social conditions; on the contrary, most social reality probably corresponds to older familiar trends. That is why many of sociology's traditions and well-established subfields will remain important and continue to constitute the heart of the discipline. Furthermore, there are good reasons why most of urban sociology has not quite engaged the characteristics and the consequences of these three trends as they are instantiated in the city: current urban data sets are quite inadequate for addressing these major trends at the level of the city Yet although these three trends may involve only part of the urban condition and cannot be confined to the urban, they are strategic in that they mark the urban condition in novel ways and, in turn, make it a key research site for major trends.

5. Globalization is also a process that produces differentiation, only the alignment of differences is of a very different kind from that associated with such differentiating notions as national character, national culture, and national society. For example, the corporate world today has a global geography, but it does not exist everywhere in the world: in fact, it has highly defined and structured spaces; it is also increasingly sharply differentiated from noncorporate segments in the economies of the particular locations (for example, a city such as New York) or countries in which it operates. There is homogenization along certain lines that cross national boundaries and sharp differentiation inside those boundaries.

6. We need to recognize the specific historical conditions for different conceptions of the "international" or the "global." There is a tendency to see the internationalization of the economy as a process operating at the center, embedded in the power of the multinational

corporations today and the colonial enterprises of the past. One could note that the economies of many peripheral countries are thoroughly internationalized because of high levels of foreign investments in many economic sectors and heavy dependence on world markets for "hard" currency. What the highly developed countries have are strategic concentrations of firms and markets that operate globally, the capability for global control and coordination, and power. This is a very different form of the international from that which we find in peripheral countries.

7. This proposition is key to my model of the global city.

8. More conceptually, we can ask whether an economic system with strong tendencies toward such concentration can have a space economy that lacks points of physical agglomeration. That is, does power—in this case economic power—have spatial correlates?

9. I see the producer services and, most especially, finance and advanced corporate services as industries producing the organizational commodities necessary for the implementation and management of global economic systems. Producer services are intermediate outputs—that is, services bought by firms. They cover financial, legal, and general management matters, innovation, development, design, administration, personnel, production technology, maintenance, transport, communications, wholesale distribution, advertising, cleaning services for firms, security, and storage. Central components of the producer services category include a range of industries with mixed business and consumer markets: insurance, banking, financial services, real estate, legal services, accounting, and professional associations. The definitive book is Bryson and Daniels 2006.

10 Methodologically speaking, this is one way of addressing the question of the unit of analysis in studies of contemporary economic processes. "National economy" is a problematic category when there are high levels of internationalization. And "world economy" is a problematic category because of the impossibility of engaging in detailed empirical study at that scale. Highly internationalized cities such as New York and London offer the possibility of examining globalization processes in great detail within a bounded setting and with all their multiple, often contradictory aspects. King (1990) notes the need to differentiate the international and the global. In many ways the concept of the global city does that.

11. A methodological tool I find useful for this type of examination is what I call circuits for the distribution and installation of economic operations. These circuits allow one to follow economic activities into terrains that escape the increasingly narrow borders of mainstream representations of the "advanced" economy and negotiate the crossing of socioculturally discontinuous spaces.

12. This invisibility of the lower-income segments is illustrated by the following event. When the stock market experienced an acute downturn in 1987 after years of enormous

growth, there were numerous press reports about a sudden and massive unemployment cri-
sis among high-income professionals on Wall Street. The other unemployment crisis on
Wall Street, affecting secretaries and blue-collar workers, was never noticed or reported on.
Yet the stock market crash created a concentrated unemployment crisis, for example, in the
Dominican immigrant community in northern Manhattan, where a lot of Wall Street's jan-
itors lived.

13. There is by now a vast literature documenting one or another of these aspects of inequality. See Fainstein, Gordon, and Harloe (1993) for the beginning of this process; see
Sassen (2006b, 2001, chap. 8) for the evidence in several countries.

14. Whether the multiplication of intercity transactions has contributed to the formation
of transnational urban systems is subject to debate (see also chap. 2 on cross-border urban
networks). The growth of global markets for finance and specialized services; the need for
transnational servicing networks in response to sharp increases in international investment;
the reduced role of the government in the regulation of international economic activity and
the corresponding ascendancy of other institutional arenas, notably global markets and corporate headquarters—all of these factors point to the existence of transnational economic
arrangements with locations in more than one country. These cities are not merely compet-
ing with one another for market share, as is often asserted or assumed; there is a division of
labor that incorporates cities of multiple countries, and in this regard we can speak of a
global system (for example, in finance) as opposed to simply an international system (see
Sassen 2001, chaps. 1–4, 7). We can see here the incipient formation of a transnational urban system.

15. Furthermore, the pronounced orientation to the world markets evident in such cities
raises questions about the articulation with their nation-states, their regions, and the larger
urban economic and social structure. Cities have typically been deeply embedded in the
economies of their region, indeed often reflecting the characteristics of the latter—and they
still do reflect those characteristics. But cities that are strategic sites in the global economy
tend in part to disconnect from their region. This disconnecting conflicts with a key proposition in traditional scholarship on urban systems—namely, that these systems promote the
territorial integration of regional and national economies.

16. More generally, we are seeing the formation of new types of labor-market segmentation. Two characteristics stand out. One is the weakening role of the firm in structuring the
employment relationship: more is left to the market. The other is what could be described
as the shift of labor-market functions to the household or the community. For definitive sociological treatments of these types of issues, see Mingione (1991 and Venkatesh 2006).

17. Linking informalization and growth takes the analysis beyond the notion that the
emergence of informal sectors in cities like New York and Los Angeles is caused by the

presence of immigrants and their propensity to replicate survival strategies typical of third world countries. Linking informalization and growth also takes the analysis beyond the notion that unemployment and recession in general may be the key factors promoting informalization in the current phase of highly industrialized economies. It may point to characteristics of advanced capitalism that are not typically noted. For analyses of conjunctural and structural patterns see Komlosy et al. (1997), Tabak and Chrichlow 2000 on the informal economy in many countries.

18. This newer case brings out more brutally than did the Fordist contract the economic significance of these types of actors, a significance veiled or softened by the provision of the family wage in the case of the Fordist contract.

19. Another important localization of the dynamics of globalization is that of the new stratum of professional women. Elsewhere I have examined the residential and commercial impact of the increase in the number of top-level professional women on high-income gentrification in global cities as well as on the reurbanization of middle-class family life (see Sassen 2001, chap. 9).

20. This language is increasingly constructing immigration as a devalued process insofar as it describes people from generally poorer, disadvantaged countries in search of the better life that the receiving country can offer; it contains an implicit valorization of the receiving country and a devalorization of the sending country.

21. There are many different forms that such contestation and slippage can assume. Global mass culture homogenizes and is capable of absorbing an immense variety of local cultural elements. But the process is never complete. The opposite—full-fledged domination—is the case when employment in lead sectors no longer inevitably constitutes membership in a labor aristocracy. Thus third world women working in export-processing zones are not empowered: capitalism can work through difference. Yet another case is that of "illegal" immigrants, here we see that national boundaries have the effect of creating and criminalizing difference. These kinds of differentiation are central to the formation of a world economic system (Wallerstein 1990).

22. Tokyo now has several mostly working-class concentrations of legal and illegal immigrants coming from China, Bangladesh, Pakistan, Brazil, Peru, and the Philippines. This is quite remarkable in view of Japan's legal and cultural closure to immigrants. Is it simply a function of poverty in those countries? By itself that is not enough of an explanation, since those countries have had poverty for a long time. I posit that the internationalization of the Japanese economy, including specific forms of investment in the countries from which the immigrants are coming, and Japan's growing cultural influence there have built bridges between those countries and Japan and have reduced their subjective distance from Japan (see Sassen 2001, 307–15; Tsuda 2003; Komai 1995; Farrer 2007).

23. An interesting question concerns the nature of internationalization today in ex-colonial cities. King's analysis of the distinctive historical and unequal conditions under which the notion of the international was constructed (1990, 78) is extremely important. King shows us how during the time of empire some of the major old colonial centers were far more internationalized than the metropolitan centers. The notion of internationalization as used today is assumed to be rooted in the experience of the center. This assumption brings up a parallel contemporary blind spot well captured in Stuart Hall's (1991) finding that contemporary postcolonial and postimperialist critiques have emerged in the former centers of empires and are silent on a range of conditions evident today in ex-colonial cities or countries. Spivak (1999), Mbembe (2001), Mamdami (1996) have written great accounts. Yet another such blind spot is disregarding the possibility that the international migrations now directed largely to the center from former colonial territories—and neo-colonial territories in the case of the United States, and, most recently, Japan—might be the correlate of the internationalization of capital that began with colonialism (Sassen 1988).

24. For a different combination of these elements, see, for example, Dunn (1994) and Drainville (2004).

25. Body-Gendrot (1999) shows how the city remains a terrain for contest, characterized by the emergence of new actors, often successively younger. It is a terrain on which the constraints and the institutional limitations of governments in addressing the demands for equity engender social disorders. Body-Gendrot argues that urban political violence should not be interpreted as a coherent ideology but rather as an element of temporary political tactics permitting vulnerable actors to enter in an interaction with the holders of power on terms that will be somewhat favorable to the weak.

CHAPTER 5   THE MAKING OF INTERNATIONAL MIGRATIONS

1. Of all subjects covered in this book, none has the vast number of small empirical studies we find on immigration. Their diversity and empirical detail make it even less possible to do full justice to this scholarship. The chapter cites several overviews of the scholarship as well as studies with particularly extensive discussions of specific issues of concern in this chapter.

CHAPTER 6   EMERGENT GLOBAL CLASSES

1. For examples of how this social structure fits into arbitrage markets, see Beunza and Stark (2004) and MacKenzie (2005). For examples of how other industries are using the social organization of groups and professionals to generate profits, see, for example, Grabher (2001, 2002) and Girard and Stark (2002). While none of these authors speaks of class,

they all provide key elements for understanding the transformed organizational context for the formation of a professional class.

Chapter 7   Local Actors in Global Politics

1. While the Internet is a crucial medium in political practices, it is important to emphasize that in the 1990s, and particularly in the mid-1990s, we entered a new phase in the history of digital networks, one in which powerful corporate actors and high-performance networks began to strengthen the role of private digital space and alter the structure of public-access digital space (Sassen 1996, chap. 2, 1999a). Digital space has emerged not simply as a means for communicating but also as a major new theater for capital accumulation and the operations of global capital. Yet civil society—in all its incarnations—also began to emerge as an increasingly energetic presence in cyberspace in the mid-1990s. (For a variety of angles, see, for example, Rimmer and Morris-Suzuki 1999, Poster 1997; Frederick 1993; Miller and Slater 2000) The greater the diversity of cultures and groups, the better for the larger political and civic potential of the Internet and the more effective the resistance to the risk that the corporate world might set the standards. (For cases of ICT use by different types of groups, see, for example, Buntarian et al. 2000; Allison 2002; Women-Action 2000; Yang 2003; Camacho 2001, Esterhuysen 2000; Dean et al. 2006)

2. In centuries past, for instance, organized religions had extensive, often global networks of missionaries and clerics. But they depended in part on the existence of a central authority (see generally Maglish and Buultjens 1993).

3. The case of the Federation of Michoacan Clubs in Illinois illustrates this mix of dynamics. These are associations of often very poor immigrants who are beginning to engage in cross-border development projects and in the process are mobilizing additional resources and political capital in their countries of origin and in the countries to which they have immigrated (Espinoza and Gzesh 1999).

4. There are several organizations that have taken on the work of adjusting to these constraints or providing adequate software and other facilities to disadvantaged NGOs. For instance, Bellanet (2002), a nonprofit set up in 1995, aims at helping such NGOs gain access to online information and disseminating information to the South. To that end it has set up Web-to-e-mail servers that can deliver Web pages by e-mail to users confined to low bandwidths, and it has developed multiple service lines For example, Bellanet's Open Development service line seeks to enable collaboration among NGOs through the use of Open Source software, open content, and open standards; it therefore customized the Open Source PHP-Nuke software to set up an online collaborative space for the Medicinal Plants Network. Bellanet has adopted Open Content for all forms of content on its Web site, which is freely available to the public, and supports the development of an open standard

for project information (international development markup language, or IDML). The value of such open standards is that they enable information sharing.

5. In a study of the Web sites of international and national environmental NGOs in Finland, the United Kingdom, the Netherlands, Spain, and Greece, Tsaliki (2002, 15) concluded that the Internet is mainly useful for intra- and interorganizational collaboration and networking, mostly complementing already-existing media techniques for promoting issues and raising awareness. But see various cases in Dean et al. 2006.

6. See Human Rights Internet, http://www.hri.ca, Greenpeace, http://www.greenpeace .org; Oxfam International, http://www.oxfam.org.

7. A very different case is Oxfam America's effort to help its staff in the global South submit information electronically quickly and effectively, not easy aims in countries with unreliable, slow connections and other obstacles to working online. The aim is to help staff in the global South manage and publish information efficiently To that end Oxfam adopted a server-side content management system and a client-side article builder called Publ-x that allows end users to create or edit articles in extendable markup language (XML) while off-line and submit them to the server when the work has been completed; an editor on the server side is then promptly notified, ensuring that the information immediately becomes public.

8. Elsewhere I have posited that we can conceptualize these "alternative" networks as countergeographies of globalization because they are embedded in some of the major dynamics and capabilities constitutive of economic globalization yet are not part of the formal apparatus or objectives of this apparatus, such as the formation of *global* markets (Sassen 2002). As already discussed (chap. 4) The existence of a global economic system and its associated institutional supports for cross-border flows of money, information, and people have enabled the intensifying of transnational and translocal networks and the development of communications technologies that can escape conventional surveillance practices (for one of the best critical and knowledgeable accounts, see, for example, World Information Order 2002; Lovink and Zehle 2006). These countergeographies are dynamic and changing in their locational features. And they comprise a broad range of activities, including a proliferation of criminal activities.

9. New Tactics in Human Rights, *The New Tactics Workbook: New Tactics in Human Rights: A Resource for Practitioners*, Center for Victims of Torture, http://www.newtactics. org/main.php/Tools for Action/The New Tactics Workbook.

10. Electronic Civil Disobedience, http://thing.net/~rdom.ecd/ecd.html.

11. It must be noted, however, that even in this campaign, centered as it was on the global South and determined as it was to communicate with global South organizations, the latter were often unable to access the sites (Kuntze, Rottmann, and Symons 2002).

12. There are many less-well-known campaigns. For instance, when Intel announced that it would include unique serial numbers in its Pentium III processing chips, advocacy groups objected to this invasion of privacy. Three groups in different locations set up a joint Web site called Big Brother Inside (http://www.bigbrotherinside.org) to provide an organizational space for advocacy groups operating in two countries, thereby also enabling them to use the place-specific resources of the different localities (Leizerov 2000). In 1997, the Washington, D.C.–based group Public Citizen put on its Web site an early draft of the Multiple Agreement on Investment (MAI, a confidential document negotiated by the OECD behind closed doors), launching a global campaign that brought the negotiations to a halt about eight months later. And these campaigns do not always directly engage questions of power. For instance, Reclaim the Streets started in London as a way to contest the Criminal Justice Act in the United Kingdom, which granted the police broad powers to seize sound equipment and otherwise discipline ravers One of the organization's tactics was to hold street parties in cities around the world: through Internet media, participants could exchange notes and tactics for dealing with the police and create a virtual space for coming together. Finally, perhaps one of the most significant developments is the Independent Media Center, a broad global network of ICT-based alternative media groups located all around the world Other such alternative media groups are MediaChannel.org, Z Communications, Protest net, and McSpotlight.

13. With other objectives in mind, one can also use a similar mix of conditions to explain in part the growth of transnational economic and political support networks among immigrants (for example, Michael Peter Smith 1994; Robert C. Smith 2006; Cordero-Guzmán, Smith, and Grosfoguel 2001; Espinoza and Gzech 1999).

14. Some of these issues are well developed in Adam's (1996) study of the Tiananmen Square uprisings of 1989, the popular movement for democracy in the Philippines in the mid-1980s, and the U.S. civil rights movement in the 1950s (but see also Zhao 2004). Protest, resistance, autonomy, and consent can be constructed at scales that can escape the confines of territorially bounded jurisdictions

15. One might distinguish a third type of political practice along these lines, one that turns a single event into a global media event that in turn serves to mobilize individuals and organizations around the world in support of the initial action and/or around similar such occurrences elsewhere. Among the most powerful of these actions, and now emblematic of this type of politics, are the Zapatistas' initial and subsequent actions. Also, the possibility of a single human rights case becoming a global media event has been a powerful tool for human rights activists.

16. The Internet may continue to be a space for democratic practices, but it will be so partly as a form of resistance to overarching powers of the economy and hierarchical power (for example, Calabrese and Burgelman 1999; see also Warf and Grimes 1997, Lovink 2003, May and Sell 2005), rather than as the space of unlimited freedom that is part of its

romantic representation. The images we need to bring to this representation must increasingly deal with contestation and resistance to commercial and military interests rather than simply freedom and interconnectivity.

17. One instance of the need to bring in the local is the issue of what databases are available to locals. Thus the World Bank's Knowledge Bank, a development gateway aimed at spurring ICT use and applications to build knowledge, is too large, according to some (Wilks 2001). A good example of a useful type and size database is Kubatana.net, an NGO in Zimbabwe that provides Web-site content and ICT services to national NGOs. It focuses on national information in Zimbabwe rather than global concerns.

18. The possibility of forms of globality that are not cosmopolitan has become an issue in my current work. It stems in part from my critique of the largely unexamined assumption that forms of politics, thinking, and consciousness that are global are ipso facto cosmopolitan (see Sassen 2006a, chaps. 6 and 7).

Chapter 8 Emergent Global Formations

1. This text is based on the Alexander von Humboldt Lecture in Human Geography, delivered at the University of Nijmegen, the Netherlands, on November 3, 2004. That lecture was based on a larger project (Sassen 2006a).

2 Elsewhere I have examined the implications of this divergence within the world of migrations (Sassen 1998). On professionals see Smith and Farell 2006.

3. Finally—and I cannot resist—we might say that a spent, used-up, sparsely populated area—for instance, a completely logged forest such that the forest has ceased to exist—represents an instance of "dead land" on what may well continue to be very dynamic global circuits—for example, the logging multinational now operating at sites in other countries or in the same country. The point is that one of the key articulations of that site remains that global logging circuit, and to (analytically) keep a dead site on the circuits that caused its death is part of a critical social science. Why render it invisible?

4. There are two other categories that may partially overlap with "internationalization as Americanization" but are important to distinguish, at least analytically. One is multilateralism, and the other is what Ruggie (1993) has called multiperspectival institutions.

5. The Project on International Courts and Tribunals (PICT) was founded in 1997 by the Center on International Cooperation (CIC), New York University, and the Foundation for International Environmental Law and Development (FIELD). Since 2002, PICT has been a common project of the CIC and the Centre for International Courts and Tribunals, University College London; see http://www.pict-pcti.org.

6. Elsewhere I examine some of these issues, particularly the future of financial centers given electronic trading and the new strategic alliances between the major financial centers (Sassen 2006a, chaps. 5 and 7).

7. Another view of these issues can be found in the Aspen Institute Roundtable on Information Technology, an annual event in Aspen, Colorado, that brings together the chief executive officers of the main software and hardware firms as well as the key venture capitalists in the sector; the overall sense of these insiders is one of the limits to the medium even at the height of the dot.com boom and that it will not replace other types of markets but rather complement them (see Bollier 1998).

8. Much of my work on global cities has been an effort to conceptualize and document the fact that the global digital economy requires massive concentrations of material and social resources in order to be what it is (see, for example, Sassen 2001) Finance is an important intermediary in this regard: it represents a capability for liquefying various forms of nonliquid wealth and for raising the mobility (that is, the hypermobility) of that which is already liquid. But to do so, even finance needs significant concentrations of material resources

9. A good example of the securitization of real estate is the creation of mortgage-backed securities (MBSs). These are produced when individual mortgages, after their origination, are bundled together with other mortgages. The groups of individual mortgages are then sold as single units to investors, and MBSs can be sold repeatedly in domestic and international secondary markets.

REFERENCES

Abbott, Andrew. 1988. *The System of Professions: An Essay on the Division of Expert Labor*. Chicago: University of Chicago Press.

———. 2004. *Methods of Discovery: Heuristics for the Social Sciences*. New York: W.W. Norton & Co.

Abrahamson, Mark. 2004. *Global Cities*. Oxford, UK: Oxford University Press.

Abu-Lughod, Janet L. 1989. *Before European Begemony: The World System A.D. 1250–1350*. New York: Oxford University Press.

———. 1994. *From Urban Village to East Village: The Battle for New York's Lower East Side*. Cambridge, Mass : Blackwell.

———. 1999a. *New York, Chicago, Los Angeles: America's Global Cities*. Minneapolis: University of Minnesota Press.

———, ed. 1999b. *Sociology for the Twenty-first Century: Continuities and Cutting Edges*. Chicago: University of Chicago Press.

Adams, Julia, Elisabeth S. Clemens, and Ann S. Orloff. 2005. *Remaking Modernity: Politics, History, and Sociology*. Durham. Duke University Press.

Adams, Paul C. 1996. "Protest and the Scale Politics of Telecommunications." *Political Geography* 15 (5): 419–41.

Agnew, John A. 2005. *Hegemony: The New Shape of Global Power*. Philadelphia: Temple University Press.

Albrow, Martin. 1996. *The Global Age: State and Society Beyond Modernity*. Cambridge, UK: Polity Press.

Alderson, Arthur S., and Jason Beckfield. "Power and Position in the World City System." *American Journal of Sociology* 109 (4): 811–51.

Alexander, Jeffrey C. 2006. *The Civil Sphere*. Oxford: Oxford University Press.

Alker, Hayward R. 2005. "Designing Information Resources for Transboundary Conflict Early Warning Networks." In Latham and Sassen 2005, 215–40.

Allen, John, Doreen B. Massey, and Michael Pryke. 1999. *Unsettling Cities: Movement/Settlement*. London, New York: Routledge in association with The Open University.

Allison, Julianne Emmons, ed. 2002. *Technology, Development, and Democracy: International Conflict and Cooperation in the Information Age*. Albany: State University of New York Press.

Althusser, Louis. 1971. "Ideology and Ideological State Apparatuses." In *Lenin and Philosophy and Other Essays*. New York: Monthly Review Press.

Aman, Alfred C. 1995. "A Global Perspective on Current Regulatory Reform: Rejection, Relocation, or Reinvention?" *Indiana Journal of Global Legal Studies* 2 (2): 429–64.

———. 1998. "The Globalizing State: A Future-Oriented Perspective on the Public/Private Distinction, Federalism, and Democracy." *Vanderbilt Journal of Transnational Law* 31: 769–870.

Amen, Mark M., Kevin Archer, and M. Martin Bosman, eds. 2006. *Relocating Global Cities: From the Center to the Margins*. New York: Rowman & Littlefield.

Amin, Ash, ed. 1994 *Post-Fordism: A Reader*. Cambridge, Mass.: Blackwell.

———. 2002. "Spatialities of Globalisation." *Environment & Planning A* 34 (3): 385–99.

Anderson, Chris. 2006. *The Long Tail: Why the Future of Business Is Selling Less of More*. New York. Hyperion.

Alexander, Jeffrey C. 2006. *The Civil Sphere*. Oxford: Oxford University Press.

Anderson, Elijah. 1990. *Streetwise: Race, Class, and Change in an Urban Community*. Chicago: University of Chicago Press.

Anderson, Jon W. 2003. "New Media, New Publics: Reconfiguring the Public Sphere of Islam." *Social Research* 70 (3): 887–906.

Aneesh, A. 2006. *Virtual Migration: The Programming of Globalization*. Durham, N.C.: Duke University Press.

Anheier, Helmut K , Marlies Glasius, and Mary Kaldor. 2002. *Global Civil Society Yearbook 2002*. Oxford: Oxford University Press.

Anonymous. 1999. "Sri Lankan Migrant Workers Remit Rs. 60 Billion in 1998." *Xinhua News Agency-Ceis*. Woodside, February 12.

Appadurai, Arjun, ed. 2000. *Globalization. A Special Issue of Public Culture*. Vol. 12, No. 1 Durham, N.C : Duke University Press.

Appleyard, R. T., ed. 1999. *Emigration Dynamics in Developing Countries, Vol. IV: The Arab Region* Aldershot: Ashgate.

Arquilla, John, and David F. Ronfeldt. 2001. *Networks and Netwars: The Future of Terror, Crime, and Militancy*. Santa Monica, Calif.: Rand.

Arrighi, Giovanni. 1994. *The Long Twentieth Century*. New York: Verso.

———. 1999. "Globalization and Historical Macrosociology." In Abu-Lughod 1999b, 117–133.

———, and Beverly J. Silver. 1999. *Chaos and Governance in the Modern World System*. Minneapolis: University of Minnesota Press.

Atton, Chris. 2003. "Reshaping Social Movement Media for a New Millennium." *Social Movement Studies* 2: 3–15.

Avgerou, Chrisanthi 2002. *Information Systems and Global Diversity*. Oxford: Oxford University Press.

———, Robin Mansell, Danny Quah, and Roger Silverstone. 2007. *Oxford Hand-*

book on Information & Communication Technologies. Oxford: Oxford University Press.

Bach, Jonathan, and David Stark. 2005. "Recombinant Technology and New Geographies of Association." In Latham and Sassen 2005.

Bada, Xochitl, Jonathan Fox, and Andrew Selee. 2006. *Invisible No More: Mexican Migrant Civic Participation in the United States.* Washington, D.C.: The Woodrow Wilson International Center for Scholars.

Bank for International Settlements. 2004 *BIS Quarterly Review: International Banking and Financial Market Developments.* Basel: BIS Monetary and Economic Development.

Barlow, Andrew L. 2003. *Between Fear and Hope: Globalization and Race in the United States.* Lanham, Md.: Rowman & Littlefield.

Barry, Andrew, and Don Slater. 2002. "Introduction: The Technological Economy." *Economy and Society* 31: 175–93.

Bartlett, Anne. 2007. "The City and the Self. The Emergence of New Political Subjects in London." In *Deciphering the Global: Its Spaces, Scales and Subjects,* ed. Saskia Sassen, 219–40. New York and London: Routledge.

Basch, Linda, Nina Glick Schiller, and Cristina Szanton Blanc. 1994. *Nations Unbound: Transnational Projects, Post-Colonial Predicaments, and Deterritorialized Nation-States.* Amsterdam: Gordon & Breach Science Publishers.

Battistella, G., and M.M.B. Assis. 1998. *The Impact of the Crisis on Migration in Asia.* Quezon City, Philippines: Scalabrini Migration Center.

Baubock, Rainer. 1994 *Transnational Citizenship: Memberships and Rights in International Migration* Aldershot, UK: Edward Elgar.

Bauchner, Joshua S. 2000. "State Sovereignty and the Globalizing Effects of the Internet: A Case Study of the Privacy Debate." *Brooklyn Journal of International Law* 26: 689–722.

Beck, Ulrich. 2000. *What Is Globalization?* Translated by Patrick Camiller. Cambridge Polity Press / Blackwell.

———, and Elizabeth Beck-Gernsheim. 2001. *Individualization: Institutionalized Individualism and Its Social and Political Consequences.* London: Sage.

———. 2006 *Cosmopolitan Vision.* Cambridge: Polity.

Bellanet 2002. *Report on Activities 2001–2002* http://home.bellanet.org (site now discontinued)

Benayoun, Chantal, and Dominique Schnapper. 2006. *Diasporas et Nations.* Paris: Odile Jacob

Beneria, Lourdes. 2003. *Global Tensions: Challenges and Opportunities in the World Economy.* New York: Routledge.

———, and Shelley Feldman, eds. 1992. *Unequal Burden: Economic Crises, Persistent Poverty. and Women's Work.* Boulder, Colo.. Westview.

Benhabib, Seyla. 2002. *Democractic Equality and Cultural Diversity: Political Identities in the Global Era.* Princeton, N.J.. Princeton University Press.

Benkler, Yochai. 2006. *The Wealth of Networks: How Social Production Transforms Markets and Freedom.* New Haven, Conn. Yale University Press.

Bennett, W. L. 2003. "Communicating Global Activism: Strengths and Vulnerabilities of Networked Politics." *Information, Communication & Society* 6 (2): 143–68.

Bestor, Theodore. 2001. "Supply-Side Sushi: Commodity, Market, and the Global City." *American Anthropologist* 103 (1): 76–95.

Berle, Adolf, and Gardiner Means. 1932. *The Modern Corporation and Private Property.* Reprint, New York. Harcourt, Brace & World, 1968.

Berman, Paul Schiff. 2002. "The Globalization of Jurisdiction." *University of Pennsylvania Law Review* 151: 314–17.

Beunza, Daniel, and David Stark. 2004. "Tools of the Trade: The Socio-technology of Arbitrage in a Wall Street Trading Room." *Industrial and Corporate Change* 13 (2): 369–400.

Bevir, Mark, and Frank Trentmann, eds. 2004. *Markets in Context.* Cambridge: Cambridge University Press.

Bhachu, Parminder. 1985. *Twice Migrants: East African Sikh Settlers in Britain.* London: Tavistock.

Block, Fred 1977. "The Ruling Class Does Not Rule " In *Revising State Theory: Essays in Politics and Postindustrialism.* Reprint, Philadelphia: Temple University Press, 1987.

———. 1994. "The Roles of the State in the Economy." In Smelser and Swedberg 1994, 691–710.

Body-Gendrot, Sophie. 2000. *The Social Control of Cities? A Comparative Perspective.* Oxford: Blackwell.

Bok, Derek Curtis 1993. *The Cost of Talent: How Executives and Professionals Are Paid and How It Affects America.* New York· Free Press.

Bolin, Richard L., ed 1998. *The Global Network of Free Zones in the 21st Century.* Flagstaff, Ariz.: The Flagstaff Institute.

Bollier, David, rapporteur. 1998. *The Global Advance of Electronic Commerce: Reinventing Markets, Management, and National Sovereignty.* Washington, D.C.: Aspen Institute

———. 2001. *Public Assets, Private Profits: Reclaiming the American Commons in an Age of Market Enclosure.* Washington, D.C.· New America Foundation

Bonilla, Frank, Edwin Melendez, Rebecca Morales, and Maria de los Angeles Torres, eds. 1998. *Borderless Borders: U.S. Latinos, Latin Americans, and the Paradox of Interdependence.* Philadelphia: Temple University Press.

Bonilla-Silva, Eduardo. 2003. *Racism without Racists: Color-blind Racism and the Persistence of Racial Inequality in the United States.* Lanham, Md.. Rowman & Littlefield.

Booth, William 1999. "Thirteen Charges Against Gang Importing Prostitutes." *Washington Post*, August 21.

Bose, Christine E., and Edna Acosta-Belén, eds. 1995. *Women in the Latin American Development Process.* Philadelphia: Temple University Press.

Bosniak, Linda, et al 2000. "Symposium· The State of Citizenship." Special issue, *Indiana Journal of Global Legal Studies* 7, no. 2.

Bourdieu, Pierre 1977. *Outline of a Theory of Practice.* Cambridge: Cambridge University Press.

Bourgois, Philippe. 1995. *In Search of Respect: Selling Crack in El Barrio.* Cambridge: Cambridge University Press.

Bousquet, M., and K. Wills, eds 2003. *Web Authority: Online Domination and the Informatics of Resistance.* Boulder, Colo.: Alt-x Press.

Bowker, Geoffrey C., and Susan Leigh Star. 1999. *Sorting Things Out: Classification and Its Consequences.* Cambridge, Mass.: MIT Press.

Boyd, Monica. 1989. "Family and Personal Networks in International Migration: Recent Developments and New Agendas." *International Migration Review* 23 (3): 638–70.

Boyle, James. 1997. "Foucault in Cyberspace: Surveillance, Sovereignty, and Hard-Wired Censors " Duke Law School. http://www.faculty.law.duke.edu/boylesite/foucault.htm.

Bradshaw, York, Rita Noonan, Laura Gash, and Claudia Buchmann. 1993. "Borrowing against the Future: Children and Third World Indebtness." *Social Forces* 71 (3): 629–56.

Brady, Henry E., and David Collier. 2004 *Rethinking Social Inquiry: Diverse Tools, Shared Standards.* Lanham, Md.: Rowman & Littlefield.

Braudel, Fernand. 1984. *The Perspective of the World* Vol. 3 of *Civilization and Capitalism, 15th–18th Century.* New York: HarperCollins.

Brenner, Neil 1998. "Global Cities, Glocal States: Global City Formation and State Territorial Restructuring in Contemporary Europe." *Review of International Political Economy* 5 (2): 1–37.

———. 1999. "Beyond State-Centrism? Space, Territoriality, and Geographical Scale in Globalization Studies." *Theory & Society* 28 (1): 39–78.

———. 2004 *New State Spaces: Urban Governance and the Rescaling of Statehood.* Oxford: Oxford University Press.

———, and Roger Keil. 2005. *The Global Cities Reader.* New York and London· Routledge.

Brettell, Caroline, and James F. Hollifield, eds 2000. *Migration Theory: Talking Across the Disciplines.* New York: Routledge.

Bridge, Gary, and Sophie Watson. 2000. *A Companion to the City, Blackwell Companions to Geography.* Oxford: Blackwell Publishers.

Briggs, Vernon M. 1992. *Mass Immigration and the National Interest.* Armonk, N.Y.: M. E. Sharpe.

Bronfenbrenner, Kate, Sheldon Friedman, Richard W. Hurd, Rudolph A. Oswald, and Ronald L Seeber, eds. 1998. *Organizing to Win: New Research on Union Strategies.* Ithaca, N.Y.: ILR Press.

Brubaker, Rogers. 1997. *Nationalism Reframed: Nationhood and the National Question in the New Europe.* Cambridge: Cambridge University Press.

———. 2004. *Ethnicity without Groups.* Cambridge, Mass.: Harvard University Press

Bryson, J. R., and P. W. Daniels, eds. 2006. *The Service Industries Handbook* Cheltenham, UK: Edward Elgar.

Budd, Leslie 1995. "Globalization, Territory, and Strategic Alliances in Different Financial Centers." *Urban Studies* 32 (2): 345–60.

Buechler, Simone. 2007. "Deciphering the Local in a Global Neoliberal Age: Three Favelas in Sao Paulo, Brazil." In *Deciphering the Global: Its Spaces, Scales and Subjects*, ed. Saskia Sassen, 95–112. New York and London: Routledge.

Buntarian, Nani, Cheekay Cinco, Karin Delgadillo, Dorothy Okello, Dafne Sabanes Plou, Chat Garcia Ramilo, Sonia Jaffe Robbins, Marie-Helene Mottin Sylla, and the Women'sNet Team. 2000. *Acting Locally, Connecting Globally: Stories from the Regions.* Women in Sync: Toolkit for Electronic Networking. Women's Networking Support Program Association for Progressive Communications. http://www.apcwomen.org/netsupport/sync/sync3.html.

Buntin, Jennifer. (in process) *Transnational Suburbs? The Impact of Immigration Communities on the Urban Edge* (Doctoral dissertation,) Sociology, University of Chicago, Chicago, Ill.

Burawoy, Michael. 1979. *Manufacturing Consent: Changes in the Labor Process under Monopoly Capitalism.* Chicago: University of Chicago Press.

Burawoy, Michael, Joseph A. Blum, Sheba George, Zsuzsa Gille, Teresa Gowan, Lynne Haney, Maren Klawiter, Steven H. Lopez, Seán Ó Ríain, and Millie Thayer. 2000. *Global Ethnography: Forces, Connections, and Imaginations in a Postmodern World.* Berkeley: University of California Press.

Burdett, Ricky, ed. 2006. *Cities: People, Society, Architecture.* New York: Rizzoli.

Bustamante, Jorge A., and Geronimo Martinez. 1979. "Unauthorized Immigration from Mexico: Beyond Borders but within Systems." *Journal of International Affairs* 33 (1): 265–84.

Cadena, Sylvia. 2004. Networking for Women or Women's Networking. In *A report for the Social Science Research Council's Committee on Information Technology and International Cooperation.* http://www.ssrc.org/programs/itic/publications/civsocandgov/cadena.pdf.

Cagatay, Nilufer, and Sule Ozler. 1995. "Feminization of the Labor Force: The Effects of Long-term Development and Structural Adjustment." *World Development* 23 (11): 1883–94.

Calabrese, Andrew, and Jean-Claude Burgelman 1999. *Communication, Citizenship, and Social Policy: Rethinking the Limits of the Welfare State.* Lanham, Md.: Rowman & Littlefield.

Calhoun, Craig J. 1997. *Nationalism.* Minneapolis. University of Minnesota Press.

———. 1998. *Neither Gods nor Emperors: Students and the Struggle for Democracy in China* Berkeley: University of California Press.

———, Frederick Cooper, and Kevin W. Moore. 2006. *Lessons of Empire: Imperial Histories and American Power.* New York. New Press.

Callon, Michel. 1998. "Introduction: The Embeddedness of Economic Markets in Economics." In *The Laws of the Markets*, ed. Michel Callon, 1–57. Oxford: Blackwell.

Camacho, Kemly. 2001. "The Internet: A Great Challenge for Civil Society Organizations in Central America." Acceso. http://www.acceso.or.cr/publica/gateway0600.html (site now discontinued).

Campos, Ricardo, and Frank Bonilla. 1982. *Bootstraps and Enterprise Zones: The Underside of Late Capitalism in Puerto Rico and the United States.* Beverly Hills, Calif.: Sage.

Carbonneau, Thomas E. 2004. "Arbitral Law-Making." *Michigan Journal of International Law* 25 (4): 1183–1208.

Castells, Manuel. 1977. *The Urban Question: A Marxist Approach*. Cambridge, Mass.: MIT Press.

———. 1983. *The City and the Grassroots: A Cross-Cultural Theory of Urban Social Movements*. Berkeley: University of California Press.

———. 1989. *The Informational City: Information Technology, Economic Restructuring, and the Urban-Regional Process*. Oxford: Blackwell.

———. 1996. *The Rise of the Network Society: The Information Age: Economy, Society and Culture, Volume 1*. Oxford: Blackwell.

Castles, Stephen, and Mark J Miller. 2003. *The Age of Migration: International Population Movements in the Modern World* 3rd ed. New York: Guilford Press.

Cederman, Lars-Erik, and Kraus, P. A. 2005. "Transnational Communications and the European Demos." In Latham and Sassen 2005, 283–311.

Cerny, Philip G. 1990. *The Changing Architecture of Politics: Structure, Agency, and the Future of the State*. London: Sage.

———. 2000. "Structuring the Political Arena: Public Goods, States and Governance in a Globalizing World." *In Global Political Economy: Contemporary Theories*, ed. Ronen Palan, 21–35. London: Routledge.

Chakrabarty, Dipesh. 2000. *Provincializing Europe*. Princeton, N.J.: Princeton University Press.

Chant, Sylvia H., and Nikki Craske. 2002 *Gender in Latin America* New Brunswick, N.J.: Rutgers University Press.

Charny, David. 1991. "Competition among Jurisdictions in Formulating Corporate Law Rules: An American Perspective on the 'Race to the Bottom' in the European Communities." *Harvard International Law Journal* 32 (2): 423–56

Chase-Dunn, Christopher 1984. "Urbanization in the World System: New Directions for Research." In Michael Peter Smith 1984, 111–20.

Chase-Dunn, Christopher, and Barry Gills. 2005. "Waves of Globalization and Resistance in the Capitalist World System: Social Movements and Critical Global Studies." In *Towards a Critical Globalization Studies*, ed. Richard Appelbaum and William Robinson, 45–54. New York: Routledge.

Chatterjee, Partha. 1993. *The Nation and Its Fragments*. Princeton, N.J.: Princeton University Press.

Chen, Xiangming. 2005. *As Borders Bend: Transnational Spaces on the Pacific Rim*. Oxford: Rowman & Littlefield.

Chesney-Lind, Meda, and John Hagedorn, eds. 1999. *Female Gangs in America: Essays on Girls, Gangs, and Gender*. Chicago: Lake View Press.

Chin, Christine B. N 1997. "Walls of Silence and Late Twentieth Century Representations of the Foreign Female Domestic Worker: The Case of Filipina and Indonesian Female Servants in Malaysia " *International Migration Review* 31 (2): 353–85.

Clark, Terry Nichols, and Seymour Martin Lipset. 1991. "Are Social Classes Dying?" *International Sociology* 6 (4): 397–410.

Clark, Terry Nichols, and Vincent Hoffmann-Martinot, eds. 1998. *The New Political Culture.* Oxford: Westview Press.

Cleaver, Harry M., Jr 1998. "The Zapatista Effect: The Internet and the Rise of an Alternative Political Fabric." *Journal of International Affairs* 51 (2): 621–40

Coalition to Abolish Slavery and Trafficking (CAST.) http://www.trafficked-women.org.

Cohen, Michael, Blair A. Ruble, Joseph S. Tulchin, and Allison M. Garland, eds 1996. *Preparing for the Global Future: Global Pressures and Local Forces.* Washington, D.C.: Woodrow Wilson Center Press.

Cohen, Robert. 1981. "The International Division of Labor· Multinational Corporations and Urban Hierarchy." In *Urbanization and Urban Planning in Capitalist Society*, ed. Michael Dear and Allen Scott, 287–315. New York: Methuen.

Cohen, Robin. 1991. *Contested Domains: Debates in International Labour Studies.* Atlantic Highlands, N.J.: Zed Books.

Coleman, G. 2004. "The Political Agnosticism of Free and Open Source Software and the Inadvertent Politics of Contrast." *Anthropological Quarterly* 77 (3): 507–19.

Comaroff, Jean, and John Comaroff. 2000. "Millennial Capitalism: First Thoughts on a Second Coming." *Public Culture* 12 (2): 291–343.

Consalvo, Mia, and Caroline Haythornthwaite, eds. 2006. *AoIR Internet Research Annual Volume 4.* New York: Peter Lang

———, and Susanna Paasonen, eds. 2002 *Women and Everyday Uses of the Internet: Agency and Identity.* New York: Peter Lang.

Cordero-Guzman, Hector R., Robert C. Smith, and Ramon Grosfoguel. 2001. *Migration, Transnationalization, and Race in a Changing New York.* Philadelphia: Temple University Press.

Cornelius, Wayne A. 2001. "Death at the Border: Efficacy and Unintended Consequences of US Immigration Control Policy." *Population and Development Review* 27 (4): 661–85.

———, Philip L. Martin, and James F. Hollifield. 2004. *Controlling Immigration: A Global Perspective.* 2nd ed. Stanford: Stanford University Press.

Coutin, Susan B. 2000. "Denationalization, Inclusion, and Exclusion: Negotiating the Boundaries of Belonging." *Indiana Journal of Global Legal Studies* 7 (2): 585–94.

Crede, Andreas, and Robin E. Mansell. 1998 *Knowledge Societies in a Nutshell: Information Technology for Sustainable Development.* Ottawa: International Development Research Centre (IDRC).

Creech, Heather, and Terry Willard. 2001. *Strategic Intentions: Managing Knowledge Networks for Sustainable Development.* Winnipeg, Manitoba: International Institute for Sustainable Development.

Crenshaw, Kimberlé, Neil Gotanda, Gary Peller, and Kendall Thomas, eds. 1996. *Critical Race Theory: The Key Writings That Formed the Movement.* New York: New Press.

Crichlow, Michaeline A. 2004. *Negotiating Caribbean Freedom: Peasants and The State in Development*. Lanham, M.D.: Lexington Books

Cutler, A. Claire. 2002. "The Politics of 'Regulated Liberalism'· A Historical Materialist Approach to European Integration." In *Historical Materialism and Globalisation: Essays on Continuity and Change*, ed. Mark Rupert and Hazel Smith, 257–83. London: Routledge.

———, Virginia Haufler, and Tony Porter, eds. 1999. *Private Authority and International Affairs*. Albany. State University of New York Press.

Dahrendorf, Ralf. 1959. *Class and Class Conflict in Industrial Society* Stanford, Calif.: Stanford University Press.

Datz, Giselle. 2007. "Global-National Interactions and Sovereign Debt-Restructuring Outcomes " In *Deciphering the Global: Its Spaces, Scales and Subjects*, ed. Saskia Sassen 321–50. New York and London· Routledge

David, Natacha. 1998. "Migrants Made the Scapegoats of the Crisis." *ICFTU OnLine* (International Confederation of Free Trade Unions). On Hartford Web Publishing. http.//www.hartford-hwp.com/archives/50/012.html.

Davis, Diana E. 1994 *Urban Leviathan: Mexico City in the Twentieth Century*. Philadelphia, Penn.: Temple University Press.

———, ed. 1999 *Political Power and Social Theory*. Vol. 13. Stamford, Conn.: JAI Press.

Davis, Mike. 2006. *Planet of Slums*. London: Verso

Dean, J., J. W. Anderson, and G. Lovink, 2006. *Reformatting Politics: Information Technology and Global Civil Society*. London: Routledge

Dear, Michael. 2002. "Los Angeles and the Chicago School. Invitation to a Debate." *City and Community* 1 (1): 5–32.

Delgado, Richard, and Jean Stefancic, eds. 1999. *Critical Race Theory: The Cutting Edge*. Philadelphia: Temple University Press.

Denning, Dorothy E 1999. *Information Warfare and Security*. New York: Addison-Wesley.

——— 2001. "Cyberwarriors: Activists and Terrorists Turn to Cyberspace." *Harvard International Review* 33 (2): 70–75

Der Derian, James. 2001. *Virtuous War: Mapping the Military-Industrial-Media-Entertainment Network*. Boulder, Colo.: Westview Press.

Derudder, B., and P J. Taylor, 2005 "The Cliquishness of World Cities." *Global Networks* 5 (1)· 71–91

Desfor, Gene, and Roger Keil. 2004. *Nature and the City: Making Environmental Policy in Toronto and Los Angeles*. Tempe. University of Arizona Press.

Dezalay, Yves, and Bryant G Garth. 1995. "Merchants of Law as Moral Entrepreneurs. Constructing International Justice from the Competition for Transnational Business Disputes." *Law & Society Review* 29 (1): 27–64.

———. 1996. *Dealing in Virtue: International Commercial Arbitration and the Construction of a Transnational Legal Order*. Chicago. University of Chicago Press.

Dobbin, Frank. 1994. *Forging Industrial Policy: The United States, Britain, and France in the Railway Age*. New York: Cambridge University Press.

Donk, Wim van de, Brian D. Loader, Paul G. Nixon, and Dieter Rucht, eds. 2005. *Cyberprotest: New Media, Citizens, and Social Movements*. London: Routledge.

Drainville, Andre C. 2004. *Contesting Globalization: Space and Place in the World Economy*. London: Routledge.

Drake, W. J., and E. M. Williams III. 2004. "Defining ICT Global Governance." In *SSRC Research Network on IT and Governance*. New York: SSRC. http://www.ssrc.org/programs/itic/publications/knowledge_report/memos/billdrake.pdf

———. 2006. *Governing Global Electronic Networks: International Perspectives on Policy and Power*. Cambridge, Mass.: MIT Press.

Duara, Prasenjit. 1997. *Rescuing History from the Nation: Questioning Narratives of Modern China*. Chicago: University of Chicago Press.

Duncan, O. 1959. "Human Ecology and Population Studies." In *The Study of Population: An Inventory and Appraisal*, ed. P. Hauser and O. Dudley, 678–716. Chicago: University of Chicago Press.

Duneier, Mitchell. 1999. *Sidewalk*. New York: Farrar, Straus & Giroux.

Dunn, Seamus. 1994. *Managing Divided Cities*. London: Ryburn / Keele University Press.

Dutton, William H., ed. 1999. *Society on the Line: Information Politics in the Digital Age*. Oxford: Oxford University Press.

Edwards, Richard. 1979. *Contested Terrain: The Transformation of the Workplace in the Twentieth Century*. New York: Basic Books.

Ehrenreich, Barbara, and Arlie Hochschild. 2003 *Global Woman: Nannies, Maids, and Sex Workers in the New Economy*. New York: Metropolitan Books.

Eichengreen, Barry. 2003. *Capital Flows and Crises*. Cambridge, Mass.: MIT Press.

———, and Albert Fishlow. 1996. *Contending with Capital Flows: What Is Different about the 1990s?* New York. Council on Foreign Relations.

Elmer, G. 2004. *Profiling Machines: Mapping the Personal Information Economy*. Cambridge, Mass.: MIT Press.

Ernst, Dieter. 2005. "The New Mobility of Knowledge: Digital Information Systems and Global Flagship Networks." In Latham and Sassen 2005, 89–114.

Espinoza, Vicente. 1999. "Social Networks among the Urban Poor: Inequality and Integration in a Latin American City." In *Networks in the Global Village: Life in Contemporary Communities*, ed. Barry Wellman, 147–84. Boulder, Colo.: Westview Press.

Espinoza, Victor, and Susan Gzesh. 1999. *The Federation of Michoacan Clubs in Illinois*. Chicago: Chicago-Michoacan Project.

Esterhuysen, Anriette. 2000. "Networking for a Purpose: African NGOs Using ICT." In *Rowing Upstream: Snapshots of Pioneers of the Information Age in Africa*. SANGONet (Southern African NGO Network). http://www.sn.apc.org/Rowing_Upstream/chapter1/ch1.html.

Evans, Peter. 1995. *Embedded Autonomy: States and Industrial Transformation.* Princeton, N.J.: Princeton University Press.

————. 1997. "The Eclipse of the State? Reflections on Stateness in an Era of Globalization." *World Politics* 50 (1): 62–87

Fagan, Jeffrey E 1996. "Gangs, Drugs, and Neighborhood Change." In *Gangs in America.* 2nd ed., ed. C. Ronald Huff, 39–74. Thousand Oaks, Calif.: Sage.

Fainstein, Susan S., Ian Gordon, and Michael Harloe 1992. *Divided Cities: New York and London in the Contemporary World.* Oxford: Blackwell.

Fantasia, Rick, and Kim Voss. 2004. *Hard Work: Remaking the American Labor Movement.* Berkeley: University of California Press.

Farrer, Gracia Liu. 2007. "Producing Global Economies from Below· Chinese Immigrant Transnational Entrepreneurship in Japan." 177–98. In *Deciphering the Global: Its Spaces, Scales and Subjects,* ed. Saskia Sassen. New York and London: Routledge.

Fassmann, Heinz, and Rainer Munz, eds. 1994 *European Migration in the Late Twentieth Century: Historical Patterns, Actual Trends and Social Implications.* Aldershot. Edward Edgar

Faux, Geoffrey P. 2006. *The Global Class War: How America's Bipartisan Elite Lost Our Future—and What It Will Take to Win It Back.* Hoboken, N.J.: Wiley

Feldbauer, Peter, Erich Pilz, Dieter Rünzler, and Irene Stacher. 1993. *Megastädte: Zur Rolle von Metropolen in der Weltgesellschaft.* Vienna: Bohlau.

Ferguson, Yale H, and Barry R. Jones, eds. 2002. *Political Space: Frontiers of Change and Governance in a Globalizing World* Albany: State University of New York Press.

Ferguson, Yale H., and Richard W. Mansbach. 2004. *Remapping Global Politics: History's Revenge and Future Shock. Cambridge Studies in International Relations;* 97. Cambridge: Cambridge University Press.

Fernandez, Kelly, Maria Patricia, and J. Shefner. 2005. *Out of the Shadows.* University Park: Pennsylvania State University Press.

Fincher, Ruth, and Jane M. Jacobs. 1998 *Cities of Difference.* New York. Guilford Press.

Fischer-Lescano, Andreas, and Gunther Teubner. 2004. "Regime-Collisions: The Vain Search for Legal Unity in the Fragmentation of Global Law." *Michigan Journal of International Law* 25 (4): 999–1046.

Fisher, Melissa. 2006. "Wall Street Women: Navigating Gendered Networks in the New Economy." In Fisher and Downey 2006.

————, and Greg Downey, eds. 2006. *Frontiers of Capital: Ethnographic Reflections on the New Economy.* Durham, N.C · Duke University Press.

Fligstein, Neil. 1990. *The Transformation of Corporate Control.* Cambridge, Mass.: Harvard University Press.

———— 2001. *The Architecture of Markets.* Princeton, N.J.: Princeton University Press.

Fourcade-Gourinchas, Marion, and Sarah L. Babb. 2002. "The Rebirth of the Liberal Creed: Paths to Neoliberalism in Four Countries" *American Journal of Sociology* 108: 533–79.

Frederick, Howard 1993. "Computer Networks and the Emergence of Global Civil Society." In *Global Networks: Computers and International Communications*, ed. Linda M. Harasim, 283–95. Cambridge, Mass : MIT Press

Friedman, Elisabeth Jay. 2005. "The Reality of Virtual Reality: The Internet and Gender Equality Advocacy in Latin America." *Latin American Politics and Society* 47: 1–34.

Friedmann, John. 1995. "World City Formation· An Agenda for Research and Action." In Knox and Taylor 1995, 21–47.

———. 2005. *China's Urban Transition*. Minneapolis: University of Minnesota Press.

———, and G Wolff. 1982. "World City Formation: An Agenda for Research and Action." *International Journal of Urban and Regional Research* 15 (1): 269–83.

Fujita, Kuniko, and Richard Child Hill, eds. 1993. *Japanese Cities in the World Economy*. Philadelphia, Penn.: Temple University Press.

Fujita, Masahisa, Paul Krugman, and Anthony J. Venables. 2004. *The Spatial Economy: Cities, Regions, and International Trade*. Cambridge, Mass.: MIT Press.

Garcia, D. Linda. 2002. "The Architecture of Global Networking Technologies." In Sassen 2002, 39–69.

Garrett, Geoffrey. 1998. "Global Markets and National Politics: Collision Course or Virtuous Circle?" *International Organization* 52: 787–824.

GaWC (Globalization and World Cities—Study Group and Network) (Ongoing). http·//www.lboro.ac.uk/gawc/.

Geddes, Andrew. 2003. *The Politics of Migration and Immigration in Europe*. Thousand Oaks, Calif.: Sage Publications.

Georges, E. 1990. *The Making of a Transnational Community: Migration, Development, and Cultural Change in the Dominican Republic*. New York. Columbia University Press.

Gereffi, Gary. 1994. "The Organization of Buyer-Driven Commodity Chains." In Gereffi and Korzeniewicz 1994, 95–122

———. 1995. "Global Production Systems and Third World Development." In *Global Change, Regional Response: The New International Context of Development*, ed. Barbara Stallings, 100–142. New York: Cambridge University Press.

———, and Miguel Korzeniewicz. 1994. *Commodity Chains and Global Capitalism*. Westport, Conn.: Praeger.

———, John Humphrey, and Timothy Sturgeon. 2005. "The Governance of Global Value Chains." *Review of International Political Economy (Special Issue: Aspects of Globalization)*. 12 (1). 78–104

Giddens, Anthony 1984. *The Constitution of Society: Outline of the Theory of Structuration*. Berkeley: University of California Press.

———. 1987. *The Nation-State and Violence*. Berkeley: University of California Press.

———. 1990. *The Consequences of Modernity*. Oxford: Polity Press.

Gill, Stephen. 1996. "Globalization, Democratization, and the Politics of Indifference." In Mittelman 1996, 205–28.

Gillett, Sharon Eisner, and Mitchell Kapor. 1996. "The Self-governing Internet: Coordination by Design." Paper presented at the Workshop on Coordination and Administration of the Internet, John F. Kennedy School of Government, Harvard University, Cambridge, Mass., September 8–10. http://ccs.mit.edu/ccswp197.html.

Girard, Monique, and David Stark. 2002. "Distributing Intelligence and Organizing Diversity in New-Media Projects " *Environment & Planning A* 34 (11): 1927–49.

Glaeser, Andreas. 2000 *Divided in Unity: Identity, Germany, and the Berlin Police* Chicago: University of Chicago Press

Glaeser, Edward L , and Joshua D. Gottlieb. 2006. "Urban Resurgence and the Consumer City." *Urban Studies* 43 (8)· 1275–99.

Goldsmith, Jack L., and Tim Wu. 2006. *Who Controls the Internet?: Illusions of a Borderless World*. New York: Oxford University Press

Gottdiener, Mark. 1985. *The Social Production of Urban Space*. Austin: University of Texas Press.

Gould, Mark 1996 "Governance of the Internet: A UK Perspective." Paper presented at the Workshop on Coordination and Administration of the Internet, John F. Kennedy School of Government, Harvard University, Cambridge, Mass. September 8–10. http://aranea.law.bris.ac.uk/HarvardFinal.html (site now discontinued).

Grabher, Gernot. 2001. "Ecologies of Creativity. The Village, the Group, and the Heterarchic Organisation of the British Advertising Industry." *Environment & Planning A* 33 (2)· 351–74.

———. 2002. "Cool Projects, Boring Institutions: Temporary Collaboration in Social Context." *Regional Studies* 36 (3): 205–14

Graham, Stephen, and Simon Marvin. 1996. *Telecommunications and the City: Electronic Spaces, Urban Places*. London: Routledge.

Graham, Stephen, ed. 2004 *Cybercities Reader*. London. Routledge.

Grasmuck, Sherri, and Patricia R. Pessar. 1991. *Between Two Islands: Dominican International Migration*. Berkeley: University of California Press.

Grusky, David, and Jesper Sorensen. 1998. "Can Class Analysis Be Salvaged?" *American Journal of Sociology* 103 (5): 1187–1234.

Grusky, David, Kim Weeden, and Jesper Sorensen. 2000. "The Case for Realism in Class Analysis." *Political Power & Social Theory* 14: 291–305.

Gu, Felicity Rose, and Zilai Tang. 2002. "Shanghai: Reconnecting to the Global Economy " In Sassen 2002, 273–307.

Gugler, Josef. 2004. *World Cities beyond the West: Globalization, Development, and Inequality*. Cambridge· Cambridge University Press.

Habermas, Jürgen. 1989. *The Structural Transformation of the Public Sphere: An Inquiry into a Category of Bourgeois Society*, trans by Thomas Burger with Frederick Lawrence. Cambridge. MIT Press.

Hagedorn, John, ed. 2006. *Gangs in the Global City: Exploring Alternatives to Traditional Criminology*: Chicago: University of Illinois Press.

Hajnal, Peter I., ed. 2002. *Civil Society in the Information Age*. Aldershot: Ashgate.

Hall, Peter. 1966. *The World Cities*. New York: McGraw-Hill.

Hall, Peter A., 1989. *The Political Power of Economic Ideas: Keynesianism across Nations*. Princeton, N.J.: Princeton University Press.

———, and David Soskice, eds. 2001. *Varieties of Capitalism: The Institutional Foundations of Comparative Advantage*. New York: Oxford University Press.

Hall, Rodney Bruce. 1999. *National Collective Identity: Social Constructs and International Systems*. New York: Columbia University Press.

———, and Thomas J. Biersteker. 2002. *The Emergence of Private Authority in Global Governance*. Cambridge: Cambridge University Press.

Hall, Stuart. 1988. "Brave New World." *Marxism Today*. October 24–29

——— 1991. *Myths of Caribbean Identity*. Coventry: Centre for Caribbean Studies, University of Warwick.

Hamilton, Nora, and Norma Chinchilla. 2001. *Seeking Community in a Global City: Salvadorans and Guatemalans in Los Angeles*. Philadelphia: Temple University Press.

Hamzic, Edin, and Maeve Seehan. 1999. "Kosovo Sex Slaves in SoHo Flats." *Sunday Times* (London), July 4.

Hansen, Randall, and Patrick Weil, eds. 2002. *Dual Nationality, Social Rights and Federal Citizenship in the U.S. and Europe: The Reinvention of Citizenship*. New York: Berghahn Books.

Hardt, Michael, and Antonio Negri. 2000. *Empire* Cambridge, Mass.: Harvard University Press.

Harvey, David. 1973. *Social Justice and the City*. Baltimore: Johns Hopkins University Press.

———. 1982. *Limits to Capital*. Oxford: Blackwell.

———. 1989. *The Condition of Postmodernity*. Oxford: Blackwell.

Harvey, Rachel. 2007. "The Sub-National Constitution of Global Markets." In *Deciphering the Global: Its Spaces, Scales and Subjects*, ed. Saskia Sassen, 199–216. New York and London: Routledge.

Haussermann, Hartmut, and Walter Siebel. 1987. *Neue Urbanität*. Frankfurt: Suhrkamp.

Hechter, Michael. 2001. *Containing Nationalism*. Oxford: Oxford University Press.

Helleiner, Eric. 1999. "Sovereignty, Territoriality, and the Globalization of Finance." In *States and Sovereignty in the Global Economy*, ed. David A Smith, Dorothy J. Solinger, and Steven C. Topik, 138–57. London: Routledge.

———, and Andreas Pickel. 2005. *Economic Nationalism in a Globalizing World. Cornell Studies in Political Economy*. Ithaca, N.Y.: Cornell University Press.

Henderson, Jeffrey. 2005. "Governing Growth and Inequality: The Continuing Relevance of Strategic Economic Planning." In *Towards a Critical Globalization Studies*, ed. Richard Appelbaum and William Robinson, 227–36. New York: Routledge.

Heyzer, Noeleen. 1994. "Introduction: Creating Responsible Policies for Migrant Women Domestic Workers." In *The Trade in Domestic Workers: Causes, Mechanisms, and Conse-*

quences of International Migration, ed. Noleen Heyzer, Geertje Lycklama à Nijeholt, and Nedra Weerakoon. London: Asian and Pacific Development Centre / Zed Books.

Hill, Matthew J. 2007. "Reimagining Old Havana: World Heritage and the Production of Scale in Late Socialist Cuba." In *Deciphering Globalization: Its Scales, Spaces and Subjects*, ed. Saskia Sassen, 59–76. New York and London: Routledge.

Himanen, Pekka. 2001. *The Hacker Ethic and the Spirit of the Information Age*. New York: Random House

Hindman, Heather. 2007. "Outsourcing Difference: Expatriate Training and the Disciplining of Culture." In *Deciphering Globalization: Its Scales, Spaces and Subjects*, ed. Saskia Sassen, 153–76. New York and London: Routledge.

Hobsbawm, Eric. 1994. *The Age of Extremes: A History of the World, 1914–1991*. New York: Vintage Books.

Holston, James. 1996. *Cities and Citizenship*. Chicago: University of Chicago Press.

Hondagneu-Sotelo, Pierrette. 1994. *Gendered Transitions: Mexican Experiences of Immigration*. Berkeley: University of California Press.

————, ed 2003. *Gender and U.S. Immigration: Contemporary Trends*. Berkeley: University of California Press

Hoogvelt, Ankie. 1997. *Globalization and the Postcolonial World: The New Political Economy of Development*. Baltimore: Johns Hopkins University Press.

Howard, Philip N. 2006. *New Media Campaigns and the Managed Citizen* New York. Cambridge University Press.

————, and Steve Jones. 2004. *Society Online: The Internet in Context*. London: Sage.

Howell, James C., John P. Moore, and Arlen Egley Jr. 2002. "The Changing Boundaries of Youth Gangs." In Huff 2002, 3–18.

Howitt, Richard 1993. "A World in a Grain of Sand: Towards a Reconceptualization of Geographical Scale." *Australian Geographer* 24 (1): 33–44

————. 1998. "Recognition, Reconciliation and Respect. Steps Towards Decolonisation?" *Australian Aboriginal Studies* 1: 28–34.

Indiana Journal of Global Legal Studies. 1996. "Feminism and Globalization: The Impact of the Global Economy on Women and Feminist Theory (Special Issue)." *Indiana Journal of Global Legal Studies* 4 (1)

————. 1998. "Symposium: The Internet and the Sovereign State; The Role and Impact of Cyberspace on National and Global Governance." *Indiana Journal of Global Legal Studies* 5 (2).

———— 2003. "Symposium· Globalization and Governance. The Prospects for Democracy." *Indiana Journal of Global Legal Studies* 10 (1).

International Monetary Fund (IMF). (annual). *International Financial Statistics*. Washington, D.C.: IMF.

————. 2005. *International Financial Statistics*. Washington, D C.: IMF.

International Organization for Migration (IOM). 1996. *Trafficking in Migrants*. Geneva: IOM.

————. 1997. *Trafficking in Women to Japan for Sexual Exploitation: A Survey on the Case of Filipino Women*. Geneva: IOM.

————. 2006. *Trafficking in Migrants*. Geneva: IOM.

Iredale, R., C. Hawksley, and K. Lyon, eds. 2002. *Migration Research and Policy Landscapes: Case Studies of Australia, the Philippines and Thailand*. Wollongong: Asia-Pacific Migration Research Network.

Isbister, John. 1996. *The Immigration Debate: Remaking America*. West Hartford, Conn.: Kumarian Books.

Isin, Engin F., ed. 2000. *Democracy, Citizenship, and the Global City* London: Routledge.

Iyotani, Toshio, Naoki Sakai, and Brett de Bary, eds. 2005. *Deconstructing Nationality*. Ithaca, N.Y.. Cornell University East Asia Program.

Izquierdo Martín, A. Javier. 2002. "Crimes, Fault, and Nobel Prizes. Scientific Authority, Economic Risk, and Moral Responsibility in the Long-Term Capital Management Financial Scandal." *Política y Sociedad* 39 (2): 339–59.

Jacobson, David, ed. 1998. *The Immigration Reader: America in a Multidisciplinary Perspective*. Oxford: Blackwell.

Jacobson, David, and Galya Benarieh Ruffer. 2006. "Scope. Global or National?: Social Relations on a Global Scale." In *Dialogues on Migration Policies*, ed. Marco Giugni and Florence Passy. Lexington, Mass.: Lexington Books.

Jessop, Bob. 1982. *The Capitalist State: Marxist Theories and Methods*. New York: New York University Press.

————. 1990. *State Theory: Putting Capitalist States in Their Place*. University Park: Pennsylvania State University Press.

————. 1999. "Reflections on Globalization and Its (Il)logic(s)." In Olds et al. 1999, 19–38.

Johnson, D., and D. Post, 1996. "Law and Borders—The Rise of Law in Cyberspace." *Stanford Law Review* 48: 1367–402

Johnson, Jennifer L. 2007 "Deregulating Markets, Reregulating Crime: Extralegal Policing and the Penal State in Mexico." In *Deciphering Globalization: Its Scales, Spaces and Subjects*, ed. Saskia Sassen, 263–80. New York and London: Routledge.

Jones, Katherine T 1998 "Scale as Epistemology." *Political Geography* 17 (1): 25–28.

Joppke, C., and E. Morawska, eds. 2002. *Towards Assimilation and Citizenship: Immigration in Liberal Nation-States*. London: Palgrave.

Judd, Denis R. 1998. "The Case of the Missing Scales: A Commentary on Cox." *Political Geography* 17 (1): 29–34.

Kaplan, Josh. 2007. "The Transnational Human Rights Movement and States of Emergency in Israel/Palestine." In *Deciphering Globalization: Its Scales, Spaces and Subjects*, ed. Saskia Sassen, 281–300. New York and London: Routledge.

Kasinitz, Philip. 1992. *Caribbean New York*. Ithaca, N.Y.: Cornell University Press.

Keane, John. 2003. *Global Civil Society?* Cambridge: Cambridge University Press.

Khagram, S., J. V. Riker, and K. Sikkink, eds. 2002. *Restructuring World Politics: Transnational Social Movements, Networks, and Norms*. Minneapolis: University of Minnesota Press.

King, Anthony D. 1990. *Urbanism, Colonialism, and the World Economy: Culture and Spatial Foundations of the World Urban System*. London: Routledge.

King, R , G. Lazaridis, and C. Tsardanidis, eds 2000. *Eldorado or Fortress? Migration in Southern Europe*. London: Macmillan.

Kirsch, Max, ed. 2006. *Inclusion and Exclusion in the Global Arena*. New York: Routledge.

Kitschelt, Herbert, Peter Lange, Gary Marks, and John D. Stephens. 1999. *Continuity and Change in Contemporary Capitalism*. Cambridge: Cambridge University Press.

Klein, Hans. 2004. "The Significance of ICANN." In *SSRC Information Technology & International Cooperation Program*. New York: SSRC. http://www ssrc org/programs/itic/publi cations/knowledge_report/memos/kleinmemo4.pdf.

Klinenberg, Eric. 2003. *Heat Wave: A Social Autopsy of Disaster in Chicago (Illinois)*. Chicago: University of Chicago Press.

Knorr Cetina, Karin, and Urs Bruegger. 2000 "The Market as an Object of Attachment: Exploring Postsocial Relations in Financial Markets." *Canadian Journal of Sociology* 25 (2): 141–68.

————. 2002. "Global Microstructures: The Virtual Societies of Financial Markets." *American Journal of Sociology* 107 (4): 905–50

Knorr Cetina, K., and A. Preda, eds. 2004. *The Sociology of Financial Markets*. Oxford: Oxford University Press.

Knox, Paul L., and Peter J. Taylor, eds. 1995 *World Cities in a World-System*. Cambridge: Cambridge University Press.

Kofman, Eleonore, Annie Phizacklea, Parvati Raghuram, and Rosemary Sales. 2000. *Gender and International Migration in Europe: Employment, Welfare and Politics*. London and New York: Routledge.

Komai, H. 1995. *Migrant Workers in Japan* London: Kegan Paul International.

Komlosy, Andrea, Christof Parnreiter, Irene Stacher, and Susan Zimmermann, eds. 1997. *Ungeregelt und Unterbezahlt: Der Informelle Sektor in der Weltwirtschaft*. Frankfurt: Brandes & Apsel / Sudwind.

Kondo, A. 2001. *Citizenship in a Global World*. Basingstoke: Palgrave.

Koo, Hagen. 2001. *Korean Workers: The Culture and Politics of Class Formation* Ithaca, N.Y. and London: Cornell University Press.

Koopmans, Ruud 2004 "Movements and Media: Selection Processes and Evolutionary Dynamics in the Public Sphere." *Theory and Society* 33· 367–91.

Korbin, Stephen J. 2001. "Territoriality and the Governance of Cyberspace." *Journal of International Business Studies* 32. 687–704.

Koser, Khalid, and Helma Lutz. 1998 *The New Migration in Europe: Social Constructions and Social Realities*. Basingstoke: Macmillan Press.

Kothari, Uma. 2006. *A Radical History of Development Studies: Individuals, Institutions and Ideologies*. London: Zed Books.

Koval, John P., Larry Bennett, Michael I. J. Bennett, Fassil Demissie, Roberta Garner, and Kiljoong Kim. 2006. *The New Chicago: A Social and Cultural Analysis*. Philadelphia: Temple University Press.

Krasner, Stephen D. 2004. "Globalization, Power, and Authority." In Mansfield and Sisson 2004, 60–81.

Kratke, Stefan. 1991. *Strukturwandel der Städte: Städtesystem und Grundstücksmarkt in der "Post-Fordistischen" Ära* Frankfurt: Campus.

Krause, Linda, and Patrice Petro. 2003. *Global Cities: Cinema, Architecture, and Urbanism in a Digital Age*. New Brunswick, N.J.. Rutgers University Press.

Kuntze, Marco, Sigrun Rottmann, and Jessica Symons. 2002. *Communications Strategies for World Bank and IMF-Watchers: New Tools for Networking and Collaboration* London: Bretton Woods Project and Ethical Media. http.//www.brettonwoodsproject.org/strategy/Commosrpt.pdf.

Kyle, D., and R. Koslowski. 2001. *Global Human Smuggling*. Baltimore and London: Johns Hopkins University Press.

Laguerre, Michel S. 2000. *The Global Ethnopolis: Chinatown, Japantown and Manilatown in American Society*. London: Macmillan.

Lamont, Michele. 2000. *The Dignity of Working Men: Morality and the Boundaries of Race, Class, and Immigration*. New York· Russell Sage Foundation.

Lannon, John. 2002. "Technology and Ties That Bind: The Impact of the Internet on Non-Governmental Organizations Working to Combat Torture." Masters thesis, University of Limerick, Ireland. http·//homepage.eircom.net/,sljohnlannon/TechTies.pdf (site now discontinued).

Lao-Montes, Agustin, and Arlene M. Davila. 2001. *Mambo Montage: The Latinization of New York*. New York: Columbia University Press.

Lardner, James, and David A. Smith. 2005. *Inequality Matters: The Growing Economic Divide in America*. New York: The New Press, in collaboration with Demos Institute.

Latham, Robert, and Saskia Sassen, eds 2005. *Digital Formations: IT and New Architectures in the Global Realm*. Princeton, N.J.: Princeton University Press.

Latham, Robert, and Saskia Sassen 2005 "Introduction. Digital Formations: Constructing an Object of Study." In Latham and Sassen 2005.

Latour, Bruno, ed. 1991. "Technology Is Society Made Durable." In *A Sociology of Monsters*, ed. J. Laws. London: Routledge.

———. 1996. *Aramis or the Love of Technology*. Cambridge, Mass.: Harvard University Press.

Laumann, Edward O., and David Knoke. 1987 *The Organizational State: Social Choice in National Policy Domains*. Madison: University of Wisconsin Press.

Lebert, Joanne. 2003. "Writing Human Rights Activism: Amnesty International and the Challenges of Information and Communication Technologies." In *Cyberactivism: Online*

Activism in Theory and Practice, ed. Martha McCaughey and Michael Ayers, 209–32. London: Routledge.

Lechner, Frank J., and John Boli. 2005. *World Culture: Origins and Consequences*. Malden, Mass.. Blackwell.

Lefebvre, Henri. 1991. *The production of space*. Translated by D. Nicholson-Smith. Oxford: Blackwell. Original ed., 1974.

Leidholdt, Dorchen A. 2005. "Combatting Trafficking in Persons· An International Perspective. The Economics of Sex Slavery." Testimony presented to the Subcommittee on Domestic and International Monetary Policy, Trade and Technology House of Representatives, June 22, 2005.

Leizerov, Sagi 2000. "Privacy Advocacy Groups versus Intel: A Case Study of How Social Movements Are Tactically Using the Internet to Fight Corporations." *Social Science Computer Review* 18: 461–83.

Lessig, Lawrence. 1999. *Code and Other Laws of Cyberspace*. New York: Basic Books.

Levitt, Peggy. 2001. *The Transnational Villagers*. Berkeley: University of California Press.

Levitt, Steven D., and Sudhir Alladi Venkatesh. 2000. "An Economic Analysis of a Drug-Selling Gang's Finances." *Quarterly Journal of Economics* 115 (3) 755–89.

Lewis Mumford Center for Comparative Urban and Regional Research. 2000. "Segregation and Income in U.S. Cities." http://mumford.albany.edu/census/index.html.

Lievrouw, L A., and S Livingstone, eds 2002. *Handbook of New Media: Social Shaping and Consequences of ICTs*. London: Sage Publications.

Likosky, Michael, ed 2002 *Transnational Legal Processes: Globalisation and Power Disparities*. London: Buttersworths Lexis-Nexis.

Lim, L.L., and N. Oishi. 1996. "International Labor Migration of Asian Women." *Asian and Pacific Migration Journal* 5 (1)

Lin, Lap-Chew, and Marjan Wijers. 1997. *Trafficking in Women, Forced Labour, and Slavery-Like Practices in Marriage, Domestic Labour, and Prostitution*. Utrecht: Foundation against Trafficking in Women, and Bangkok: Global Alliance against Traffic in Women

Lloyd, Richard D. 2005. *Neo-Bohemia. Art and Commerce in the Postindustrial City* New York: Routledge.

Lo, Fu-Chen, and Yue-man Yeung. 1996. *Emerging World Cities in Pacific Asia*. Tokyo and New York. United Nations University Press.

Lovink, Geert. 2002. *Dark Fiber: Tracking Critical Internet Culture*. Cambridge, Mass.· MIT Press.

———. 2003 *My First Recession: Critical Internet Culture in Transition*. Rotterdam· VP2/NAi Publishing.

Lovink, Geert, and Soehnke Zehle 2006 *Incommunicado Reader*. Amsterdam. Institute of Network Cultures.

Low, Setha M. 1999. *Theorizing the City: the New Urban Anthropology Reader*. New Brunswick, N.J.: Rutgers University Press.

Lowell B. L., Findlay A., and Stewart E. 2004. *Brain Strain· Highly Skilled Migration Flows from Developing Countries.* London: ippr.http://www.ippr.org/research/index.php?current=19&project=183.

Lucas, Linda, ed. 2005. *Unpacking Globalisation: Markets, Gender and Work.* Kampala, Uganda: Makerere University Press.

Lukes, Steven. 2005. *Power: A Radical View.* New York: Palgrave Macmillan.

MacKenzie, Donald. 1999. "Technological Determinism." In *Society on the Line: Information Politics in the Digital Age,* ed. W. H. Dutton. Oxford: Oxford University Press.

———. 2003. "Long-Term Capital Management and the Sociology of Arbitrage." *Economy & Society* 32 (3): 349–80.

———. 2004. "Social Connectivities in Global Financial Markets." *Environment & Planning D: Society & Space* 22 (1). 83–101.

———, and Boelie Elzen. 1994. "The Social Limits of Speed: The Development and Use of Supercomputers." *IEEE Annals of the History of Computing* 16: 46–61.

———, and Judy Wajcman. 1999. *The Social Shaping of Technology.* Milton Keynes: Open University Press.

———, and Yuval Millo. 2003. "Constructing a Market, Performing Theory: The Historical Sociology of a Financial Derivatives Exchange." *American Journal of Sociology* 109 (1): 107–45.

Mahler, Sarah. 1995. *American Dreaming: Immigrant Life on the Margins.* Princeton, N.J.: Princeton University Press.

Mahler, S. 2000. "Constructing International Relations: The Role of Transnational Migrants and Other Non-State Actors." *Identities: Global Studies in Culture and Power* 7: 197–232.

Mahoney, James, and Dietrich Rueschmeyer. 2003. *Comparative Historical Analysis in the Social Sciences.* Cambridge: Cambridge University Press.

Maimbo, Samuel Munzele, and Dilip Ratha. 2005. *Remittances: Development Impact and Future Prospects.* Washington D.C.: World Bank.

Mamdani, Mahmood. 1996. *Citizen and Subject: Contemporary Africa and the Legacy of Late Colonialism.* Princeton, N.J.: Princeton University Press.

Mann, Michael. 1986 *A History of Power from the Beginning to A.D. 1760.* Vol. 1 of *The Sources of Social Power.* Cambridge: Cambridge University Press.

———. 1997. "Has Globalization Ended the Rise and Rise of the Nation-State?" *Review of International Political Economy* 4 (3). 472–96.

Manovich, Lev. 2001. *The Language of New Media.* Cambridge, Mass.: MIT Press.

Mansell, Robin, and Brian S. Collins, eds. 2005. *Trust and Crime in Information Societies.* Northampton, Mass.: Edward Elgar.

Mansfield, Edward D., and Richard Sisson, eds. 2004. *The Evolution of Political Knowledge: Democracy, Autonomy, and Conflict in Comparative and International Politics.* Columbus: Ohio State University

Marcotullio, Peter, and Fu-Chen Lo. 2001. *Globalization and the Sustainability of Cities in the Asia Pacific Region.* New York: United Nations University Press.

Marcuse, Peter, and Ronald van Kempen, eds. 2000. *Globalizing Cities: A New Spatial Order?* Oxford· Blackwell.

Marres, Noortje, and Richard Rogers 2000. "Depluralising the Web, Repluralising Public Debate· The Case of GM Food on the Web." In *Preferred Placement: Knowledge Politics on the Web*, ed. R. Rogers. Masstricht: Jan van Eyck Editions.

Martin, Philip L. 1993 *Trade and Migration: NAFTA and Agriculture.* Washington, D.C.: Institute for International Economics.

———. 2002. *Immigration and the Changing Face of Rural and Agricultural America.* Washington, D.C.: Urban Institute.

Martinotti, Guido. 1993. *Metropoli: La Nuova Morfologia Sociale della Città.* Bologna: Il Mulino.

Massey, Doreen B. 1984. *Spatial Divisions of Labor: Social Structures and the Geography of Production.* New York: Methuen.

Massey, Douglas S., and Luin Goldring. 1994. "Continuities in Transnational Migration: An Analysis of Nineteen Mexican Communities." *American Journal of Sociology* 99 (6): 1492–1553.

Massey, Douglas S., Joaquin Arango, Hugo Graeme, Ali Kouaouci, Adela Pellegrino, and J. Edward Taylor. 1993. "Theories in International Migration: A Review and Appraisal." *Population & Development Review* 19 (3): 431–66.

Mathiason, John R., and Charles C. Kuhlman 1998. "International Public Regulation of the Internet: Who Will Give You Your Domain Name?" Paper presented to the panel "Cyber-hype or the Deterritorialization of Politics? The Internet in a Post-Westphalian Order" at the annual meeting of the International Studies Association, Minneapolis, March 29–30. http://www.intlmgt.com/pastprojects/domain.html (site now discontinued).

May, Christopher, and Susan K. Sell. 2005. *Intellectual Property Rights: A Critical History.* Boulder, Colo : Lynne Rienner Publishers.

Mazlish, Bruce, and Ralph Buultjens, eds. 1993. *Conceptualizing Global History.* Boulder, Colo.· Westview Press.

Mbembe, J. A. 2001. *On the Postcolony.* Berkeley: University of California Press

McMichael, Philip. 2004. *Development and Social Change: A Global Perspective.* 3rd ed. Thousand Oaks, Calif: Pine Forge Press.

Mele, Christopher. 1999. "Cyberspace and Disadvantaged Communities: The Internet as a Tool for Collective Action." In *Communities in Cyberspace*, ed. Marc A. Smith and Peter Kollock, 290–309. London: Routledge.

Menjivar, Cecilia. 2000. *Fragmented Ties· Salvadoran Immigrant Networks in America.* Berkeley: University of California Press.

Meyer, Carrie A. 1997. "The Political Economy of NGO's Information Sharing." *World Development* 25 (7): 1127–40.

Meyer, David R. 2002 "Synergy between Hong Kong's Global Networks of Capital and Its Telematics." In Sassen 2002a, 249–71

Meyer, John, J. Boli, G. Thomas, and F. Ramirez. 1997. "World Society and the Nation-state." *American Journal of Sociology* 103:1.

Miles, Malcolm, Tim Hall, and Iain Borden. 2003. *The City Cultures Reader.* 2nd ed. London: Routledge

Milkman, Ruth, and Kim Voss. 2004. *Rebuilding Labor: Organizing and Organizers in the New Union Movement.* Ithaca, N.Y.: Cornell University Press.

Miller, Daniel, and Don Slater 2000. *The Internet: An Ethnographic Approach.* Oxford. Berg.

Mills, Kurt. 2002. "Cybernations: Identity, Self-Determination, Democracy and the 'Internet Effect' in the Emerging Information Order." *Global Society* 16 (1): 69–87.

Mingione, Enzo. 1991. *Fragmented Societies: A Sociology of Economic Life beyond the Market Paradigm.* Oxford· Blackwell.

Mintz, Beth, and Michael Schwartz. 1985. *The Power Structure of American Business.* Chicago, Ill.: University of Chicago Press.

Mitchelson, Ronald L, and James O. Wheeler. 1994. "The Flow of Information in a Global Economy: The Role of the American Urban System in 1990." *Annals of the Association of American Geographers* 84 (1): 87–107.

Mittelman, James H., ed. 1996. *Globalization: Critical Reflections.* Boulder, Colo.: Lynne Rienner.

———. 2000. *The Globalization Syndrome: Transformation and Resistance.* Princeton, N.J.: Princeton University Press.

Mizruchi, Mark, and Stearns, Linda. 1994. "Money, Banking, and Financial Markets." In Smelser and Swedberg 1994.

Moghadam, Valentine M. 2005. *Globalizing Women: Transnational Feminist Networks.* Baltimore, Md.. Johns Hopkins University Press.

Monberg, J. 1998. "Making the Public Count: A Comparative Case Study of Emergent Information Technology-Based Publics." *Communication Theory* 8 (4): 426–54.

Moore, Joan. 1998. "Introduction: Gangs and the Underclass; A Comparative Perspective." In *People and Folks: Gangs, Crime, and the Underclass in a Rustbelt City,* ed John Hagedorn and Perry Macon. Chicago: Lakeview Press.

Morita, Kiriro, and Saskia Sassen. 1994. "The New Illegal Immigration in Japan, 1980–1992." *International Migration Review* 28 (1). 153–63

Morokvasic, Mirjana. 1984. "Birds of Passage Are Also Women . . ." *International Migration Review* 18 (4): 886–907.

Morrill, Richard. 1999. "Inequalities of Power, Costs, and Benefits across Geographic Scales: The Future Uses of the Hanford Reservation." *Political Geography* 18 (1): 1–23.

Moyer, Brian C., Mark A. Planting, Paul V Kern, and Abigail M. Kish. 2004. "Improved Annual Industry Accounts for 1998–2003: Integrated Annual Input-Output Accounts and Gross-Domestic-Product-by-Industry Accounts." *Survey of Current Business* 84 (6): 21–57.

Mueller, Milton 1998. "The 'Governance' Debacle: How the Ideal of Internetworking Got

Buried by Politics." Paper presented at INET (annual conference of the Internet Society), Geneva, July 22. http://www.isoc.org/inet98/proceedings/5a/5a_1.htm.

———. 2004. *Ruling the Root: Internet Governance and the Taming of Cyberspace.* Cambridge, Mass.: MIT Press

Munger, Frank, ed. 2002. *Laboring below the Line: The New Ethnography of Poverty, Low-Wage Work, and Survival in the Global Economy.* New York: Russell Sage Foundation.

Naim, Moises. 2006. *Illicit: How Smugglers, Traffickers, and Copycats Are Hijacking the Global Economy.* New York: Anchor Books.

Naples, Nancy A., and Manisha Desai. 2002. *Women's Activism and Globalization: Linking Local Struggles and Transnational Politics.* New York: Routledge.

Nash, June C., and Maria Patricia Fernandez-Kelly. 1983. *Women, Men, and the Internacional Division of Labor.* Albany: State University of New York Press.

Nashashibi, Rami. 2007. "Ghetto Cosmopolitanism: Making Theory at the Margins." In *Deciphering the Global: Its Spaces, Scales and Subjects,* ed. Saskia Sassen, 241–62. New York and London: Routledge.

Net Critique. Lovink, Geert, and Pit Schultz, compilers. *Netzkritik: Materialian zur Internet-Debatte.* Berlin: Edition ID-Archiv.

Neuwirth, Robert. 2004. *Shadow Cities: A Billion Squatters, A New Urban World.* London: Routledge.

Newman, Katherine S. 1999. *Falling from Grace: Downward Mobility in the Age of Affluence.* Berkeley: University of California Press.

Nijman, Jan. 1996. "Breaking the Rules: Miami in the Urban Hierarchy." *Urban Geography* 17 (1): 5–22.

Notzke, Claudia. 1995. "A New Perspective in Aboriginal Nature Resource Management. Co-management." *Geoforum* 26 (2): 187–209.

Novak, William J. 1996. *The People's Welfare: Law and Regulation in Nineteenth-Century America* Chapel Hill: University of North Carolina Press.

Noyelle, Thierry J, and Anna B. Dutka. 1988. *International Trade in Business Services: Accounting, Advertising, Law, and Management Consulting* Cambridge, Mass: Ballinger.

Nyberg Sorensen, N., and K. Fog Olwig, eds. 2002. *Work and Migration: Life and Livelihoods in a Globalizing World (Transnationalism).* London: Routledge.

Offe, Claus. 1984. *Contradictions of the Welfare State.* Ed. John Keane. Cambridge, Mass.: MIT Press.

Okuda, M. 2000. "Asian Newcomers in Shinjuku and Ikebukuro Area, 1988–98: Reflections on a Decade of Research." *Asian and Pacific Migration Journal* 9 (3).

Okunishi, Y. 1996. "Labor Contracting in International Migration: The Japanese Case and Implications for Asia." *Asian and Pacific Migration Journal* 5 (2–3).

Olds, Kris, Peter Dicken, Philip F. Kelly, Lilly Kong, and Henry Wai-chung Yeung, eds. 1999. *Globalization and the Asian Pacific: Contested Territories.* London: Routledge.

Olesen, Thomas. 2005. "Transnational Publics: New Space of Social Movement Activism and the Problem of Long-Sightedness." *Current Sociology* 53: 419–40.

Ong, Aihwa. 1999. *Flexible Citizenship: The Cultural Logics of Transnationality*. Durham, N.C.: Duke University Press.

Ó Riain, Seán. 2000. "States and Markets in an Era of Globalization." *Annual Review of Sociology* 26: 187–213.

Organization for Economic Cooperation and Development (OECD). 2000. *International Direct Investment Statistics Yearbook 1999*. Paris: OECD.

Orozco, Manuel. 2002. *International Norms and Mobilization of Democracy: Nicaragua in the World*. Aldershot, UK: Ashgate.

———, B. Lindsay Lowell, Micah Bump, and Rachel Fedewa. 2005. *Transnational Engagement, Remittances and their Relationship to Development in Latin America and the Caribbean*. Washington, D.C.: Institute for the Study of International Migration, Georgetown University.

Pace, William R, and Rik Panganiban. 2002. "The Power of Global Activist Networks: The Campaign for an International Criminal Court." In Hajnal 2002, 109–25.

Paddison, Ronan, ed. 2001. *Handbook of Urban Studies*. Thousand Oaks, Calif.: Sage.

Padilla, Felix. 1992. *The Gang as an American Enterprise*. New Brunswick, N.J : Rutgers University Press.

Pakulski, Jan, and Waters, Malcolm. 1996. "The Reshaping and Dissolution of Social Class in Advanced Society." *Theory & Society* 25 (5): 667–91.

Palan, Ronan, ed. 2000. *Global Economy: Contemporary Theories*. London: Routledge.

Palumbo-Liu, David. 1999. *Asian/American: Historical Crossings of a Racial Career*. Palo Alto, Calif.: Stanford University Press.

Panitch, Leo. 1996. "Rethinking the Role of the State." In Mittelman 1996, 83–113.

Papademetriou, Demetrios G., and Philip L. Martin. 1991. *The Unsettled Relationship: Labor Migration and Economic Development*. New York: Greenwood Press.

Pare, Daniel J. 2003. *Internet Governance in Transition: Just Who Is the Master of This Domain?* Lanham, Md.: Rowman & Littlefield.

Park, Robert E , and Ernest W Burgess. 1925. *The City: Suggestions for Investigation of Human Behavior in the Urban Environment*. Reprint, Chicago: University of Chicago Press, 1967.

Parkin, Frank. 1979. *Marxism and Class Theory: A Bourgeois Critique*. New York: Columbia University Press

Parnreiter, Christof 1995. "Uprooting, Globalization, and Migration: Selected Questions." Special Issue on Migration. *Journal für Entwicklungspolitik* 11 (3): 245–60.

———. 2002. "Mexico: The Making of a Global City." In Sassen 2002, 145–82.

Parr, John, and Leslie Budd. 2000. "Financial Services and the Urban System: An Exploration Source." *Urban Studies* 37 (3): 593–610.

Parreñas, Rhacel Salazar. 2001. *Servants of Globalization: Women, Migration, and Domestic Work*. Palo Alto, Calif.: Stanford University Press.

————. 2005. *Children of Global Migration: Transnational Families and Gendered Woes*. Stanford, Calif.: Stanford University Press.

Parsa, Ali, and Ramin Keivani. 2002. "The Hormuz Corridor· Building a Cross-border Region between Iran and the United Arab Emirates." In Sassen 2002, 183–207

Passel, J. S., R. Capps, and M. Fix. 2004. *Undocumented Immigrants: Facts And Figures*. Washington, D.C.: Urban Institute. http·//www.urban.org/UploadedPDF/1000587_undoc_immigrants_facts.pdf.

Pauly, Louis. 2002. "Global Finance, Political Authority and the Problem of Legitimation." In *The Emergence of Private Authority and Global Governance*, ed R. B. Hall and T. J. Biersteker Cambridge: Cambridge University Press.

Payne, Anthony, ed. 2006. *Key Debates in New Political Economy*. London and New York: Routledge.

Pearce, N. 2004. "Diversity versus Solidarity· A New Progressive Dilemma?", *Renewal*, Vol 12 (3). http://www renewal.org.uk/vol12no32004diversityversussolidarity htm.

Péraldi, Michel, and Évelyne Perrin, eds. 1996. *Réseaux productifs et territoires urbains: Cultures urbaines, marchés, entreprises, et réseaux* Toulouse, France: Presses Universitaires du Mirail.

Persky, Joseph, and Wim Wiewel. 1994. "The Growing Localness of the Global City." *Economic Geography* 70 (2): 129–43.

Pessar, P. R., and S. J. Mahler. 2003. "Transnational Migration· Bringing Gender In " *International Migration Review* 37 (3): 812–846

Peterson, Marina 2007. "Translocal Civilities: Chinese Modern Dance at Downtown Los Angeles Public Concerts " In *Deciphering Globalization: Its Scales, Spaces and Subjects*, ed. Saskia Sassen, 41–58. New York and London: Routledge.

Picciotto, Sol. 1992. *International Business Taxation: A Study in the Internationalization of Business Regulation*. New York: Quorum Books.

Pierson, Paul. 2004. *Politics in Time: History, Institutions, and Social Analysis*. Princeton, N.J.. Princeton University Press.

Pieterse, Jan Nederveen. 2004. *Globalization and Culture: Global Melange*. Lanham, MD· Rowman & Littlefield.

Pijl, Kees van der 1998. *Transnational Classes and International Relations*. London: Routledge.

Piore, Michael, and Charles Sabel. 1984. *The Second Industrial Divide: Possibilities for Prosperity*. New York: Basic Books.

Piven, Frances Fox, and Cloward, Richard. 1971. *Regulating the Poor: The Functions of Public Welfare*. New York· Pantheon Books.

Pogge, Thomas. 1992. "Cosmopolitanism and Sovereignty." *Ethics* 103. 48–75

Pollack, Mark A., and Gregory C. Shaffer. 2001. *Transatlantic Governance in the Global Economy*. Lanham, Md.: Rowman & Littlefield

Porter, Michael E. 1990. *The Competitive Advantage of Nations*. New York: Free Press.

Portes, Alejandro. 2000. "The Resilient Importance of Class. A Nominalist Interpretation." *Political Power & Social Theory* 14. 249–84.

————, and John Walton. 1981. *Labor, Class, and the International System*. New York: Academic Press.

————, and Ruben G. Rumbaut. 1996. *Immigrant America: A Portrait*. Berkeley: University of California Press.

Portnoy, Brian. 2000. "Constructing Competition: The Political Foundations of Alliance Capitalism." PhD diss., University of Chicago.

Post, David G. 1995. "Anarchy, State, and the Internet: An Essay on Law-Making in Cyberspace." *Journal of Online Law*. Article 3. http://www.wm.edu/law/publications/jol/articles/post.shtml.

Poster, Mark. 1997. "Cyberdemocracy: Internet and the Public Sphere." In *Internet Culture*, ed. David Porter, 201–18. London: Routledge.

————. 2004. "Consumption and digital commodities in the everyday." *Cultural Studies* 18: 409–23.

Postone, Moishe. 1993. *Time, Labor, and Social Domination: A Reinterpretation of Marx's Critical Theory*. Cambridge: Cambridge University Press.

Potts, L. 1990. *The World Labor Market: A History of Migration* London: Zed.

Poulantzas, Nicos. 1973. *Political Power and Social Classes*. Translated by Timothy O'Hagen. London: New Left Books.

Powell, Walter, and Paul DiMaggio, eds. 1991. *The New Institutionalism in Organizational Analysis*. Chicago: University of Chicago Press.

Pryke, Michael, and J. Allen. 2000. "Monetized Time-Space: Derivatives—Money's 'New Imaginary'?" *Economy and Society* 29: 329–44

Przeworksi, Adam. 1985. *Capitalism and Social Democracy*. Cambridge: Cambridge University Press.

Pyle, Jean L., and Kathryn Ward. 2003. "Recasting Our Understanding of Gender and Work During Global Restructuring." *International Sociology* 18 (3): 461–89.

Rantanen, Terhi. 2005. *The Media and Globalization*. Thousand Oaks, Calif.: Sage

Redden, Guy. 2001. "Networking Dissent: The Internet and the Anti-globalisation Move-ment." *MotsPluriels* 18. http://www.arts.uwa.edu.au/MotsPluriels/MP1801gr.html.

Reidenberg, Joel R. 1996. "Governing Networks and Rule-Making in Cyberspace." *Emory Law Journal* 45: 912–300.

————. 1998. "Lex Informatica: The Formulation of Information Policy Rules Through Technology." *Texas Law Review* 76: 553–94. http://reidenberg.home.sprynet.com/lex_informatica.pdf.

Revista Internacional de Filosofia. 2006. "Inmigracion, Estado y Ciudadania. Simposio." *Revista Internacional de Filosofia* 27 (July).

Rex, J. and, D Mason, eds. 1986. *Theories of Race and Ethnic Relations*. Cambridge, Mass.: Cambridge University Press.

Rheingold, Howard. 2003. *Smart Mobs*. Cambridge, Mass.: Perseus.

Ribas-Mateos, Natalia. 2005. *The Mediterranean in the Age of Globalization: Migration, Welfare, and Borders.* Somerset, N.J.. Transaction.

Ricca, S. 1990. *Migrations Internationales en Afrique.* Paris· L'Harmattan.

Riemens, Patrice, and Geert Lovink. 2002. "Local Networks: Digital City Amsterdam." In Sassen 2002, 327–45.

Rimmer, Peter J, and Tessa Morris-Suzuki. 1999. "The Japanese Internet: Visionaries and Virtual Democracy." *Environment & Planning A* 31 (7): 1189–1206.

Robertson, Roland. 1992. *Globalization: Social Theory and Global Culture.* Thousand Oaks, Calif.· Sage.

Robin, Corey. 2004 *Fear: The History of a Political Idea* Oxford and New York· Oxford University Press.

Robinson, S. 2004. "Towards a Neoapartheid System of Governance with IT Tools," *SSRC IT & Governance Study Group.* New York· SSRC. http://www.ssrc.org/programs/itic/publications/knowledge_report/memos/robinsonmemo4.pdf, accessed 18 Mar. 06.

Robinson, William. 2004. *A Theory of Global Capitalism: Transnational Production, Transnational Capitalists, and the Transnational State.* Baltimore: Johns Hopkins University Press

Rodriguez, Nestor. 1999. "U.S. Immigration and Changing Relations between African Americans and Latinos." In *The Handbook of International Migration: the American Experience,* ed. Charles Hirschman, Philip Kasinitz, and Josh DeWind. New York: Russell Sage Foundation.

———, and Joe Feagin. 1986. "Urban Specialization in the World System: An Investigation of Historical Cases." *Urban Affairs Quarterly* 22 (2): 187–220.

Rogers, Richard. 2004. *Information Politics on the Web* Cambridge, Mass.: MIT Press.

Ronfeldt, David, John Arquilla, Graham E. Fuller, and Melissa Fuller. 1998. *The Zapatista Social Netwar in Mexico.* Santa Monica, Calif.. Rand.

Rosenau, James N. 1992. "Governance, Order, and Change in World Politics." In *Governance without Government: Order and Change in World Politics,* ed. James N Rosenau and Ernst Otto Czempiel, 1–29 Cambridge: Cambridge University Press.

———. 1997. *Along the Domestic-Foreign Frontier: Exploring Governance in a Turbulent World.* Cambridge: Cambridge University Press.

———, and J. P. Singh, eds. 2002. *Information Technologies and Global Politics: The Changing Scope of Power and Governance* Albany, N.Y.: State University of New York Press.

Roulleau-Berger, Laurence. 2003. *Youth and Work in the Post-industrial City of North America and Europe.* Boston: Brill Academic Publishers.

Rowe, Peter G., and Seng Kuan. 2004. *Shanghai: Architecture & Urbanism for Modern China.* New York· Prestel.

Rudolph, Christopher. 2006. *National Security and Immigration: Policy Development in the United States and Western Europe since 1945* Stanford. Stanford University Press.

Ruggie, John Gerard. 1993. "Territoriality and Beyond: Problematizing Modernity in International Relations." *International Organization* 47· 139–74.

Rutherford, Jonathan. 2004. *A Tale of Two Global Cities: Comparing the Territories of Telecommunications Developments in Paris and London*. Aldershot: Ashgate.

Rutherford, Kenneth R. 2002. "Essential Partners: Landmines-Related NGOs and Information Technologies." In *Civil Society in the Information Age*, ed. Peter I. Hajnal 2002, 95–107.

Sachar, Arie. 1990. "The Global Economy and World Cities." In *The World Economy and the Spatial Organization of Power*, ed. Arie Sachar and Sture Oberg, 149–60. Aldershot: Avebury.

Sack, Warren. 2005. "Discourse Architecture and Very Large-Scale Conversation." In Latham and Sassen 2005, 242–82.

Sadiq, Kamal 2007. "Illegal Immigrants as Citizens in Malaysia." In *Deciphering Globalization: Its Scales, Spaces and Subjects*, ed. Saskia Sassen, 301–20 New York and London: Routledge.

Safa, Helen 1995. *The Myth of the Male Breadwinner: Women and Industrialization in the Caribbean*. Boulder, Colo.: Westview Press.

Saidam, Sabri. 2004. "On Route to an E-Society: Human Dependence on Technology and Adaptation Needs." In *SSRC Committee on Information Technology and International Cooperation*. http://www.ssrc.org/programs/itic/publications/knowledge_report/memos/sabri.pdf.

Salacuse, Jeswald. 1991. *Making Global Deals: Negotiating in the International Marketplace*. Boston: Houghton Mifflin.

Salzinger, Leslie. 2003a. *Genders in Production: Making Workers in Mexico's Global Factories*. Berkeley and Los Angeles: University of California Press.

———. 2003b. "Market Subjects: Traders at Work in the Dollar/Peso Market." Paper presented at the annual meeting of the American Sociological Association, Atlanta, August 18.

Samers, Michael. 2002. "Immigration and the Global City Hypothesis: Towards an Alternative Research Agenda." *International Journal of Urban & Regional Research* 26 (2): 389–402.

Sampson, Robert, and Stephen W Raudenbush. 2002. "Seeing Disorder: Neighborhood Stigma and the Social Construction of 'Broken Windows.' " *Social Psychology Quarterly* 67 (4): 319–42.

Santos, Milton, Maria Adélia Aparecida de Souza, and Maria Laura Silveira. 1994. *Território: Globalização e Fragmentação*. São Paulo: Editora Hucitec.

Sassen, Saskia. 1988. *The Mobility of Labor and Capital: A Study in International Investment and Labor Flow* Cambridge: Cambridge University Press.

———. 1991 (2nd ed. 2001). *The Global City*. Princeton, N.J.: Princeton University Press.

———. 1996 *Losing Control? Sovereignty in an Age of Globalization. The Schoff Lectures*. New York: Columbia University Press.

―――. 1998. *Globalization and Its Discontents: Essays on the New Mobility of People and Money.* New York: New Press.

――― 1999a. "Beyond Sovereignty: De Facto Transnationalism in Immigration Policy." *European Journal of Migration Law* 1 (1): 177–98.

―――. 1999b "Digital Networks and Power." In *Spaces of Culture: City, Nation, World,* eds. M. Featherstone and S. Lash, 49–63. London: Sage.

―――. 1999c. *Guests and Aliens.* New York: New Press.

―――. 2000a. "Women's Burden: Countergeographies of Globalization and the Feminization of Survival." *Journal of International Affairs* 53 (2): 503–24.

―――. 2000b. "Digital Networks and the State: Some Governance Questions." *Theory Culture & Society. Special Section on Globalization and Sovereignty* 17 (4) 19–33

―――, ed. 2002 *Global Networks, Linked Cities.* New York: Routledge.

―――. 2006a. *Territory, Authority, Rights: From Medieval to Global Assemblages.* Princeton, N.J.: Princeton University Press.

―――. 2006b *Cities in a World Economy.* 3rd ed. Thousand Oaks, Calif.: Pine Forge/Sage.

―――. 2006c. "A State of Decay." *Open Democracy,* March 5. http://www.opendemocracy .net/debates/article.jsp?id=3&debateId=137&articleId=3500.

Sassen-Koob, Saskia. 1982. "Recomposition and Peripheralization at the Core." *Contemporary Marxism* 5: 88–100.

―――. 1984. "The New Labor Demand in Global Cities." In Michael Peter Smith 1984, 139–71.

Satler, Gail. 2006 *Two Tales of a City: Rebuilding Chicago's Architectural and Social Landscape, 1986–2005.* DeKalb: Northern Illinois University Press.

Sayad, Abdelmalek. 2004. *The Suffering of the Immigrant.* Oxford: Polity Press.

Savitch, H. V 1996. "Cities in a Global Era: A New Paradigm for the Next Millennium " In Michael Cohen et al. 1996, 25–38.

Schiffauer, Werner, Gerd Baumann, Riva Kastoryano, and Steven Vertovec. 2006 *Civil Enculturation: Nation-State, Schools, and Ethnic Difference in Four European Countries.* New York: Berghahn Books.

Schiffer Ramos, Sueli. 2002. "Sao Paulo: Articulating a Cross-Border Regional Economy." In *Global Networks/Linked Cities,* ed. Saskia Sassen, 209–36. New York and London: Routledge.

Schnapper, Dominique. 2001. *Exclusions aux Coeur de la Cite.* Paris: Anthropos.

―――. 2006. *Providential Democracy: An Essay on Contemporary Equality.* New Brunswick, N.J.: Transaction Publishers.

Scholte, Jan Aart. 2005. *Globalization a Critical Introduction* (2nd ed.). New York: Palgrave Macmillan.

Schuler, Doug. 1996. *New Community Networks: Wired for Change.* Boston, Mass.: Addison-Wesley.

————, and Peter Day, eds. 2004. *Community Practice in the Network Society: Local Action, Global Interaction*. London: Routledge.

Scott, Allen J. 2000. *Global City-Regions: Trends, Theory, Policy*. Oxford: Oxford University Press.

Scott, Matthew J. O. 2001. "Danger—Landmines! NGO-Government Collaboration in the Ottawa Process." In *Global Citizen Action*, ed. Michael Edwards and John Gaventa, 121–33. Boulder, Colo.: Lynne Rienner.

Seidman, Gay. 1994. *Manufacturing Militance: Workers' Movements in Brazil and South Africa, 1970–1985* Berkeley: University of California Press.

Sennett, Richard. 1998. *The Corrosion of Character: The Personal Consequences of the New Capitalism*. New York: Norton.

————. 2003. *Respect in an Age of Inequality*. New York: Norton.

Seol, D. H. and J. D. Skrentny. 2004. "South Korea: Importing Undocumented Workers." In Cornelius et al., op. cit.

Sewell, William H. 2005. *Logics of History: Social Theory and Social Transformation*. Chicago: University of Chicago Press.

Shannon, Susan. 1999. "The Global Sex Trade: Humans as the Ultimate Commodity." *Crime & Justice International* 15 (May): 5–25.

Sharp, John. 1997. "Communities of Practice: A Review of the Literature." http://www.tfriend.com/cop-lit htm.

Short, John R and Yeong-Hyun Kim. 1999. *Globalization and the City*. Essex· Addison Wesley Longman.

Silver, Beverly J. 2003. *Forces of Labor: Workers' Movements and Globalization since 1870*. Cambridge: Cambridge University Press.

Silvern, Steven E. 1999. "Scales of Justice: Law, American Indian Treaty Rights and Political Construction of Scale." *Political Geography* 18 (6). 639–68.

Simmonds, Roger, and Gary Hack. 2000. *Global City Regions: Their Emerging Forms*. New York: E & FN Spon.

Sinclair, Timothy J. 1994. "Passing Judgment: Credit Rating Processes as Regulatory Mechanisms of Governance in the Emerging World Order." *Review of International Political Economy* 1 (1): 133–59.

————. 2005. *The New Masters of Capital: American Bond Rating Agencies and the Politics of Creditworthiness*. Ithaca, N.Y.: Cornell University Press.

Siochru, Sean O., Bruce Girard, and Amy Mahan. 2002. *Global Media Governance: A Beginner's Guide*. Lanham, Md.: Rowman & Littlefield.

Skeldon, R. 1992. "International Migration within and from the East and Southeast Asian Region: A Review Essay." *Asian and Pacific Migration Journal* 1 (1).

————. 1997. "Hong Kong. Colonial City to Global City to Provincial City?" *Cities* 14 (5): 265–71.

Sklair, Leslie. 1991. *Sociology of the Global System*. New York: Harvester Wheatsheaf.

———. 1995. Sociology of the Global System. Baltimore: Johns Hopkins University Press.

———. 2001. *The Transnational Capitalist Class*. Oxford: Blackwell.

Skocpol, Theda. 1979. *States and Social Revolutions*. Cambridge. Cambridge University Press.

———. 1985. "Bringing the State Back In: Strategies of Analysis in Current Research." In *Bringing the State Back In*, ed. Peter Evans, Dietrich Rueschemeyer, and Theda Skocpol, 3–43. Cambridge: Cambridge University Press.

———, and Kenneth Finegold. 1982. "State Capacity and Economic Intervention in the Early New Deal." *Political Science Quarterly* 97 (2) 255–78

———, Peter B. Evans, and Dietrich Rueschemeyer, eds. 1985. *Bringing the State Back In* New York: Cambridge University Press.

Slaughter, Anne-Marie. 2004. *A New World Order*. Princeton, N.J.: Princeton University Press.

Small, Mario Luis. 2004. *Villa Victoria: The Transformation of Social Capital in a Boston Barrio*. Chicago. University of Chicago Press.

Smelser, Neil J., and Richard Swedburg, eds. 1994 *The Handbook of Economic Sociology* Princeton, N.J.: Princeton University Press.

Smith, David A. 1995. "The New Urban Sociology Meets the Old: Re-reading Some Classical Human Ecology." *Urban Affairs Review* 30 (3): 432–57.

———, and Michael Timberlake. 2002. "Hierarchies of Dominance among World Cities: A Network Approach." In Saskia Sassen 2002a, 117–41.

———, Dorothy J. Solinger, and Steven C. Topik, eds 1999. *States and Sovereignty in the Global Economy*. London: Routledge.

Smith, Joan, and Immanuel Wallerstein, eds. 1992. *Creating and Transforming Households: The Constraints of the World-Eonomy*. Cambridge and Paris. Cambridge University Press and Maison des Sciences de l'Homme.

Smith, Michael Peter, and Adrian Favell. 2006 "The Human Face of Global Mobility. International Highly Skilled Migration in Europe, North America and the Asian Pacific." Special Issue. *Comparative Urban and Community Research*. (8).

Smith, Michael Peter, ed. 1994. "Can You Imagine? Transnational Migration and the Globalization of Grassroots Politics." *Social Text* 39: 15–34.

———. 1984. *Cities in Transformation: Class, Capital and the State*. Beverly Hills, Calif.: Sage

Smith, Peter J. 2001. "The Impact of Globalization on Citizenship: Decline or Renaissance." *Journal of Canadian Studies* 36: 116–40.

Smith, Robert C. 1997. "Transnational Migration, Assimilation, and Political Community." In *The City and the World: New York's Global Future*, ed Margaret Crahan and Alberto Vourvoulias-Bush. New York: Council on Foreign Relations.

————. 2006. *Mexican New York: Transnational Worlds of New Immigrants*. Berkeley and Los Angeles: University of California Press.

Soja, Edward W. 2000. *Postmetropolis: Critical Studies of Cities and Regions*. Malden, Mass.. Blackwell.

Spivak, Gayatri Chakravorty. 1999. *A Critique of Postcolonial Reason: Toward a History of the Vanishing Present*. Cambridge, Mass.: Harvard University Press.

Stasiulis, D. K., and N. Yuval-Davis, eds 1995. *Unsettling Settler Societies*. London: Sage.

Steger, Manfred B. 2003. *Globalization: A Very Short Introduction*. Oxford: Oxford University Press.

Steinmetz, George. 2005. *The Politics of Method in the Human Sciences: Positivism and its Epistemological Others*. Durham, N.C.: Duke University Press.

Stren, Richard. 1996. "The Study of Cities: Popular Perceptions, Academic Disciplines, and Emerging Agendas." In Michael Cohen, et al., 392–420.

Suarez-Orozco, Carola, and Marcelo M. Suarez-Orozco. 2002. *Children of Immigration*. Cambridge, Mass.. Harvard University Press.

Suarez-Orozco, Marcelo M., and Mariela Paez. 2002. *Latinos: Remaking America*. Berkeley, Calif.: University of California Press.

Sum, Ngai-Ling. 1999. "Rethinking Globalisation: Re-articulating the Spatial Scale and Temporal Horizons of Trans-border Spaces." Olds et al. 1999, 129–45.

Susser, Ida. 2002. "Losing Ground: Advancing Capitalism and the Relocation of Working Class Communities." In *Locating Capitalism in Time and Space: Global Restructurings, Politics, and Identity*, ed. David Nugent, 247–90. Stanford, Calif.: Stanford University Press.

Suttles, Gerald D. 1968. *The Social Order of the Slum: Ethnicity and Territory in the Inner City*. Chicago: University of Chicago Press.

Swyngedouw, Erik. 1997. "Neither Global nor Local: 'Glocalization' and the Politics of Scale." In *Spaces of Globalization: Reasserting the Power of the Local*, ed. Kevin Cox, 137–66. New York: Guilford Press.

Tabak, Frank and Michaeline A. Chrichlow, eds. 2000. *Informalization: Process and Structure*. Baltimore, Md.: The Johns Hopkins Press.

Tait, Vanessa. 2005. *Poor Workers' Unions: Rebuilding Labor from Below*. Cambridge, Mass.: South End Press.

Taylor-Gooby, Peter. 2004. "Open Markets and Welfare Values: Welfare Values, Inequality, and Social Change in the Silver Age of the Welfare State." *European Societies* 6 (1): 29–48.

Taylor, Peter. 1995. "World Cities and Territorial States· The Rise and Fall of Their Mutuality." In Knox and Taylor 1995, 28–62.

————. 1996. "Embedded Statism and the Social Sciences: Opening Up to New Spaces." *Environment & Planning A* 28 (11): 1917–28.

————. 2000. "World Cities and Territorial States under Conditions of Contemporary Globalization." *Political Geography* 19 (5): 5–32.

————. 2004. *World City Network: A Global Urban Analysis*. London: Routledge.

————. 2006. *Cities in Globalization: Practices, Policies, and Theories*. London: Routledge

————, D.R.F. Walker, and J. V. Beaverstock. 2002. "Firms and Their Global Service Networks." In Sassen 2002.

Tennant, Evalyn W. 2007. "Locating Transnational Activists: The United States Anti-Apartheid Movement and the Confines of the National." In *Deciphering the Global: Its Spaces, Scales and Subjects*, ed. Saskia Sassen, 117–36. New York and London: Routledge.

Teubner, Gunther. 2004. "Societal Constitutionalism: Alternatives to State-Centered Constitutional Theory." In *Transnational Governance and Constitutionalism*, ed. Christian Joerges, Inger-Johanne Sand, and Gunther Teubner, 3–29. Oxford: Hart

Thaler, Henri Lustiger. 2004. "The Rift in the Subject. A Late Global Modernist Dilemma." *Current Sociology* 52 (4). 615–31.

Thierer, Adam D., and Clyde Wayne Crews. 2003. *Who Rules the Net?: Internet Governance and Jurisdiction*. Washington, D.C.: Cato Institute.

Thrift, Nigel. 1987. "The Fixers: The Urban Geography of International Commercial Capital." In *Global Restructuring and Territorial Development*, ed. J. W. Henderson and Manuel Castells, 219–47 London: Sage.

————. 2005. *Knowing Capitalism*. Thousand Oaks, Calif.: Sage.

————, and Andrew Leyshon. 1994. "A Phantom State? The De-traditionalization of Money, the International Financial System, and International Financial Centers." *Political Geography* 13 (4): 299–327.

Tilly, Charles. 1990. *Coercion, Capital, and European States, A.D. 990–1992*. Cambridge: Blackwell.

————. 1999. *Durable Inequality*. Berkeley. University of California Press.

————. 2005. *Identities, Boundaries, and Social Ties*. Boulder, Colo.: Paradigm Publishers.

Timberlake, Michael, ed. 1985. *Urbanization in the World Economy*. Orlando, Fla.: Academic Press.

Tinker, Irene, ed. 1990. *Persistent Inequalities: Women and World Development*. New York. Oxford University Press.

Tomlinson, John. 1999. *Globalization and Culture*. Chicago, Ill.: University of Chicago Press.

Trachtman, Joel. 1993. "International Regulatory Competition, Externalization, and Jurisdiction." *Harvard International Law Journal* 34 (1): 47–104.

Tsaliki, Liza. 2002. "Online Forums and the Enlargement of the Public Space: Research Findings from a European Project" *Public* 9: 95–112

Tsuda, Takeyuki. 1999. "The Permanence of 'Temporary' Migration: The Structural Embeddedness of Japanese-Brazilian Immigrant Workers in Japan " *Journal of Asian Studies* 58 (3): 687–722.

————. 2003. *Strangers in the Ethnic Homeland: Japanese Brazilian Migration in Transnational Perspective*. New York: Columbia University Press.

Tsuzuki, K. 2000. "*Nikkei* Brazilians and local residents: a study of the H Housing Complex in Toyota City." *Asian and Pacific Migration Journal* 9 (3).

Tuijl, Peter Van, and Lisa Jordan. 1999. "Political Responsibility in Transnational NGO Advocacy." http://www.bicusa.org/bicusa/issues/misc_resources/138.php.

Tunstall, Kate E. 2006. *Displacement, Asylum, Migration: The 2004 Amnesty Lectures.* Oxford: Oxford University Press.

United Nations Conference on Trade and Development (UNCTAD). (annual). *World Investment Report: Trends and Determinants.* New York: UNCTAD.

———. 1999. *World Investment Report: Foreign Direct Investment and the Challenge of Development.* New York: UNCTAD.

United Nations Development Programme (UNDP). 2005. *A Time For Bold Ambition: Together We Can Cut Poverty in Half.* New York: UNDP.

U.S. Department of State. 2004. *Trafficking in Persons Report,* released by the Office to Monitor and Combat Trafficking in Persons. Washington, D.C.: U.S. Department of State.

Venkatesh, Sudhir Alladi. 1997. "The Social Organization of Street Gang Activity in an Urban Ghetto." *American Journal of Sociology* 103 (1): 82–111.

———. 2006. *Off The Books: the Underground Economy of the Urban Poor.* Cambridge, Mass.: Harvard University Press.

Vertovec, S. 2003. "Migration and Other Modes of Transnationalism: Towards Conceptual Cross-Fertilization," *International Migration Review* 37 (3): 641–665.

———, and C. Peach. 1997. *Islam in Europe: The Politics of Religion and Community.* London: Macmillan Press, Ltd.

Von Petz, Ursula, and Klaus M. Schmals, eds 1992. *Metropole, Weltstadt, Global City: Neue Formen der Urbanisierung.* Dortmund, Germany: Dortmunder Beitrage zur Raumplanung, Universitat Dortmund.

Walker, R.B.J. 1993. *Inside/Outside: International Relations as Political Theory.* Cambridge: Cambridge University Press.

Wallace, C., and D. Stola, eds. 2001. *Patterns of Migration in Central Europe.* Basingstoke/ New York: Palgrave.

Wallerstein, Immanuel. 1974. *Capitalist Agriculture and the Origins of the European World-Economy in the Sixteenth Century.* Vol. 1 of *The Modern World-System.* New York: Academic Press.

———. 1990 "Culture as the Ideological Battleground of the Modern World-System " In *Global Culture: Nationalism, Globalization, and Modernity,* ed. Mike Featherstone, 31–55. London: Newbury Park.

Walton, John 1982. "The International Economy and Peripheral Urbanization." In *Urban Policy under Capitalism,* ed. Norman I. Fainstein and Susan S. Fainstein, 119–35. Beverly Hills, Calif.: Sage.

Ward, Kathryn, ed. 1990. *Women Workers and Global Restructuring.* Ithaca, N.Y.: ILR Press, School of Industrial and Labor Relations, Cornell University.

Warf, Barney, and John Grimes. 1997. "Counterhegemonic Discourses and the Internet." *Geographical Review* 87 (2): 259–74.

Warkentin, Craig. 2001. *Reshaping World Politics: NGOs, the Internet, and Global Civil Society.* Lanham, Md.: Rowman & Littlefield.

Waters, M. C. 1999. *Black Identities: West Indian Immigrant Dreams and American Realities.* New York and Cambridge, Mass.: Russell Sage Foundation

Weber, Max 1944. *From Max Weber*, ed. Hans Gerth and C. Wright Mills. New York: Oxford University Press.

Weber, Steven. 2005 "The Political Economy of Open Source Software and Why It Matters." In Latham and Sassen 2005, 178–212.

Weiss, Linda. 1998. *The Myth of the Powerless State.* Ithaca, N.Y.: Cornell University Press.

Wellman, Barry, and Caroline A Haythornthwaite 2002. *The Internet in Everyday Life.* Malden, Mass.: Blackwell Publishers.

White, Gregory. 1999. "Encouraging Unwanted Immigration: A Political Economy of Europe's Efforts to Discourage North African Immigration." *Third World Quarterly* 20 (4): 839–54.

Whittel, A. 2001. "Toward a Network Sociality." *Theory, Culture & Society* 18 (6): 51–7, 76

Wievorka, Michel 2004. *La Violence.* Paris: Balland.

Wihtol de Wenden, C., and R. Leveau. 2001. *La Beurgeoisie: les trois ages de la vie associative issue de l'immigration.* Paris: CNRS Editions.

Whyte, William H, Jr. 1956. *The Organization Man.* New York. Doubleday Anchor.

Wilks, Alex. 2001. "A Tower of Babel on the Internet? The World Bank's Development Gateway." Bretton Woods Project http://www.brettonwoodsproject.org/topic/knowl edgebank/k22gatewaybrief.pdf.

Williams, Jody, and Stephen Goose. 1998. "The International Campaign to Ban Landmines." In *To Walk without Fear: The Global Movement to Ban Landmines*, ed. Maxwell A. Cameron, Robert J. Lawson, and Brian W. Tomlin, 20–47. Ontario· Oxford University Press.

Williamson, T., G. Alperovitz, and D. L. Imbroscio. 2002. *Making a Place for Community. Local Democracy in a Global Era.* New York: Routledge.

Wilson, W. J. 1997. *When Work Disappears.* New York. Alfred A. Knopf.

WomenAction. 2000. *Alternative Assessment of Women and Media Based on NGO Reviews of Section J, Beijing Platform for Action* WomenAction. http://www.womenaction.org/ csw44/altrepeng.htm.

Wong, D. 1996 "Foreign Domestic Workers in Singapore." *Asian and Pacific Migration Journal* 5 (1).

Woodall, Pam. 1995. "The World Economy: Who's in the Driving Seat?" *The Economist* 337 (7935): 5–18, 44.

Woolgar, S., ed. 2002. *Virtual Society? Technology, Cyberpole, Reality* Oxford: Oxford University Press

World Bank. 2006. *Global Economic Prospects: Economic Implications of Remittances and Migration*. Washington, D.C.: The World Bank.

———. 2005. *Increasing Aid and Its Effectiveness*. Washington, D.C.: The World Bank. http://siteresources.worldbank.org/INTGLOBALMONITORING/Resources/ch5_GMR 2005.pdf.

World Information Order. 2000. *World-Information Files: The Politics of the Info Sphere*. Vienna: Institute for New Culture Technologies, and Berlin: Center for Civic Education. http://world-information.org.

Wright, Erik Olin. 1979 *Class, Crisis, and the State*. New York: Verso.

———. 1985. *Classes*. New York: Verso.

Wright, Talmadge. 1997. *Out of Place: Homeless Mobilizations, Subcities, and Contested Landscapes*. Albany: State University of New York Press.

Yaeger, Patricia, ed. 1996. *Geography of Identity*. Ann Arbor: University of Michigan Press.

Yamamoto, Satomi. 2006. "Habituating Migration: The Role of Intermediary in the Case of Filipina Nurses' Migration to the U.S." Department of Sociology, University of Illinois, Champaign, Urbana, IL. Unpublished manuscript.

Yang, Guobin. 2003. "Weaving a Green Web: The Internet and Environmental Activism in China." In *China Environment Series* 6, 89–92. Washington D.C.: Woodrow Wilson International Centers for Scholars.

Young, Iris Marion. 2002. *Inclusion and Democracy*. Oxford: Oxford University Press.

Yuval-Davis, Nira. 1999. "Ethnicity, Gender Relations, and Multiculturalism." In *Race, Identity, and Citizenship*, ed. Rodolfo D. Torres, Louis F Miron, and Jonathan Xavier Inda, 112–25. Oxford: Blackwell.

Zeitlin, Maurice. 1974. "Corporate Ownership and Control: The Large Corporation and the Capitalist Class." *American Journal of Sociology* 79 (5): 1073–1119.

Zhao, Dingxin. 2004. *The Power of Tiananmen: State-society Relations and the 1989 Beijing Student Movement*. Chicago, Ill.: University of Chicago Press.

Zlolniski, Christian. 2006. *Janitors, Street Vendors, and Activists. The Lives of Mexican Immigrants in Silicon Valley*. Berkeley: University of California Press.

Zolberg, Aristide R. 2006. *A Nation by Design: Immigration Policy in the Fashioning of America*. New York: Russell Sage Foundation.

———, and Peter Benda, eds. 2001. *Global Migrants, Global Refugees*. New York and Oxford: Berghahn Books.

Zukin, Sharon. 1991 *Landscapes of Power: From Detroit to Disney World*. Berkeley: University of California Press.

INDEX